Children's Literature

Volume 11

Volume 11

Annual of
The Modern Language Association
Division on Children's Literature
and The Children's Literature
Association

Yale University Press
New Haven and London
1983

Children's Literature

Editor-in-Chief: Francelia Butler
Editor: Compton Rees
Book Review Editor: David L. Greene
Editorial Correspondent: Jack Zipes (Frankfurt, Germany)
Advisory Board: Robert Coles, M.D., Elizabeth A. Francis, Martin Gardner, Alison Lurie, William T. Moynihan, Samuel Pickering, Jr., Albert J. Solnit, M.D.
Editorial Assistants: Richard Wayne Rotert, John David Stahl, E. Charles Vousden
Board of Directors: The Children's Literature Foundation: Francelia Butler, Rachel Fordyce, John C. Wandell

Editorial Correspondence should be addressed to:
The Editors, *Children's Literature*
Department of English
University of Connecticut
Storrs, Connecticut 06268

Manuscripts submitted should conform to the *MLA Handbook.* An original on non-erasable bond and a copy are requested. Manuscripts must be accompanied by a self-addressed envelope and return postage.

Volumes 1–7 of *Children's Literature* can be obtained directly from the Children's Literature Foundation, Box 370, Windham Center, Connecticut 06280.

Library of Congress catalog card number: 79-66588
ISBN: 0-300-02991-8 (cloth), 0-300-02992-6 (paper)

Set in Baskerville type by Coghill Composition Co., Inc., Richmond, Va. Printed in the United States of America by Vail-Ballou Press, Binghamton, N.Y.

10   9   8   7   6   5   4   3   2   1

Contents

"Quite Contrary": Frances Hodgson Burnett's The Secret Garden

Elizabeth Lennox Keyser

> When Mary Lennox was sent to Misselthwaite Manor to live with her uncle everybody said she was the most disagreeable-looking child ever seen.[1]

Thus begins Frances Hodgson Burnett's *The Secret Garden*. Ann Thwaite, Burnett's biographer, remarks that "the most original thing about [*The Secret Garden*] was that its heroine and one of its heroes were both thoroughly unattractive children."[2] And Marghanita Laski has written, "I do not know of any children's book other than *The Secret Garden* that frankly poses this problem of the introspective unlikeable child in terms that children can understand."[3] Burnett herself describes Mary Lennox as wondering "why she had never seemed to belong to anyone even when her father and mother had been alive. Other children seemed to belong to their fathers and mothers, but she had never seemed to really be anyone's little girl. . . . She did not know that this was because she was a disagreeable child; but then, of course, she did not know she was disagreeable. She often thought that others were, but she did not know that she was so herself" (p. 12). Unattractive, unlikeable, disagreeable—these are the ways in which the critics and the author herself characterize Mary Lennox and the way in which the critics at least characterize Colin Craven. But I want to examine closely what the term "disagreeable" really means in connection with the heroine, Mary, and to distinguish between the ways in which the two children are unattractive or unlikeable.

Mary initially "disagrees" with the adult characters in the story not only because her looks and manners fail to please them but also because she refuses to accept their authority. From the outset, however, she is by no means "thoroughly unattractive" to the narrator, who, in the passage quoted above, conveys sympathy as well as antipathy for Mary by mingling the child's point of view with the omniscient. Nor is Mary "thoroughly unattractive" even to

1

the critic who so labels her, for that critic obviously finds a powerful attraction in that very unattractiveness. As the book proceeds, Mary becomes at least moderately agreeable, both to others in the novel and to the narrator, who grants her a grudging approval. But as Mary ostensibly "improves," her role in the book diminishes, and she loses for the reader her main appeal. Instead the other "thoroughly unattractive" child, Master Colin, increasingly gains the center of the stage.

Colin, I would argue, is never as unattractive to the narrator as Mary, nor is he ever as attractive to the reader. Unlike Mary, who is never described as more than "almost pretty" even when she gains flesh and color, Colin, though far more fretful and selfish, is described from the beginning as having a "sharp, delicate face the color of ivory" and great black-fringed eyes like those of his dead mother (p. 124). The narrator tells us that Colin, having had the advantage of "wonderful books and pictures," is more imaginative than Mary, and as he recovers his health he acquires both extraordinary physical beauty and a charismatic power. At the end of *The Secret Garden* we see Colin besting Mary in a footrace, and, indeed, he has already run away with, or been allowed to dominate, the final third of the book.

The race is not always to the swift, however. Ask an adult what he or she remembers from a childhood reading of *The Secret Garden*.[4] Memories will differ, of course. But what I remembered before I re-read it recently was Mary's first finding and awakening the garden and then, in a reversal of the "Sleeping Beauty" story, her finding and awakening Colin. I remembered Mary exploring the winding paths and gardens within gardens, and indoors the winding corridors with their many locked rooms. And I remembered Mary as stubborn and defiant in her attitude toward adult authority and even toward Colin, but also tender and nurturing. I remembered Colin, too, but always as lying in his room being comforted by Mary or being wheeled by her into the garden. And I remembered his first faltering steps, supported by Mary, but I did not remember his digging, his running, and his calisthenics. And I certainly did not remember his expounding on magic and science.

In fact, if my memory serves me, the more conventionally attractive that Colin grew and the more he came to dominate the book, the less memorable both he, and it, became.

Burnett seems to have intended to evoke sympathy for both Mary and Colin while at the same time portraying them as genuinely disagreeable children—children who treat others hatefully and are hated in turn because, having never known love, they feel hatred for themselves. She then apparently meant to show their transformation from self-hating and hateful to loving and lovable through the acquisition of self-esteem. For reasons which I will suggest later, however, Burnett makes Mary too attractive in her disagreeableness and Colin too unattractive in his agreeableness. As Mary becomes less disagreeable, she becomes, after a certain point, less interesting. And Colin, as he becomes more agreeable in some ways, becomes something of a prig and a bore. But before speculating as to why Burnett allows both characters to get out of control, let us consider how Mary, despite—or rather because of—authorial severity, becomes such a compelling figure.

An early example of Mary's unpleasantness earns her the nickname "Mistress Mary Quite Contrary." As a little boy named Basil watches Mary "making heaps of earth and paths for a garden," he suggests that they make a rockery. She spurns his offer, but what strikes us is not so much Mary's ill temper at what she takes to be his interference as her attempt, literally and metaphorically, to make something grow from barren ground. Although the narrator later tells us that Mary is less imaginative than Colin, we, having witnessed her persistent efforts to bring forth life, tend to disbelieve the narrator or at least to question her use of the word *imagination*. True, Mary must overcome the distrustfulness that makes her contrary with well-meaning people like Basil. And she succeeds by admitting first Dickon and then Colin to her secret garden. After admitting Dickon, she tells him about the incident with Basil. He replies, in characteristic fashion, "There doesn't seem to be no need for no one to be contrary when there's flowers an' such like" (p. 108). But Dickon is, in some respects, more naive than Mary, who knows there is more to the world than flowers and friendly wild things. Sometimes, as it was for Mary in India, contrariness is necessary for self-preservation; and sometimes, as for Mary in England, it is even necessary for self-renewal.[5]

We can sympathize with Mary even though she is not a "nice sympathetic child" in part because of the deprivation she has endured. Her mistreatment of the Indian servants, though shocking, seems excusable, since she has been left almost entirely to their care by an apathetic, invalid father and a vain, frivolous mother. When, after her parents' death, she is passed from one reluctant guardian to another, her suspiciousness seems justified. And when, on arriving at Misselthwaite Manor, she overhears the housekeeper, Mrs. Medlock, being warned to keep her out of her uncle's sight and confined to her own two rooms, we can understand why Mary "perhaps never felt quite so contrary in all her life" (p. 23). Yet while we can see that Mary's unhappiness gives rise to her naughtiness,[6] the narrator, by saying that Mary never belonged to anyone because she was a disagreeable child, implies that the reverse is true. In fact, the narrator's refusal to intervene on behalf of Mary, as she does on behalf of Colin, forces us into the position of defending her ourselves.

If Mary's contrariness consisted of mere sullenness, we might agree with the narrator and the adult characters' assessment of her. But there is, as I have suggested, a positive side to her contrariness, which is supported by other characters in the book as well. On her first morning at Misselthwaite, Mary awakens to find the servant Martha in her room. There had been no reciprocity in Mary's relationship with her Indian servants. She could verbally, and even physically, abuse her ayah with impunity. On meeting Martha, however, Mary wonders how she would react to being slapped. Something tells her that Martha would slap her right back. Sure enough, when Mary calls her a "daughter of a pig," as she was wont to insult her ayah, Martha reproves her. The way Martha reacts to and affects Mary resembles the way in which Mary later reacts to and affects Colin. When Martha forces Mary to make at least some effort to dress herself, the narrator comments: "If Martha had been a well-trained fine young lady's maid she would have been more subservient and respectful and would have known that it was her business to brush hair, and button boots, and pick things up and lay them away. She was, however, only an untrained Yorkshire rustic" (p. 30). When Mary later tells Colin that she hates him and contradicts him when, in a bid for her pity, he says he feels a lump on his back, the narrator similarly comments: "A nice sympathetic child could neither have thought nor said such things" (p. 175). But in fact both the untrained Yorkshire rustic and "savage little Mary" have a salutary effect on those who are used to being coddled, and the ironic treatment of Mary's antitypes—the well-trained maid, the fine young lady, and the nice sympathetic child—suggests both the author's need to condemn plainspokenness and her even stronger desire to condone it.

Martha insists that the reluctant Mary play out-of-doors, where she meets another character whose contrariness matches her own. Ben Weatherstaff, the crusty gardener, "had a surly old face, and did not seem at all pleased to see her—but then she was displeased with his garden and wore her 'quite contrary' expression, and certainly did not seem at all pleased to see him" (p. 34). But when Mary mentions a robin and Ben describes how it was abandoned by its parents, she is able for the first time to recognize and admit her own loneliness. Like Martha, Ben Weatherstaff is given to plainspokenness. He says to Mary: "We was wove out of th' same cloth. We're neither of us good lookin' an' we're both of us as sour as we look. We've got the same nasty tempers, both of us, I'll warrant" (p. 40). Mary is taken aback and contrasts him, like Martha, with the native servants who always "salaamed and submitted to you, whatever you did." But Ben's bluntness, too, helps Mary both to know herself and to see herself as others see her.

Dickon, with his intuitive understanding of nature, and his mother, with her equally wonderful understanding of human nature, not only aid Mary but also counter the asperity of the narrator toward her. But in doing justice to Dickon and his mother, one tends to forget that it is Ben who befriends the robin, whose plight was analogous to Mary's and Colin's, and that it is Ben who kept the garden alive during the ten years it was locked up. It is also Ben who, along with Martha, piques Mary's curiosity about the garden but refuses to satisfy it, thus arousing by *his* contrariness all her stubborn determination to seek it out. And during the time that Mary searches for an entrance to the garden, Ben and Martha provide her with the insights necessary to appreciate her eventual discovery. In the chapter in which Mary finds the key, Martha forces Mary to consider the possiblity that perhaps she does not really like herself. In the chapter in which Mary finds the gate, Martha, with her gift of a skipping-rope, persuades Mary that she is likeable and that she, in turn, is capable of liking others. Thus encouraged, Mary actively seeks and gains Ben's approval, so that by the time "the robin shows the way," Ben and Martha have already helped her find the key to her own heart.

Contrariness then, of the kind that Mary gradually loses, originates in sourness, irritability, an unwillingness to be interested or pleased. But the kind of contrariness that Mary retains, at least until Colin comes to dominate the book, arises from emotional honesty and reliance on one's own judgment.[7] Mary finds both the garden and Colin largely because "she was not a child who had been trained to ask permission or consult her elders about things" (p. 66) Despite repeated denials by Martha that Mary hears crying in the night, and despite repeated warnings from Mrs. Medlock against exploring the house, Mary continues to believe the evidence of her own senses and to search for the source of the cries she hears. What she finds is a boy very similar to herself. Like Mary, Colin has been rejected by his father and has become used to overhearing terrible things about himself, many of which he now believes. Even more than Mary, he has become a tyrant to those who are paid to wait on him. Given everything he ever requested, never forced to do what he didn't wish, he is the object of pity but also of dislike and disgust. But because Mary has also played the tyrant out of misery, acting the little ranee to her ayah, and because she is not afraid to impose her will on others, she is able to do for Colin what no doctor or even Dickon can.

Mary not only encourages Colin to believe that he can live; she persuades him that he need not live as a chronic invalid. In order to do so Mary must oppose her contrariness to Colin's own and act in a way not "nice" by conventional standards. When Colin unjustly accuses Mary of neglecting him, she becomes angry but, after reflection, relents. When she awakens to hear Colin in hysterics, however, she becomes enraged at the way her emotions, and those of everyone else in the house, are being manipulated. In expressing to Colin what no nice child would say or, according to the narrator, even feel—namely, that Colin is an emotional rather than a physical cripple whose self-centeredness has made him an object of contempt and loathing—Mary is actually expressing what everyone, including the reader, is feeling or would feel in similar circumstances. Her "savagery," as the narrator calls it, her ability to set aside the civilized veneer which has thinly disguised everyone else's hostility towards Colin, has a purgative effect on the entire household. And by disclosing what the nurse and doctor have long known but feared to say, that Colin is only weak from lying in bed and indulging in self-pity, Mary relieves him of his morbid fear and sets him on the road to recovery.

Gradually, with Mary's and Dickon's help, Colin gains enough strength to enter the garden. But although Dickon plants the suggestion that Colin will one day be able to walk, it is plain-spoken Ben Weatherstaff who brings him to his feet. Like Mary, Weatherstaff will express the unmentionable thoughts in everyone's minds: on finding the children in the secret garden, he blurts out, "But tha'rt th' poor cripple" (p. 222). And he is condemned as "ignorant" and "tactless" (p. 223) just as Mary is castigated for being "savage" and not "nice." But his bluntness also has a salutary effect on Colin. "The strength which Colin usually threw into his tantrums rushed through him now in a new way. . . . His anger and insulted pride made him forget everything but this one moment and filled him with a power he had never known before, an almost unnatural strength" (p. 223). Though "magic" later enables him to run and perform calisthenics, it is his passionate desire to refute Ben that enables him to take his first steps.

After watching Colin stand and walk, and after examining his legs, Ben decides that Colin, far from being "th' poor cripple," " 'lt make a mon yet" (p. 224). From that point on Colin's athletic prowess, his leadership ability, his interest in science, and his magical powers all seem meant to prove Ben right. In the early chapters the narrator often reminded us of Mary's unattractiveness and unpleasantness; now she stresses Colin's beauty and charisma. At one point the narrator intervenes to tell us that Colin "was somehow a very convincing sort of boy," and it is doubtless this convincing quality that is meant to convince *us* of Colin's ascendancy over Ben, Dickon, and even Mary. Whereas earlier Colin had been a peevish little tyrant, he now becomes a benevolent despot, a combination rajah and priest. Colin, "fired by recollections of fakirs and devotees in illustrations," arranges the group cross-legged in a circle under a tree which makes "a sort of temple" (p. 241). Later Colin heads the rajah's procession "with Dickon on one side and Mary on the other. Ben Weatherstaff walked behind, and the 'creatures' trailed after them" (p. 243). It has been argued that "in this Eden, nature dissolves class—gardner and Pan-boy share the broadly human vocation of nursing the invalid boy to straight health."[8] These doings in the garden, however, suggest a definite hierarchy, one that includes sex as well as class.

During Colin's lectures, "Mistress Mary" is described as feeling "solemnly enraptured" and listening "entranced" (pp. 241–42). Although we are doubtless meant to be as charmed by Colin as the other characters are and to see in his domination of the little group the promise of his future manhood, we are in fact disenchanted to find Mary little more than a worshipful Huck to the antics of Colin's Tom Sawyer. Yet Mary and Huck are the truly imaginative and convincing children who do not, like Colin and Tom, need the stimulus of books in order to have real adventures and solve real problems. Huck's escape from Pap and his flight down the river with Jim, Mary's discoveries of Colin and the garden, and, above all, her self-discoveries, make Tom's "evasion" and Colin's "magic" anticlimactic. And just as Jim loses stature because of the indignities inflicted on him by Tom, so the roles of Martha and Ben Weatherstaff, so important to Mary's development, diminish. Martha, as remarkable in her way as Dickon and their mother, simply disappears from the final chapters; but since she is the first person for whom Mary feels anything like trust and affection, it is hard to believe that Mary would forget her. Ben, like Mrs. Sowerby a party to the secret in the garden, is treated condescendingly by Colin— and by the author. When Ben makes a joke at the expense of

Colin's "scientific discoveries," Colin snubs him, a snub which Ben—acting out of character—takes humbly (p. 245). But at least at the end of Twain's book we are left with its true hero. In *The Secret Garden* Burnett shifts from Mary's to Colin's point of view shortly after the scene in which Mary confronts him with his cowardice and hypochondria. From there on Mary slips into the background until she disappears entirely from the final chapter. The novel ends with the master of Misselthwaite and his son, Master Colin, crossing the lawn before their servants' admiring eyes.

Perhaps the analogy between Mary and Huck can do more than suggest why the final third of *The Secret Garden* is so unsatisfying. Huck is a memorable, even magical, creation not only because he is a very convincing boy (so is Tom, for that matter), but because he is, at the same time, unconventional. He resists being civilized in a way that Tom, for all his infatuation with outlaws, does not. Mary, too, is a more memorable creation than Colin because she is both recognizably human and refreshingly different. Thwaite and Laski have tried to link this difference with her unpleasantness, but I believe it lies more in her freedom from sex-role stereotypes.[9] (This, of course, is why girls have always found Jo March so appealing, especially in Part 1 of *Little Women*.)

From the first Mary is an independent, self-contained, yet self-assertive child. Unlike Colin, she discovers and enters the secret garden all by herself, and she defies adult authority in order to find, befriend, and liberate Colin. Unlike her mother, she is never vain of her appearance; she is proud when she finds herself getting plump, rosy, and glossy-haired, but only because these are signs of her growing strength. When she receives a present from Mr. Craven, she is delighted to find books rather than dolls, and she works and exercises in the garden along with Colin and Dickon. She does not wish to have a nurse or governess but seems to thrive on an active life out-of-doors. Early in the relationship with Colin she is the leader, and even when he is able to run about, it is she who, on a rainy day, suggests that they explore his house. Colin, when we first meet him, is a hysterical invalid, and his father, as the name "Craven" signifies, is a weak and cowardly man, still mourning after ten years his dead wife and, in doing so, neglecting their living son. It is as though Burnett so generously endowed Mary at the expense of Colin and his father that she had to compensate for it by stressing Mary's disagreeable traits and exaggerating Colin's charm. And in the final chapter Colin's ascendancy suggests that if he becomes a "mon," as Ben predicts, then Mary will have to become a woman—quiet, passive, subordinate, and self-effacing. Huck at the end of *Huckleberry Finn* cannot escape civilization; Mary cannot escape the role that civilization has assigned her.

Burnett's ambivalence toward Mary and her indulgence of Colin probably reflect lifelong conflicts. As a child Burnett was encouraged by her widowed mother to cultivate genteel and ladylike manners. And as a young married woman she is described by Thwaite as "obviously trying her best . . . to appear as the nineteenth century's ideal of womanhood" (p. 52). Often, especially during these early years, Burnett regarded her writing as a necessary, even sacrificial task, performed for the sake of her husband, struggling to establish himself as an ophthalmologist, and their sons. Yet Burnett continued to write long after Dr. Swan Burnett was well able to support his family. By then, however, writing, and the fame and fortune which attended it, seems to have become a psychological necessity. Her favorite image of herself was that of a fairy godmother, and the power as well as the magnanimity of that role must have appealed to her. So like many successful women writers, including Louisa May Alcott and Burnett's prolific friend Mrs. Humphry Ward, she tried to rationalize her writing as unselfish service, and, when she could not ignore its self-assertive and self-serving role, punished herself with ill health. And finally, again like other women writers (great ones such as the Brontës and George Eliot as well as minor ones such as Alcott and Ward), she chastened her self-assertive female characters.[10]

The Secret Garden, written in 1911 toward the end of a long, successful career, seems to suggest not only self-condemnation and self-punishment in its treatment of Mary but an attempted reparation for wrongs Burnett may have felt she inflicted on the males closest to her. Most obviously, the idealized Colin seems to represent her elder son, Lionel, and his recovery a wish-fulfilling revision of what actually happened. After the extraordinary success of *Little Lord Fauntleroy* in 1886, Burnett began to spend much of each year abroad. Although she was a doting mother, able from her earnings to give her sons whatever their hearts desired, she may have felt that even these luxuries, like those Colin's father provides for him, could not compensate for her absence. And when, during one of these absences, Lionel became consumptive, her guilt must have been intensified. To assuage it she nursed Lionel devotedly and especially prided herself on protecting him from the knowledge that he was dying.[11] But in a notebook entry, written a few months after Lionel's death, she asks: "Did I do right to hide from you that you were dying? It seemed to me that I *must* not give you the terror of knowing."[12] The situation in *The Secret Garden* is significantly reversed: Colin is kept in ignorance not of his imminent death but of his capacity for life; Mary, by breaking the conspiracy of silence, enables him to live.

The figure of Colin is reminiscent not only of Lionel but also of Swan Burnett and of Mrs. Burnett's second husband, Stephen Townesend. Swan, himself crippled in his youth, became a successful eye specialist, but the marriage seems never to have been a happy one. Two years after their divorce, Burnett married Townesend, a doctor and aspiring actor ten years younger than herself. Burnett had long attempted to use her theatrical connections to further his acting career, especially after Townesend helped her to nurse Lionel through his fatal illness. As her son Vivian wrote: "This was one of the few solaces that Dearest had in her dark hours, making her feel that surely some good had come out of her wish to help her older—disappointed—Stephen boy."[13] And as Burnett wrote to her friend Kitty Hall, "If I had done no other one thing in my life but help Lionel to die as he did, I should feel as if I ought to be grateful to God for letting me live to do it—but if I can help Stephen to *live,* that will be another beautiful thing to have done."[14] As these quotations suggest, Burnett's interest in Stephen Townesend was largely maternal, a desire to play fairy godmother as she had in the lives of her sons. To use her fortune and influence

to aid a struggling young man would somehow justify her possession of it. But although Stephen, unlike Lionel, survived, she never
succeeded in helping either him or their marriage to "live."

Thus *The Secret Garden,* far from combining "the ideal remembered holiday in a golden age . . . with a classless, reasonable, and
joyous Utopia for the future," reflects its author's ambivalence
about sex roles.[15] On the one hand, she vindicates Mary's self-
assertiveness and her own career by allowing Mary to bring the
garden, Colin, and, eventually, Mr. Craven back to life. On the
other hand, she chastens herself and Mary by permitting the
narrator to intervene only to reprove her and by making her
subordinate to Colin in the final chapters of the book. By idealizing
Colin at the expense of Mary she seems to be affirming male
supremacy, and the final version of the master of Misselthwaite
with his son, Master Colin, further suggests a defense of patriar-
chal authority. While Mr. Craven can be seen as the neglectful,
erring parent of either sex—and thus still another means by which
Burnett atones for her material failings—he, like the peevish
invalid Colin, can also be viewed as an expression of her impatience
with male weakness. And her attempts to glorify Colin are unsuc-
cessful enough to make us wonder if even here her ambivalence—
even her resentment and hostility—does not show through. For all
her efforts to make Mary disagreeable and to efface her, Mary
remains a moving and memorable creation, whereas Colin's
"magic" never amounts to more than a mere trick. Mary, like the
author herself, seems to have both gained and lost from her
contrariness, and *The Secret Garden* succeeds and fails accordingly.

Notes

1. Frances Hodgson Burnett, *The Secret Garden* (1911; rpt. New York: Dell,
1977), p. 1. All further references will be to this edition and will be cited parenthetically in the text.

2. *Waiting for the Party: The Life of Frances Hodgson Burnett 1849–1924* (New
York: Charles Scribner's Sons, 1974), p. 221.

3. *Mrs. Ewing, Mrs. Molesworth, and Mrs. Hodgson Burnett* (London: Arthur
Barker, 1950), p. 88. Although Laski sees Mary and Colin as original, she also places
them in the tradition of Charlotte Yonge's Ethel May, the heroine of *The Daisy Chain*
(1856).

4. Madelon S. Gohlke, in "Re-reading *The Secret Garden*," *College English,* 41 (1980), 894–902, insists that *The Secret Garden* withstands the test of adult rereading. On subjecting the book to the same test, however, I find that only the part I remember most vividly from childhood—that in which Mary predominates—meets my adult criteria.

5. When the cholera epidemic strikes the Lennox compound, Mary is the only one who neither flees nor dies. In the midst of death and destruction she remains calm and self-possessed, partly out of ignorance, of course, but largely out of toughness. Burnett tells us that "as she was a self-absorbed child she gave her entire thought to herself" (p. 8). It is this self-absorption that insulates her from fear during the epidemic and from desolation on learning of her parents' death.

6. Clarissa M. Rowland, in "Bungalows and Bazaars: India in Victorian Children's Fiction," *Children's Literature,* 2 (1973), identifies the connection between naughtiness and unhappiness as a theme of Victorian children's fiction set in India (p. 194).

7. In "Little Girls without Their Curls," pp. 14–31, U. C. Knoepflmacher argues that the guise of fantasy enables Juliana Ewing, in "Amelia and the Dwarfs," and Burnett herself, in "Behind the White Brick," to indulge more fully a wish for female aggression in defiance of Victorian taboos than is possible in a realistic fiction such as *The Secret Garden.* I would argue, however, that because less "anarchic," Mary's aggressiveness or contrariness, at least that which she retains until Colin comes to dominate the book, has more social value than that of Amelia or Jem/Baby and thus her "domestication" represents a loss rather than a gain.

8. Fred Inglis, *The Promise of Happiness: Value and Meaning in Children's Fiction* (Cambridge: At the University Press, 1981), p. 112.

9. Inglis, in his chapter on sex roles in children's fiction, praises Burnett for endowing her heroines with the intelligence and independence of Elizabeth Bennet (ibid., p. 165), but this seems true of Mary only in the first two-thirds of the story.

10. Another interesting topic for exploration would be Burnett's use of the Brontë novels in her children's fiction. The Yorkshire setting of *The Secret Garden,* of course, resembles that of *Jane Eyre* and *Wuthering Heights,* but Mary has elements of Jane Eyre and both Catherines, Dickon resembles a more benign little Heathcliff, and Colin seems a blend of Rochester, Linton Heathcliff, and Hareton Earnshaw. As Inglis says, "The influence of the Brontës is felt on every page" (ibid., p. 112).

11. To a cousin she wrote: "It will perhaps seem almost incredible to you as it does to others when I tell you that he never did find out. He was ill nine months but I never allowed him to know that I was *really* anxious about him. I never let him know he had consumption or that he was in danger." Quoted in Vivian Burnett, *The Romantick Lady* (New York: Scribner's, 1930), pp. 211–12.

12. Ibid., p. 214.

13. Ibid., p. 212.

14. Ibid., pp. 222–23.

15. Inglis, p. 113.

Little Girls without Their Curls: Female Aggression in Victorian Children's Literature

U. C. Knoepflmacher

The expression of anger by female writers has become of increasing interest to literary critics. We are now far more aware of the rich implications—cultural, biographical, artistic—that this subject entails, especially for our understanding of nineteenth-century women writers who faced simultaneously new freedoms and new restraints on their creativity. Still, when, in *The Madwoman in the Attic,* Gilbert and Gubar insist on separating the "decorous and ladylike facade" of Jane Austen or Maria Edgeworth from the more overt (and hence somehow more valued) depiction of aggressive impulses by those who " 'fell' into the gothic/Satanic mode,"[1] even the most comprehensive discussion of the subject remains slightly distorted.

The decorous and lady-like women who dominated the field of Victorian children's literature—such as Mrs. Gatty, Mrs. Ewing, Mrs. Molesworth, Jean Ingelow, Frances Hodgson Burnett, and others—were hardly gothic Satanists. As gentlewomen writing for middle-class juveniles, they, even more than an Austen or an Edgeworth, needed to maintain restraint and decorum. Paradoxically, the mode of fantasy also freed the same aggressive impulses that their fictions ostensibly tried to domesticate. Especially after 1865, with the playful anarchy of Lewis Carroll's *Alice's Adventures in Wonderland* before them as a foil as well as a model, women writers began to portray little girls who were allowed to express hostility without the curbs on female rebelliousness that had been placed earlier, in children's literature as well as in adult fiction.[2] The fairy-tale realms depicted in Juliana Horatia Ewing's "Amelia and the Dwarfs" (1870), in Burnett's *The Secret Garden* (1911), and in Burnett's earlier, less well-known, but delightful fantasy, "Behind the White Brick" (1874), thus serve a double purpose. The surreal setting is enlisted, on the one hand, to mute the hostile behavior of girls on the road to socialization and maturity; on the other hand, however, it permits their creators to turn their own satiric energies against the deficiencies or complacencies of a society that frowned on expressions of female anger.

In the ensuing discussion I shall first look at "Amelia and the Dwarfs" and at the Irish folktale "Wee Meg Barnileg and the Fairies," on which Ewing based her story of an Alice-like descent into a claustrophobic underground. I shall then proceed to *The Secret Garden* and, after briefly noting the treatment of Mary Lennox, return to Burnett's "Behind the White Brick," which responds to *Through the Looking-Glass* just as Ewing's story had indirectly responded to *Alice's Adventures in Wonderland*. Like Jean Ingelow, who countered Alice in *Mopsa the Fairy* (1869), and Madeleine L'Engle, who still evokes Carroll in *A Wrinkle in Time* (1962), Ewing and Burnett follow—yet also subvert—their male predecessor by transporting their intemperate heroines into realms of open aggression.

I

Ewing's Amelia, repeatedly called "a very observing child,"[3] will be humiliated by underground creatures who correspond to her own anarchic unconscious, in a way similar to Carroll's "curious" Alice. As Nina Auerbach has shown, the aggression that Alice meets in Wonderland mirrors her own repressed anarchism, an anarchism suggested by her repeated identification with the predatory cat Dinah, who kills bats and mice and birds;[4] it is Alice's long-suppressed outburst of anger at her primary female rival, the Queen of Hearts, that finally dissolves her dream and returns her to an unquestioning world of teacups and governesses. But if Carroll relies on mere inference to suggest the aggressive behavior, above ground, of a superficially dutiful Victorian little girl, Ewing devotes the first half of her tale to a careful documentation of Amelia's conduct as an aggressive little monster who deftly tyrannizes and exploits stupidly impotent Victorian adults. Indeed, it is Ewing's ability to identify with the naughty Amelia and, moreover, to make her readers empathize with this "very observing" child that gives the story its initial force. Whereas Carroll remains ambivalent about the girl-child he both worships and wants to humiliate, the author of "Amelia and the Dwarfs" apparently recognizes her own irrepressible self in the resourceful, manipulative creature who makes adults her playthings. The wittiest of Mrs. Margaret Gatty's ten children, an inveterate parodist who mocked both her clergyman father and her earnest, naturalist mother in some of her youthful productions, Julie Gatty chose to marry Major Ewing because he was "very clever" and "*so* unlike Trollope's heroes . . . and all the prigs and reprobates, and fidgets, and selfish unchivalrous used-up growling Britons one meets in books of the period."[5] Somehow she managed to keep her satirical tendencies under control when she established herself as the chief contributor to her mother's *Aunt Judy's Magazine.*

Ewing subtly criticized her own class by elevating Wee Meg Barnileg, the farmer's daughter in the Scottish folktale, into the bourgeois yet antibourgeois Amelia of "Amelia and the Dwarfs." In expanding both the plot of "Wee Meg" and the character of its protagonist, she not only depicted the domestication of an unruly *enfant terrible,* but also managed, in the process, to pour some of Meg-Amelia's anarchic powers onto priggish and over-civilized Victorian adults incapable of repressing the child's hostility. What is more important, Ewing validates that hostility by blaming Amelia's bland and uncomprehending parents for their permissiveness. Ostensibly as interested in presenting Amelia's moral reformation as the folktale had been, she nonetheless taps the very aggression that story attempts to exorcise.

Ewing begins her tale by insisting that it has been transmitted by a line of female storytellers—it is her "godmother's grandmother," whose own grandmother had actually seen a fairy "rade" in the North, who is credited at the outset for the imaginative vitality of "this pleasant tale, with a good moral" (p. 159). Essentially amoral, Amelia herself possesses that imaginativeness and vitality in superabundance. The little girl thus is immediately distinguished from her parents:

> They were an easy-going, good-humored couple; "rather soft,"
> my godmother said, but she was apt to think anybody soft who
> came from the southern shires, as these people did. Amelia,

who had been born farther north, was by no means so. She had a strong, resolute will, and a clever head of her own, though she was but a child. She had a way of her own too, and had it very completely. Perhaps because she was an only child, or perhaps because they were so easy-going, her parents spoiled her. [pp. 159–60]

In "Wee Meg Barnileg and the Fairies," where the parents are also called "a soft good-natured pair,"[6] neither they nor Meg are strongly individualized. In "Amelia and the Dwarfs," however, the softness of the couple is soon exposed as a soft-headedness that Amelia, like the narrator herself, deliciously exploits.

When Amelia embarrasses her mother in a home they are visiting by noting, bluntly and unsparingly, that an ottoman is really just "a box covered with chintz" or an old china basin has really been "broken and mended," her mamma can at best mutter "reprovingly, 'My *dear* Amelia.' " Her maternal ineptness is evident from the limited range of remonstrances:

Sometimes the good lady said, "You *must* not." Sometimes she tried—"You must *not*." When both these failed, and Amelia was balancing the china bowl on her finger ends, her mamma would get flurried, and when Amelia flurried her, she always rolled her r's, and emphasized her words, so that it sounded thus:

"My dear-r-r-r Ramelia! You MUST NOT."

At which Amelia would not so much as look around, till perhaps the bowl slipped from her fingers, and was smashed into unmendable fragments. Then her mamma would exclaim, "Oh, dear-r-r-r, oh dear-r-r-r Ramelia!" and the lady of the house would try to look as if it did not matter, and when Amelia and her mother departed, would pick up the bits, and pour out her complaints to her lady friends, most of whom had suffered many such damages at the hands of this "very observing child." [p. 161]

Nor is Amelia's mother any more effective in checking her irrepressible daughter when entertaining friends at her own home.

For Amelia now proves to be as skillful in breaking polite conversations as in destroying Victorian gimcrackery:

> She would take up her position near some one, generally the person most deeply engaged in conversation, and either lean heavily against him or her, or climb on to his or her knees, without being invited. She would break in upon the most interesting discussions with her own little childish affairs, in the following style—
>
> "I've been out to-day. I walked to the town. I jumped across three brooks. Can you jump? Papa gave me six-pence to-day. I am saving up my money to be rich. You may cut me an orange; no, I'll take it to Mr. Brown, he peels it with a spoon and turns the skin back. Mr. Brown! Mr. Brown! Don't talk to mamma, but peel me an orange, please. Mr. Brown! I'm playing with your finger-glass."
>
> And when the finger-glass full of cold water had been upset on to Mr. Brown's shirt-front, Amelia's mamma would cry— "Oh dear, oh dear-r Ramelia!" and carry her off with the ladies to the drawing room. [p. 162]

It is in the drawing room, however, that Amelia exhibits her greatest powers of disruption. She tramples on the hems of ladies' gowns, breaks a bracelet by pretending not to understand the working of a clasp, and even exercises her talents as a blackmailer on discovering younger women whispering to each other in a "quiet corner."

> The observing child was sure to spy them, and run on to them, crushing their flowers and ribbons, and crying—"You two want to talk secrets, I know. I can hear what you say. I'm going to listen, I am. And I shall tell, too." When perhaps a knock at the door announced the nurse to take Miss Amelia to bed, and spread a general rapture of relief. [pp. 162–63]

Ewing relishes Amelia's destructive tactics, for they allow her to expose the codes of passivity maintained by genteel Victorians, forced to stifle their natural desire to retaliate. She mocks these self-shackling adults for being "so very well-bred and amiable, that they never spoke their minds to either the mother or the daughter about what they endured from the latter's rudeness, willfulness, and powers of destruction" (p. 163). Yet Amelia soon meets an antagonist wholly unbound by such codes of civility:

> At last one day Amelia was tormenting a snow-white bull-dog (who was certainly as well-bred and amiable as any living creature in the kingdom), and she did not see that even his patience was becoming worn out. His pink nose became crimson with increased irritation, his upper lip twitched over his teeth, behind which he was rolling as many warning Rs as Amelia's mother herself. She finally held out a bun towards him, and just as he was about to take it, she snatched it away and kicked him instead. This fairly exasperated the bull-dog, and as Amelia would not let him bite the bun, he bit Amelia's leg. [pp. 163–64]

The bulldog's response is natural, direct, and eminently healthy. When a doctor examines Amelia, whose wound is not at all deep, he finds her kissing the dog, who, far "from looking mad, . . . looked a great deal more sensible than anybody in the house." Least sensible, of course, is Amelia's mother, who regards the dog's justified expression of anger—which she has never allowed herself to express—as a sure sign of rabies. But her befuddled outburst only exposes her own unacknowledged resentment of the child whom she, as a Victorian lady, is not allowed to bite. She considers shooting the bulldog "for fear he should go mad," wants to cauterize Amelia's wound for fear her daughter should go mad, yet shies away from applying chloroform for fear that it might kill the child. On articulating these wishes and fears, the agitated "poor lady" unwittingly reveals her forcibly repressed hostility. She garbles her intended meaning when she says, "Whether we shoot Amelia and burn the bull-dog—at least I mean shoot the bull-dog and burn Amelia with a red-hot poker—or leave it alone; and whether Amelia or the bull-dog has chloroform or bears it without—it seems death or madness everyway!" (p. 164).[7]

Although the bulldog's salutary bite makes Amelia behave with "utmost propriety to animals" thereafter, she still continues (quite understandably) to plague her mother and to torment "her mother's friends as much as ever." She will meet her true match only when, in the story's second half, sadistic male fairies turn on her the aggression curbed by her family and her family's friends. Pinching male dwarfs, bellicose creatures who are unbound by and contemptuous of the "soft" Victorian drawing-room world above, nonetheless avenge the outrages that Amelia has committed in that world. They humiliate their captive below, while planting a hairy "stock" above as a substitute, which her mother and the physician, but not the sagacious bulldog, mistake for a sick Amelia. Still, though degraded by her jailers and particularly by a "smutty" old dwarf enamoured of her, Amelia once again relies on her wit and resourcefulness when she manages to flee her underground prison. She is aided in her escape by a fellow captive, an old woman who teaches Amelia how to outwit the dwarfs, especialy the "grotesque and grimy old dwarf" who finds her so sexually attractive. The old woman (notably absent in the original folktale) acts both as analogue and as foil to Amelia's undiscerning mother. Confined and forced into a passive role, she can teach Amelia how to avoid her own fate by pretending to accommodate the male dwarfs while manipulating these aggressive creatures every bit as "cunningly" as she had handled the soft and passive Victorian adults in the world of surfaces above.

Once back in that world, Amelia herself opts for softness. But her new acquiescence stems from a fuller awareness of her strengths, strengths she has tested, channeled, and mastered. Her humiliating captivity and the old woman's example have produced a voluntary self-suppression rather than a lapse into her mother's weakness and passivity. Amelia relinquishes her aggression, just as the bulldog relinquishes the "incomprehensible fury" he had shown during her absence. She embraces her still-uncomprehending mother, who welcomes, yet has played no part in, Amelia's socialization. And, "in spite of the past, [she] grew up good and gentle, unselfish, and considerate for others." Even Amelia's adult acquaintances forget their former animosity: "She became so popular . . . that they said—'We will no longer call her Amelia, for it was a name we learned to dislike, but we will call her Amy, that is to say, "Beloved" ' " (p. 194).

Ewing thus completes the transformation of a little girl–anarchist into an accepted member of society. Superficially, "Amelia and the Dwarfs" would seem to endorse the "decorous and ladylike facade" that, in "adult" fictions of the nineteenth century, is imposed on an Emma Woodhouse or a Gwendolen Harleth, Amelia's fellow egotists. But Ewing is sure to show that Amelia's metamorphosis into "Amy" is above all an act of self-restraint. It is the bulldog and not her mother, confused and befuddled to the end, to whom Amelia can confide her true story. The adults in the drawing-room remain soft and ridiculous; both as child and as a grownup, Amelia remains their superior. She is chastened by her underground experiences rather than forced to submit to a Mr. Knightley or Daniel Deronda. Like her creator, then, Amelia blunts her considerable satirical energies and keeps them in reserve. To her Victorian readers, Mrs. Juliana Horatia Ewing, a pious moralist, must also have seemed an "Amy" or "Well-Beloved." But as "Amelia and the Dwarfs" so convincingly shows, Ewing could also probe far beneath the conventional facades she upheld. Beneath her social self lurked the strong anarchic imagination so neatly channeled in her retelling of an old Irish folktale.

II

Frances Hodgson Burnett's strengths were far less concealed than those of Juliana Ewing. While Ewing's invalid condition forced her to live apart, during her last years, from her dashing military husband, Burnett twice divorced the weak men she first attracted and then repelled. In March 1898, after she had instituted divorce proceedings against her first husband, Dr. Swan Burnett, the *New York Herald* rather cruelly contrasted her forceful person to the husband whose effeminate first name she had always hated: "Mrs. Burnett is a woman of pleasing appearance and much personal magnetism, while her husband is of less than ordinary stature and a cripple."[8]

The Secret Garden, written some years after Burnett's separation from her second husband—the young secretary she had married apparently as surrogate for an older son who had died of consumption—ends on an all-masculine note. Archibald Craven, the hunchback master of Misselthwaite Manor, a neurotic weakling, is amazed to discover that his once-deformed son now walks "as strongly and steadily as any boy in Yorkshire—Master Colin!"[9] Burnett, whom a contemporary described as "a masculine, matter-of-fact person," was clearly fascinated by the strong male identity attained by Colin in his dead mother's magical garden. Describing her own practices as a gardener, Burnett confessed, "I should always have preferred to have been at least two strong men in one. . . . I love to dig. I love to kneel down on the grass at the edge of the flower bed and pull out the weeds fiercely. . . . I love to fight with those who can spring up again almost in a night and taunt me. I tear them up by the roots again and again, and when at last . . . it seems as if I had beaten them for a time at least, I go away feeling like an army with banners."[10]

Yet if *The Secret Garden* ends as the story of Colin's mastery, a weak boy's recovery from an imaginary curvature of the spine, the book begins—and usually is remembered—as the story of the tough and indestructible Mary Lennox, a garden-builder from the very start. Indeed, the book was originally to be called *Mistress Mary.* And, though its opening sentence describes Mary as "the most disagreeable-looking child ever seen," (p. 1), it soon becomes evident that this asocial creature, uninterested "in anyone but herself" (p. 31), engages our sympathies even more than Amelia did. Like Amelia, who tyrannizes her governess, Mary berates her Indian ayah as "Pig! Daughter of pigs!" (p. 3). Although Burnett returns the compliment by calling Mary as "selfish a little pig as ever lived" (p. 2), she shows us that Mary's aggressiveness is her sole defense against the deprivations she has suffered by being "kept out of the way" (p. 2), by her indifferent parents. Unlike the excessively indulged Amelia, Mary is ignored by her flighty mother and her ill and absent father. She is not allowed to hate her parents openly. Yet her anger at the absent ayah, who, unbeknownst to her, has died of the plague, masks her real anger at parents who also soon will die in the same epidemic. To compensate for her desolation, she makes a pretend flowerbed by sticking "big scarlet hibiscus blossoms into little heaps of earth, all the time growing more and more angry" (p. 3).

Mary's anger proves emotionally therapeutic. It is a sign of her hardiness. While the adults around her perish, she survives. The abandoned child fearlessly stares "at a little snake gliding along and watching her with eyes like jewels" (p. 6). Deprivation has made her as tough as it has made her cousin Colin soft, we soon discover. Transported from Kipling's India to Brontë's Yorkshire, Mary will prove to be as hardy as a Mowgli or a Jane Eyre. And when, like Jane, she hears mysterious night-cries in the gothic manor house, she bravely ventures into the hidden chamber, to find not a raving Bertha Mason, the madwoman in the attic, but a whimpering, effeminate little boy, her weaker cousin and alter ego. Colin, to be sure, is also a tyrant, "a young *Rajah*." Like the aggressive Amelia who terrorizes adults, the screaming boy intimidates Mrs. Medlock the housekeeper, Martha the servant, Dr. Craven his physician, and his attendant nurse.

Knowing Mary's own aggressive powers, however, these adults enlist her to subdue the hysterical boy. Her hostility now serves a purpose. Unused to "any one's tempers but her own," Mary decides to frighten Colin as "he was frightening her" (p. 174). She stamps her foot and runs along the corridor, feeling "quite wicked" by the time she reaches Colin's door. She slaps it open and runs to the four-poster bed (p. 175):

"You stop!" she almost shouted. "You stop! I hate you! Everybody hates you! I wish everybody would run out of the house and let you scream yourself to death! You *will* scream yourself to death in a minute, and I wish you would!"

A nice sympathetic child could neither have thought nor said such things, but it just happened that the shock of hearing them was the best possible thing for this hysterical boy whom no one had ever dared to restrain or contradict. . . .

"If you scream another scream," she said, "I'll scream too—
and I can scream louder than you can and I'll frighten you, I'll
frighten you."

He actually had stopped screaming because she had startled
him so. The scream which had been coming almost choked
him. The tears were streaming down his face and he shook all
over.

"I can't stop!" he gasped and sobbed. "I can't—I can't."

"You can!" shouted Mary. "Half that ails you is hysterics
and temper—just hysterics—hysterics—hysterics!" and she
stamped each time she said it. [pp. 175–76]

Colin protests that he has felt a lump on his back; he is sure he is
to become a hunchback like his father and then, like his mother,
die. But Mary fiercely contradicts him. She orders the startled
nurse to bare the boy's back and then clinically inspects it. "There's
not a lump as big as a pin," she triumphantly declares, "except
backbone lumps, and you can only feel them because you're thin.
I've got backbone lumps myself, and they used to stick out as much
as yours do, until I began to get fatter" (p. 177). Colin is shocked
into submission by the obstinacy of this "angry unsympathetic little
girl" (p. 178). The adults that he had cowed are surprised—yet
highly pleased—by her outburst.

Burnett, too, obviously relishes Mary's "savage" behavior. The
relentless ferocity with which the little girl sets out to assure Colin
that the growth on Colin's back is imaginary seems identical to the
determined pulling of weeds that spring up at night to taunt and
choke the healthy, daylight growth of unencumbered plants.
Burnett implies that growth, whether of plants or of little girls,
involves both healthy anger and healthy nurturance. Mary can
threaten Colin with hatred, the removal of love, but she also can
and does soothe him by singing a lullaby. She soon transports the
boy to the secret garden. There, fattened by the maternal Mrs.
Sowerby, as much an ally as is the old woman in "Amelia and the
Dwarfs," he gradually attains the vitality that Mary the garden-
builder has all along possessed.

In the last third of the book Burnett cedes the garden to her little

Adam. The creator of Little Lord Fauntleroy suddenly becomes more interested in Colin's silly push-ups and acts of physical prowess than in Mary's instinctual need to actualize the imaginary gardens she had built in India. Mistress Mary, the book's seeming protagonist, slips into an increasingly subsidiary role. The garden becomes the boy's preserve, the place where his fragile mother (Mary's paternal aunt) had sustained her fatal injury. It is his to reclaim. He is the future master of Misselthwaite; he is a male. Mary's sudden subordination, though sanctioned by the plot, nevertheless remains more disturbing than Amelia's conversion into "Amy," the beloved. Her displacement, to be sure, seems more offensive to the adult than to the juvenile reader. Children, especially girls, who have the story read to them are not so perturbed, for Burnett provides them with some means whereby they can disregard, even screen out, the importance she accords to Colin's vigorous eugenic exercises.[11]

Mary's displacement by Colin may well have its roots in Frances Hodgson Burnett's need to resort to compensatory fantasies: as Elizabeth Keyser notes, the boy Mary nurses back to health is clearly a wishful embodiment of Burnett's son Lionel, for whose death she blamed herself, as well as of the weak mates who had depended on her and of the dead father whose place as the family's breadwinner she had so early had to assume. But whatever relation Colin's dominance bears to Burnett's split between the "masculine" and feminine elements she so uneasily tried to balance in her own gender-divided personality, it is noteworthy that she had already handled the figure of the aggressive little girl without relying on such male deflections in "Behind the White Brick," written more than thirty years earlier. It is significant, too, that this story, unlike the more realistic *Secret Garden,* should have been cast as a Victorian dream-fantasy like "Amelia and the Dwarfs." In fact, if Ewing's 1870 tale was, among other things, a counter-fantasy to Carroll's *Alice's Adventures in Wonderland* (1865), Burnett's 1874 story about a little girl transported to the world behind the brick wall of a chimney can be read as an extension of *Through the Looking-Glass* (1870).

In *Through the Looking-Glass,* Carroll insists on a continuity between life and dream, between Alice's bossy behavior toward the black kitten and her determination to be crowned queen of the chess-board; in Burnett's "Behind the White Brick," a dream played out behind the square of "a white brick among the black ones"[12] allows an imaginative little girl to work out the hostilities she felt before falling asleep. Jemima, whose mother always calls her "Jem" or "Mimi" but whose aunt delights in calling her by her full "ugly name," suffers further affronts from the intemperate Aunt Hetty: "It was a dreadful day to Jem. Her mother was not home, and would not be until night. She had been called away unexpectedly, and had been obliged to leave Jem and the baby to Aunt Hetty's mercies" (p. 142). Ordered to wash dishes and pick fruit and attend to her baby sister, Jem finally relaxes by turning to a book, "a certain delightful story book, about a little girl whose name was Flora" (p. 142). Yet Aunt Hetty erupts into this secret garden spot of Jem's imagination. Rushing into the room, she catches her foot on the matting, strikes her elbow against a chair, and, full of anger, flies at Jem. Seeing the book, Aunt Hetty throws it into the fireplace, where the blaze catches it at once. The provoked Jem, too, becomes ablaze. "You are a wicked woman!" she shouts, "in a dreadful passion" (p. 143). In retaliation, Aunt Hetty boxes her ears, pushes her back on a footstool, and stalks out of the room. The sobbing Jem soon cries herself to sleep. Her ensuing dream allows her to confront the unresolved anger of the female child against the female adult.

Jem follows some falling soot into the chimney and finds, behind the white brick, a fully restored Flora and her pastoral, story-book world of "delightful things"—"books and flowers and playthings and pictures, and in one corner a great cage full of love-birds" (p. 146). Flora, looking exactly as she looked in the burned book ("with lovely, soft, flowing hair, and a little fringe on her pretty round forehead, crowned with a circlet of daisies"), laughingly welcomes Jem into this sanctuary. But the dreamworld Jem now explores does not harbor only the quintessential version of "soft" Victorian femininity. It also allows the child to replay the antagonistic feelings she has experienced. If Flora symbolizes a sentimentalized feminine veneer shattered by Aunt Hetty's and Jem's sharp anger, the agent for that anger now becomes a figure far more downtrodden than Jem—her forgotten baby sister, whose depiction turns out to be totally devoid of the sentimentality associated with Victorian baby-worship.

After entering a rose-colored room ("funny as well as pretty"), Jem hears a "shrill little voice" (Aunt Hetty's voice was also described as having a "sharp ring"). She no sooner observes the voice to be "funny" than she startles to discover that it emanates from a most militant Baby:

> "Why," exclaimed Jem, beginning to feel frightened. "I left you fast asleep in your crib."
>
> "Did you?" said Baby, somewhat scornfully. "That's just the way with you grown-up people. You think you know everything, and yet you haven't discretion enough to know when a pin is sticking into one. You'd know soon enough if you had one sticking into your own back."
>
> "But I'm not grown up," stammered Jem; "and when you are at home you can neither walk nor talk. You're not six months' old."
>
> "Well, miss," retorted Baby, whose wrongs seemed to have soured her disposition somewhat, "you have no need to throw that in my teeth; you were not six months old, either, when you were my age."
>
> Jem could not help laughing.
>
> "You haven't got any teeth," she said.
>
> "Haven't I?" said Baby, and she displayed two beautiful rows with some haughtiness of manner. "When I am up here," she said, "I am supplied with the modern conveniences, and that's why I never complain." [pp. 146–47]

Yet Baby soon lists complaints, which, unlike Colin's in *The Secret Garden*, are hardly imaginary. She is more impotent than Jem and hence, she implies, has a far greater justification to be angry than her older sister does: "How would you like to have to sit and stare at things you wanted, and not to be able to reach them, or, if you did reach them, have them fall out of your hand, and roll away in the most unfeeling manner? And then be scolded and called 'cross.' It's no wonder we are bald. You'd be bald yourself" (p. 148).

Jem's most conciliatory, Flora-like manners cannot placate this little termagant. Soon, however, Baby is diverted by two other opponents. The first turns out to be a Mr. S. C., who identifies himself as the toymaker "S. Claus, Esquire, of Chimneyland." Although Jem is attracted to this rather feminized, very tiny, "rosy" gentleman, Baby decides to be offended when he patronizingly calls her "Tootsicums." Her peevish overreaction enacts Jem's more concealed resentment at being called "Jemima" by her aunt:

> Baby's manner became very acid indeed.
> "I shouldn't have thought you would have said that, Mr. Claus," she remarked. "I can't help myself down below, but I generally have my rights respected up here. I should like to know what sane godfather or godmother would give one the name of 'Tootsicums' in one's baptism. They are bad enough, I must say; but I never heard of any of them calling a person 'Tootsicums.' " [pp. 150–51]

Mr. S. C. dismisses Baby's pugnaciousness goodhumoredly. He also allows that her older sister is "a nice child, though a trifle peppery" (p. 151).

But a second opponent, even tinier, does not shy away from a fight. When a toyshop doll haughtily criticizes one of her sisters for saying "Mamma" and contends that dolls should not demean themselves by "talking to human beings" at all, Baby pounces on her, hoping to assert her seniority:

> "You know a great deal, considering you are only just finished," snapped Baby, who really was a Tartar.
> "I was FINISHED," retorted the doll. "I did not begin life as a baby!" very scornfully.
> "Pooh!" said Baby. "We improve as we get older."
> "I hope so, indeed," answered the doll. "There is plenty of room for improvement." And she walked away in great state. [pp. 154–55]

Even if the fight between the doll and Baby reenacts Jem's skirmish with Aunt Hetty, Jem still has to confront a more direct emblem of her hostilities. Taken to a Wish Room by Baby, she sees next to the physical incarnations of her kinder wishes one that causes her a most "dreadful pang of remorse." Underneath a glass shade, crouching like a stuffed animal or a preserved foetus, sits "Aunt Hetty, with her mouth stitched up so that she could not speak a word, and beneath the stand was a label bearing these words, in large black letters—'I wish Aunt Hetty's mouth was sewed up. Jem.'"

Appalled by this visible token of secret hatred, aware that "it must have hurt" her aunt, Jem wishes to unwish her wish. When the stitches disappear and Aunt Hetty looks "herself again, and even smiling" (p. 157), Jem becomes "grateful beyond measure, but Baby seemed to consider her weak minded" (p. 158). Unforgiving to the end, Baby (and that half of Burnett which remains just as implacable) contends that it served Aunt Hetty right to be thus punished.

But Jem is ready to part company with Baby. When Baby calls their mother "mean" for wishing that she turn into "a better tempered baby," Jem has had enough. She defends her mother: "'It wasn't mean,' she said. 'She couldn't help it. You know you are a cross baby—everybody says so.'" By identifying with her mother and distancing herself from Baby, who persists in her anger, Jem has signified her readiness to "fall awake." And when she does awake, with a new storybook on her lap to replace the burned one,[13] her mother stands by; "Miss Baby" is apart, crying in her crib as usual. As she kisses the startled dreamer, Jem's mother good-naturedly insists on her primacy: "Don't I look as if I was real?" (p. 160).

Burnett chooses to end on this note of domestic harmony and psychic reintegration. Still, the fusion of mother and daughter significantly differs from the ending of Ewing's "Amelia and the Dwarfs." The Amelia who turns into a docile Amy must struggle far more than the Jemima who can easily slip back into that half of her personality that had always been her mother's true Jem. Amelia outwits sadistic dwarfs in a dark netherworld she barely manages to escape; Jem merely chooses her better half in the female realm behind the white-brick patch. Unlike Amelia, she has been divided from the very start, surprised by the anger of her self-assertion. Kindled by Aunt Hetty's own anger and enacted by the regressive Baby and Doll, her aggression has all along been in conflict with her compliant tendencies. These tendencies are embodied by her absent, but returned mother; by the burned, but resurrected Flora; and, finally, by the feminized dollmaker S. Claus, a figure she had skeptically banished yet reinstated, because of her need to believe in a system that rewards good girls who nurse crippled dolls. The hardier Amelia tests herself against a hierarchy of opponents, from Mr. Brown to the bulldog to the dwarfs, only to defer, at the end, to the ineffectual mother at the very bottom rung of that ladder. Jem, on the other hand, merely needs to quell the Baby-within. Eager for a female model, she can exorcise Aunt Hetty and embrace her understanding mother.

"Amelia and the Dwarfs" and "Behind the White Brick" are alike, however, in the brilliant satirical energies they unleash. These energies are made possible by the indulged wish of female aggression in defiance of Victorian taboos. Both stories preserve and present this wish more fully than the later *Secret Garden*: Amelia's absolute powers over fumbling adults and Baby's display of her teeth in Chimneyland allow free play to the very anarchy that each work tries to domesticate. It is fantasy—a fantasy that lies in a borderland between the masochistic and the sadistic—that achieves what concessions to realism cannot attain. The sudden potency accorded to a female baby whose back has been pricked by real pins remains more pleasurable as a compensatory fantasy than Master Colin's removal of his imaginary lumps—at Mistress Mary's expense.

Notes

1. Sandra M. Gilbert and Susan Gubar, *The Madwoman in the Attic: The Woman Writer and the Nineteenth-Century Literary Imagination* (New Haven and London: Yale University Press, 1979), p. 101.

2. Charlotte Brontë may depict a Jane Eyre who bloodies the nose of John Reed and George Eliot may depict the demonism of a Maggie Tulliver who hammers nails

into the head of her fetish doll, but when these girls become women, it is a providential fire or a catastrophic flood that must be invoked as an agent of retribution.

3. Juliana Horatia Ewing, *The Brownies and Other Tales* (New York: H. M. Caldwell Company, n.d.), p. 160. Future references to "Amelia and the Dwarfs" are to this edition and are cited parenthetically in the text.

4. Nina Auerbach, "Alice and Wonderland: A Curious Child," *Victorian Studies,* 18 (1973), 31–47.

5. Quoted in Christabel Maxwell, *Mrs. Gatty and Mrs. Ewing* (London: Constable, 1949), pp. 161, 162.

6. Ruth Sawyer, ed., *The Way of the Story-Teller* (New York: Viking, 1962). p. 205.

7. The fear of chloroform displayed by Amelia's mother helps to distinguish her from Mrs. Margaret Gatty, Mrs. Ewing's mother, who had it administered to herself to set an example for the ignorant.

8. Quoted in Ann Thwaite, *Waiting for the Party: The Life of Frances Hodgson Burnett* (New York: Charles Scribner's Sons, 1974), p. 177.

9. *The Secret Garden* (1911; rpt. New York: Dell, 1977), p. 298. Future references to this edition are cited parenthetically in the text.

10. Quoted in Thwaite, p. 183. The citation is from Burnett's posthumously published *In the Garden*.

11. As Elizabeth Keyser rightly notes in her own contribution to this issue ("'Quite Contrary': Frances Hodgson Burnett's *The Secret Garden*,"), Colin's displacement of Mary and Dickon (and Ben Weatherstaff) resembles the shift that occurs in *Huckleberry Finn* when Tom Sawyer displaces Huck and Jim, who have been the mainstay of our interest and sympathy. If it is not necessarily true, as Keyser suggests, that Twain's book leaves us "with its true hero" intact (p. 9), there is no doubt that he makes us value the "imagination" that bonds Huck to Jim (and to the reader) far above Tom's game-playing "fancy." Yet unlike Twain, her great admirer and would-be collaborator on a project that never was realized, Burnett fully endorses the Tomlike game-playing of her Colin. Why, then, do child-readers remain unoffended by the book's concluding third? The responses of two of my students, both of whom first read *The Secret Garden* at the age of eight, strongly support Keyser's own recollections (pp. 2–3). Writes one: "It was the garden I pictured and Dickon; Colin did not interest me." The other one admits: "I detested Colin and strongly identified with Mary, but I simply must not have paid much attention to Colin after the scene in which Mary shouts that he would scream himself to death." By successfully screening out discordancies that an adult reader cannot as easily dismiss, the child reader can always be more selective.

12. *Little Saint Elizabeth and Other Stories* (London: Frederick Warne & Co., [1890]), p. 143. Future references to "Behind the White Brick" are cited parenthetically in the text.

13. The "beautiful scarlet and gold book" Jem finds is clearly her mother's "real" present, but it is emblematic, too, of the gift of maturity she has wrested from Chimneyland.

Alice *and the Reviewers*

Elizabeth A. Cripps

Opposite the entry in his diary for 2 October 1864, Lewis Carroll with characteristic orderliness listed the press notices of *Alice's Adventures in Wonderland:*

1865		
Reader...........................	Nov.	12
Press	Nov.	25
Guardian..........................	Dec.	13
Publisher's Circular.................	Dec.	8
Atheneum.........................	Dec.	16
Illustrated London News	Dec.	16
Ilustrated Times	Dec.	16
Pall Mall Gazette...................	Dec.	23
Spectator..........................	Dec.	23
Times	Dec.	26
London Review.....................	Dec.	23
Star		
Christmas Bookseller	Dec.	25

Monthly Packet....................	Jan.	1/66
John Bull..........................	Jan.	20
Literary Churchman.................	May	5
Sunderland Herald..................	May	25
Aunt Judy's Magazine...............	June	1
Contemporary Review (allusion)	Oct.	1

As one would expect, the list has proved to be fairly accurate and complete. There is one small slip (the *Reader*'s review actually appeared on November 18) and there are certain omissions; in particular, there is no review later than October 1866. The disparaging review in the *Scotsman* of December 22, 1866, is therefore missing. We learn of it from the novelist Henry Kingsley, the

Newspaper Notices
of Alice's Adventures in Wonderland .

1865

Reader ——————— Nov. 12
Press ———————— Nov. 25
Guardian ——————— Dec. 13
Publisher's Circular ——— Dec. 8
Athenæum ——————— Dec. 16
Illustrated London News — Dec. 16
Illustrated Times ——— Dec. 16
Pall Mall. Gazette ——— Dec. 23
Spectator ——————— Dec. 23
Times ———————— Dec. 26
London Review ———— Dec. 23
Star ————————
Christmas Bookseller ——— Dec. 25
Monthly Packet ———— Jan. 1/66
John Bull ————— Jan. 20
Literary Churchman —— May 5
Sunderland Herald ——— May 25
Aunt Judy's Magazine — June 1.
Contemporary Review (allusion) —— Oct. 1

A page from Lewis Carroll's diary. Reproduced by permission of the British Library.

brother of Charles Kingsley, who was a friend of Carroll: "The literary ability of *The Scotsman* I really *cannot* rank high with regard to works of fiction and fancy: who could trust a paper which said that the letter-press of *Alice's Adventures* was pointless balderdash!"[1]

Alice was published in July 1865, but the first edition was withdrawn—dissatisfaction with the reproduction of the illustrations led to a reprint—and the earliest reviews are of the second edition, which appeared in November.[2] The delay was fortunate: the book caught the Christmas trade as a result.

Children's books were considered in Victorian periodicals either in general reviews such as "Current Literature" in the *Spectator* or as literature specifically for children in reviews such as "Books for the Young" in the *Illustrated London Times.* They were also included in those few magazines written especially for children, such as Mrs. Gatty's *Aunt Judy's Magazine.* Consequently *Alice* appeared with some strange companions: in the *Manchester Guardian* it was considered alongside Dante's "The Vision of Hell" and in the *Illustrated London News* alongside "The Works of the Ettrick Shepherd." During late November and throughout December the reviews, for example, "Gift Books of the Season" in the *Reader* or "Christmas Stories" in the *London Review,* naturally concentrated on seasonal books. As these review titles suggest, the appearance and presentation of the books were thought to be as important as the text to the reviewers. The *Reader*'s review commented almost exclusively on these aspects (page size, quality of illustration, gilt edging, cover design, and color). Some hundred books were considered, each receiving a few phrases, invariably of commendation. Watts's *Divine and Moral Songs* was described simply as "one of the most charming of Christmas presents" and the Religious Tract Society's *Our Life* was praised as "very nicely got up as to its richly gilt binding and type and toned paper, the prose and poetry well selected, and the illustrations happy and well executed." *Alice* received more generous attention than most—two sentences of comment: "From Messrs. Macmillan & Co. comes a glorious artistic treasure, a book to put on one's shelf as an antidote to a fit of the blues; "Alice's Adventures in Wonderland" by Lewis Carroll, with forty-two illustrations by John Tenniel, sure to be run after as one of the most popular works of its class."[3]

It is a feature of the reviews generally that as much space was devoted to praising Tenniel's work as to discussing the merits and demerits of the text. This is, of course, partly because of the "gift book" aspect of the Christmas reviews, and partly because of Tenniel's brilliant conception and execution of the *Alice* illustrations. But there is also a more prosaic fact to be taken into account: the reviewers, faced with a large number of volumes to comment on, had little time to become closely acquainted with the contents. Several reviewers indicated the size of the Christmas trade in children's gift books. The *Publisher's Circular* review "New Books" aludes to "the two hundred books for children which have been sent to us this year,"[4] and the *London Review's* "Christmas Stories" begins similarly: "With December there comes a rush of story-books. A heap of these ephemeral fictions lies before us. . . ."[5]

The last comment discloses another characteristic shared by Christmas books and often commented on in the reviews—their short lifespan. Books for the Christmas market were attractively produced ephemera, for the most part; that was the expected product and what quite a number of reviewers thought *Alice* to be: "This is a very elegant piece of fancy-work wrought by a clever brain for the amusement and even instruction of children. Externally and internally it is well-suited for the season at which children receive . . . all manner of gifts, amongst which books are not the least conspicuous."[6]

The features of "these ephemeral fictions" were anatomized in the *London Review*: "All the tales are written in what we may describe as a rather "rapid" style; all have a little humour, a little sentiment, a little loving-kindness, and the other usual ingredients of Christmas literature; and all are of proper length for indolent holiday reading."[7]

Only a minority of the periodicals—the *Athenaeum,* the *London Review, Aunt Judy's Magazine*—attempted much by way of detailed evaluative comment, and even then the review articles were slight in comparison with the often massive considerations of contempo-

rary adult fiction. In view of this general situation it should come as
no surprise that *Alice* was introduced to the public without very
much éclat and received much the same share of attention as the
rest.

I wish next to consider the reviewers' comments in some detail,
grouping them under the bland or unnoticing, the genuinely
perceptive, and the hostile or dismissive.[8]

In at least a third of the reviews listed, *Alice* was received with no
more than mild acceptance as an amusing piece of nonsense. The
Times notice is typical and I quote it almost in full.

> Mr. Tenniel . . . has illustrated a little work—*Alice's Adventures
> in Wonderland,* with extraordinary grace. Look at the first
> chapter of this volume, and note the rabbit at the head of it.
> His umbrella is tucked under his arm and he is taking the
> watch out of his pocket to see what o'clock it is. The neatness of
> touch with which he is set living before us may be seen in a
> dozen other vignettes throughout the volume, the letter-press
> of which is by Mr. Lewis Carroll, and may best be described as
> an excellent piece of nonsense. No less amusing is the set of
> tales issued under the name of *The Magic Mirror* . . . [9]

Who now has heard of, much less read, W. Gilbert's *The Magic
Mirror,* judged at the time to be "no less amusing" than *Alice's
Adventures?* The *Monthly Packet* (an Anglican magazine for girls,
edited by Charlotte Yonge), the *Spectator,* the *Press,* the *Manchester
Guardian,* and the *Illustrated London News* wrote similarly bland,
approving notices, differing only as to whether it was "one long
dream of sheer nonsense" (the *Monthly Packet)* or could be said to
some degree to "inculcate good principles" (the *Press).*

A slightly larger group wrote more perceptively. Only one, *John
Bull,* hailed *Alice* as a work of undoubted genius.

> The above is *facile princeps* of the Christmas [children's]
> Books, that have come before us during the present prolific
> season, and fairly deserves a notice to itself. It is quite a work
> of genius, and a literary study; for, if the reputed author be

the true one . . . it effectually dispels the notion that first-rate mathematical talent and ability are inconsistent with genuine humour and imagination.[10]

It was observed more than once that *Alice* had as much adult appeal as child appeal: "It supplies a fund of almost equal amusement to the juvenile and adult reader,"[11] and "'Alice's Adventures in Wonderland' is a delightful book for children—or, for the matter of that, for grown-up people, provided they have wisdom and sympathy enough to enjoy a piece of down-right hearty drollery and fanciful humour."[12] Some reviewers praised the parodies and, even more, Carroll's original gift for talented nonsense writing, seen not just as trivial material to amuse the young but as a distinct branch of humor.

> But parody is confessedly an inferior form of humour, and these scraps [i.e., quotations from "You are Old, Father William" and "How Doth the Little Busy Bee"] give no idea of the author's best. The nonsense verses, *not* parody, which form "Alice's Evidence" . . . are extremely happy in the appearance of sense which is maintained in the midst of utter inconsequence.[13]

Another reviewer of *Alice* referred enthusiastically to a different aspect of its humor—"the briskness and richness of its satirical jocularity."[14]

It may surprise us a little to discover that, with an evident sense of relief among the reviewers, *Alice* was praised frequently for *not* being morally didactic or instructive. *Aunt Judy's Magazine* simply warned, "Parents and guardians . . . must not look to 'Alice's Adventures' for knowledge in disguise"; but the *Sunderland Herald* made the case explicitly.

> It has this advantage, that it has no moral, and that it does not teach anything. It is, in fact, pure sugar, throughout, and is without any of that bitter foundation of fat which some people imagine ought to be at the bottom of all children's books . . . We can confidently recommend this book as a present for any children who are in the habit of spending a part of each day in

"doing their lessons," and who may therefore be fairly allowed a little unalloyed nonsense as a reward.[15]

Carroll was also praised for his skill in creating a dreamlike experience: "Everyone knows how gravely in our dreams we take part in the most absurd transactions, unconscious of their absurdity; but it is not everyone who can reproduce this unconsciousness in waking hours, like the author of 'Alice's Adventures.' "[16] As the *John Bull* reviewer pointed out, this gift is rare, and only possessed by those retaining a childlike outlook on life themselves: "The probable impossibilities, monstrous absurdities, and incongruous situations of a childhood dream are the subject of the comedy, and must have required a childlike mind to rehabilitate them."[17]

Strongly adverse comment was rare, but some of the more powerful organs of the press did not take to *Alice*. The *Athenaeum*'s critic wrote:

Mr. Carroll has laboured hard to heap together strange adventures, and heterogeneous combinations; and we acknowledge the hard labour. Mr. Tenniel, again, is square, and grim and uncouth in his illustrations, howbeit clever, even sometimes to the verge of grandeur, as is the artist's habit. We fancy that any real child might be more puzzled than enchanted by this stiff, overwrought story.[18]

The *Spectator* liked the story in general but considered the Hatter "de trop"! The *Illustrated Times* thought the best guarantee of success to be Tenniel's drawings, the story itself being "too extravagantly absurd to produce more diversion than disappointment and irritation."[19] When Henry Kingsley declared The *Scotsman* to have dismissed *Alice* as "pointless balderdash" he exaggerated, but it had been distinctly unfavorable: "Nor is the story unreadable; but it is dull. There is no flow of animal spirits in its fun, which is forced and over-ingenious. Mr. Carroll seems to have said to himself, 'Go to now, I shall write a child's book,' and forthwith he has done it; whereas true children's literature is really of the poetical order, and must be born, not made.[20]

There are many indications of the growth in popularity of *Alice's*

Adventures between 1866 and 1871 when *Through the Looking-Glass, and What Alice Found There* was published. Several periodicals gave the book more consideration in follow-up reviews, as subsequent printings appeared, and it was translated in this period into French and German. As early as 1869 a *Spectator* article, "Alice Translated," comparing the quality of the translations with the original, referred to *Alice's Adventures* as "beyond question supreme among modern books for children."[21] This was used as an extract puffing the book in early advertisements.

In expectation of a fairly heavy demand for *Through the Looking-Glass,* Macmillan printed 9,000 copies, but by November 1871 advance orders already amounted to 7,500, and so they immediately printed 6,000 more. The book caught the Christmas trade and Carroll was able to note in his diary on January 27, 1872, after the book had been out scarcely seven weeks: "My birthday was signalized by hearing from Mr. Craik [of Macmillan's] that they have now sold 15,000 *Looking-glasses,* and have orders for 500 more!"[22]

There was no chance that *Through the Looking-Glass* would be an unobtrusive volume among the hundreds on reviewers' desks. The *Spectator* observed, "Of course everyone knows who Alice is. Does any one say no? Perhaps there may be an excuse for you, good reader. At the time of her Adventures in Wonderland you may have been on the Mountains of the Moon, in search of your own adventures—perhaps not more true than hers, and certainly not so good—"[23]

The *Athenaeum* had dismissed *Alice's Adventures* in four sentences. Its review of *Through the Looking-Glass,* in contrast, appeared in the literature section between appraisals of two prestigious nonfiction works and occupied one and a half columns. The opening remarks not only indicate the writer's awareness of the great contemporary appeal of the work but give a confident prediction of its future success:

> It would be difficult to over-estimate the value of the store of hearty and healthy fun laid up for whole generations of young people by Mr. Lewis Carroll and Mr. John Tenniel in the two

books which they have united to produce. In the first volume,
Alice won the affections of a whole child-world as she wandered through Wonderland; in the second, that now before us,
she will be sure to add fresh troops to the number of her
unknown friends, besides retaining her place in the hearts of
her old admirers.[24]

Having "got it wrong" in 1866 the *Athenaeum* offered fulsome
praise, but the review was essentially uncritical; one learns little of
the differences between the two books or of the nature of their
special appeal.

There was general agreement, among those who considered the
question, that *Through the Looking-Glass* was not so good as its
predecessor. The reasons given for this varied. It was perhaps too
contrived—"Mr. Carroll makes rather too much use here of the
Red and White pieces in the game of chess"[25]—or not so inventive.
Possibly the expectations raised by *Alice's Adventures* were so high
that no sequel could hope to meet them adequately.

A continuation of a book that has proved very popular
seldom is successful, and we cannot say that we think Alice's
last adventures by any means equal to her previous ones.
Making every allowance for the lack of novelty, and our own
more highly raised expectation, it seems to us that the parodies
are somewhat less delightfully absurd, the nonsense not so
quaint, the transitions rather more forced.[26]

The reviewer still concluded that Carroll had "surpassed all modern writers of children's books except himself."

The *Spectator* devoted quite a lot of space to comparing the
humor of the two books and decided (as W. H. Auden was to do
later) that in *Through the Looking-Glass* a discernible set of rules was
in operation, "a law of nonsense," and that it had "an increased
element of inner congruity"[27] in its imaginary world and an air of
greater maturity than *Alice's Adventures*. The story was compared
with our experience in a dreaming state, where weird scenes occur,
but with some distorted resemblance to normal life.

The reviews contained a good deal about nonsense writing as a literary genre and recognized Carroll as a brilliant exponent of it, because he had both an understanding of the dreamy thoughts of inexperienced and illogical childhood and "the trained intellect of a scholar, with a serious poetic imagination and some insight into metaphysical questions, such as are apt to beset the debatable ground between nonsense and philosophic truth."[28] This connection between nonsense and metaphysics was mentioned more than once. There is something profound in a world picture that can integrate elements apparently dissimilar to the surface view. Nonsense writing becomes an act of artistic creativity, joining in brilliant combination the most unlikely or homely materials. In this context the *Times* reviewer linked Carroll with Lear,[29] and it is significant that Lear's *More Nonsense: Pictures, Rhymes . . .* was distinguished by a two-and-a-half-column review in the *Spectator*'s Christmas 1871 issue, where nonsense writing was also lightly scrutinized.

Others reflecting on the genre to which the *Alices* belonged suggested fable, and here Carroll was compared with Hans Andersen. One reviewer supposed Andersen to be the originator of modern fable but noted that both writers owed a debt to the old stories in which beasts, birds, fish, and insects were endowed with thought and speech. Usually, though, those stories were intended to point some moral about human conduct. More markedly even than in 1865, the reviewers openly recommended *Through the Looking-Glass* because it possessed *no* moral. The *Times* reckoned that among its chief charms, "there is literally no sense in it, no lurking moral, no convert satire, no meaning, so far as we read it, of any sort whatever, . . ." a judgment echoed triumphantly by the *Examiner* in its final sentence: "And the best of all is that the book has no moral, and is nothing but a capital jumble of fun."[30]

What of the reactions of individual readers, especially children? One of the most famous approving comments about *Alice's Adventures* is that of six-year-old Greville MacDonald. Carroll had left the manuscript with his friend, George MacDonald, whose wife read the story to their children, whereupon young Greville "exclaimed that there ought to be sixty thousand volumes of it."[31] Amy Cruse, in *The Victorians and Their Books,* quotes a number of commendations by adults.[32] Henry Kingsley thought it "a charming book," and Walter Besant said that it was "one of the very few books in the world that can be read with pleasure by old and young." Yet Cruse was one of the opinion that there is little evidence that the young liked it. She cites only two child readers, one of whom told Carroll, "I think that *Through the Looking-Glass* is more stupid than *Alice's Adventures*. Don't you think so?" And one, Henry Sanderson, thought it very silly, when read to him before he was nine. This picture is contradicted by the mounting sales and by the conviction of the reviewers of *Through the Looking-Glass* that it would bring delight to many young readers. The reminiscence of one young reader in later life may be taken to be more representative: "*Alice in Wonderland* we all knew practically by heart and one of the red-letter days of my life was a birthday when I received from my father *Through the Looking-Glass*. I got through the morning some-how, and then buried myself in it all the afternoon. . . . As I handle the book now I live over again that enchanted afternoon."[33]

There is ample evidence that both *Alice* books were still popular with the young at the time of Carroll's death in 1898. The *Pall Mall Gazette*, for instance, in an article entitled "What the Children Like," gave the result of a request to children to list their favorite books. "To pass to the positive, the verdict is so natural that it will surprise no normal person. The winner is 'Alice in Wonderland'; 'Through the Looking-Glass' is in the twenty, but much lower down. Perfectly correct."[34] The lists of several children were quoted: Miss Freda Penney, age nine, put *Alice* and *Through the Looking-Glass* in third and fourth place respectively, and Miss Audrey Fuller, thirteen and a half, included both *Alices* in her list. Hans Andersen and the Brothers Grimm tied for second place. *The Arabian Nights* (children's version), Andrew Lang's fairy books, and Mrs. Molesworth were also in the twenty. This article, in its concluding remarks, confirms the anti-moralizing trend evident in a number of *Alice* reviews of the mid-1860s and the 1870s. "Of the list as a whole the most obvious point is the victory of fairy tales. . . . Aesop's absence from the elect is perhaps to be attributed to the pernicious trick of printing morals that nobody wants along with the fables."[35]

It has often been said that *Alice's Adventures* began a new epoch in children's literature. The 1977 Centenary Exhibition of the (British) Library Association was entitled "After Alice," and the Introduction to the catalogue offered this explanation. *"Alice's Adventures in Wonderland* . . . opened up a new path in imaginative children's literature. After 'Alice' books for children were never quite as they had been earlier, and the title 'After Alice' therefore seemed almost to select itself for this present survey."[36] This seems a surprising judgment in view of the contemporary reception; no one saw *Alice's Adventures* as having any special significance when the book first appeared.

Harvey Darton, in his standard history of children's books, says similarly that Carroll "changed the whole cast of children's literature," and it is clear that he is referring to a change from books intended to improve or instruct to ones intended simply to give pleasure.

> Except in the tiniest details of customary manners . . . there is not . . . an ulterior motive in the *Alices* from beginning to end. . . . The directness of such work was a revolution in its sphere. . . . Henceforth fear had gone, and with it shy disquiet. There was to be in hours of pleasure no more dread about the moral value, the ponderable, measured quality and extent of the pleasure itself.[37]

In the chapters on fairy tales in Gillian Avery's *Nineteenth Century Children, Alice* is represented as belonging to a general movement, rather than effecting a revolution.[38] The conclusion, however, states: "The great revolution came a hundred years ago when *Alice's Adventures in Wonderland* marked the beginning of the change to the book to amuse," a judgment very close to Darton's.

The new "directness" Darton refers to would seem to have been anticipated by a greater freedom in the range and content of children's books in the years immediately preceding the publication of *Alice*. In part it came about as a result of the struggle between "Peter Parley" and "Felix Summerly" in the 1840s. The original Peter Parley, Samuel Griswold Goodrich of New England, had attacked children's books early in the nineteenth century, especially those containing fairy tales and nursery rhymes, as "full of nonsense," "full of something very like lies, and . . . very shocking to the mind."[39] He decided to devote his energies to producing books for children that would redress the balance and impart useful information. Various pseudo-Parleys sprang up in England in the first half of the century; Darton identifies six. Felix Summerly, editor of *Home Treasury of Books* (1841–49), declared open warfare on Parleyism in his preface to the work.

> The character of most Children's Books published during the last quarter of a century, is fairly typified in the name of Peter Parley, which the writers of some hundreds of them have assumed. The books themselves have been addressed after a narrow fashion, almost entirely to the cultivation of the understanding of children. The many tales sung or said from time immemorial, which appealed to the other and certainly not less important elements of a little child's mind, its fancy, imagination, sympathies, affections, are almost all gone out of memory, and are scarcely to be obtained. . . . The conductor of this series purposes to produce a series of Works, the character of which may be briefly described as anti–Peter Parleyism. . . .[40]

This promising development was followed in 1846 by Howitt's and Peachey's translations of Hans Andersen's fairy tales, and with the already established popularity of the Grimms through Edgar Taylor's translation of the *Tales*—as Darton says—"the victory of fantasy was in sight." The same year saw Lear's *Book of Nonsense*. In fact, Darton lists six significant developments in children's literature as having taken place between 1837 and 1862, three years before the publication of *Alice's Adventures*. Apart from the acceptance of fairy tales and nonsense, he notes a lessening of the appeal of "useful knowledge" books; the popularity of stories of American juvenile life; the rise of boys' and girls' books; and the beginnings of the juvenile novel. The legacy inherited by writers of children's books in the 1860s, then, was one of comparative license because their predecessors had "almost—but certainly not quite—killed the Moral Tale, in the restricted sense of the term. They mitigated—

indeed, turned to joy—the Awful Warning. That was a very large contribution for one generation to make."[41] In this context, Carroll's work does not seem so *very* revolutionary.

It is worthwhile to investigate briefly the reviews of *Alice's Adventures* to see how far they indicate the range of books for children that Darton suggests. Hans Andersen's *What the Moon Saw, and other Tales* was mentioned most frequently and in general was thought to be the outstanding book of the Christmas 1865 selection. It was prized not as a traditional fairy tale but as a work of imaginative invention, appealing to adult and child alike. In fact Andersen made a distinction between "fairy tale" and "story" in his fantasy writing, which covered a much wider field than the traditional tale. It was a literary form that he urged should be taken seriously, and in this he was phenomenally successful, elevating the previously homely folk tale to a new art form. His own definition gives some idea of its scope.

> In the whole realm of poetry no domain is so boundless as that of the fairytale. It reaches from the blood-drenched graves of Antiquity to the pious legends of a child's picture-book; it takes in the poetry of the people and the poetry of the artist. . . . He who masters it must be able to put into it tragedy, comedy, naive simplicity and humour; . . . the innocence of poetry, overlooked and jeered at by the other brothers, will reach farthest in the end.[42]

Shortly after his work had appeared in translation in the 1840s, contemporary reviews make it clear that he was regarded as an exciting writer of great poetic talent. Twenty years later his reputation was still high. The *Athenaeum*, complaining of the lack of ingenuity in the current crop of children's fiction in 1865, makes one exception—Andersen. "On the quaintness and pathos of the author—only approached or excelled by . . . Hawthorne—we need not descant anew."[43] A year later there were no less than five different collections of his stories among the gift book selections and, though some complained about the generally melancholy effect of the works of the "gloomy Dane," the sentiment "One can never have too much of Hans Andersen" was more representative.

The high rating of Andersen, compared with many other writers of fantasy for children, would seem to have depended on a distinction between "imagination" and "fancy" in the minds of some reviewers, the latter term being reserved for work of a lesser order of poetic invention. For example, Madame de Chatelain's *The Sedan Chair, and Sir Wilfred's Seven Flights* was widely praised. It is a collection of original fairy tales linked by the magic sedan chair, which moves like a magic carpet from one adventure to another. The reviews also comment on re-tellings of traditional fairy stories, such as the Reverend H. Adams's *Balderscourt; or, Holiday Tales.* The basis of the plot is a string of favorite fairy tales told at a children's Christmas party.

Returning to Darton's list, there *were* boys' and girls' books in abundance mentioned in these reviews, especially annuals: *Every Boy's Annual, Old Merry's Annual,* even *Peter Parley's Annual,* to which the *Manchester Guardian* reviewer objected as "scarcely up to the mark; the original mark, we mean, of the true Peter Parley of other days."[44]

There is plenty of evidence to support Darton's claim that by the 1860s writers had "almost killed the Moral Tale." The review in the *Reader,* for instance, was atypical in mentioning only books of a theological or moral character, including Mrs. Barbauld's *Hymns for Children,* Watts's *Divine and Moral Songs,* Keble's *Evening Hymns,* and various publications by the Religious Tract Society. Much more common was fun at the moral tale's expense. The *London Review,* one of the fullest in its treatment of current children's fiction and one of the most perceptive, opened its review "Children's Books" in the December 1866 issue:

> It is impossible to open the . . . first books on our list [Mrs. Sherwood's *Charles Lorraine; or the Young Soldier,* and *Little Henry and his Bearer]* without being carried back to our own childhood. Surely we have heard of Mrs. Sherwood before, and the opening words of the preface are anything but modern. Children's books nowadays do not talk of their authors being actuated by a high moral purpose, inculcating important lessons as to the difference between theoretical and practical

piety, and warning others against those temptations, which, by flattering youth's vanity, soon lead to the overthrow of the homely virtues which had once been his consolation and happiness. We do not even employ these words, when we write for men. Much less can we expect children to spell through them.[45]

Peter Parley was said to have "wisely advanced with the times" in the *Illustrated Times* Christmas 1865 review, and its critic enjoyed laughing at the anonymous *Ellen Montgomery's Bookshelf* for its cautionary tales: "The teaching is, of course, all that can be desired; and, if little Sibyl or Chryssa overdoes prudence by one strawberry, Aunt gives them at least a page on the vanity of things earthly."[46]

In this broad context, then, *Alice's Adventures* would seem to have appeared neither epoch-making nor even supremely talented to most of those professionally engaged in reviewing children's books in the mid-1860s. In less than a decade, however, Carroll became recognized by most as preeminent among writers for children, a place he appears to have held throughout the rest of the century.

Notes

1. S. M. Ellis, *Henry Kingsley, 1830–1876* (London: Grant Richards, 1931), p. 75.
2. For an account of this, see *The Diaries of Lewis Carroll*, ed. R. L. Green (London: Cassell, 1953), pp. 217, 233; *The Letters of Lewis Carroll*, ed. M. N. Cohen (London: Macmillan, 1979), p. 82; and W. H. Bond, "The Publication of *Alice's Adventures in Wonderland*," *Harvard Library Bulletin*, 10, No. 3 (Autumn, 1956), 309–12.
3. *The Reader*, Nov. 18, 1865, p. 567.
4. *The Publisher's Circular*, Dec. 8, 1865, p. 686.
5. *The London Review*, Dec. 23, 1865, p. 674.
6. *Illustrated London News*, Dec. 16, 1865, p. 590.
7. *The London Review*, p. 675.
8. All the reviews of *Alice's Adventures in Wonderland* have now been reprinted in *Jabberwocky*. See *Jabberwocky—The Journal of the Lewis Carroll Society*, vol. 9, nos. 1–4, 1979–80.
9. *The Times*, Dec. 26, 1865, p. 5.
10. *John Bull*, Jan. 20, 1866, pp. 43–44.
11. Ibid.
12. *The London Review*, p. 674.
13. *Pall Mall Gazette*, Dec. 23, 1865, pp. 9–10.
14. *John Bull*, Jan. 20, 1866, pp. 43–44.
15. *The Sunderland Herald*, May 25, 1866, p. 2.

16. *The Manchester Guardian*, supplement no. 1045, Dec. 13, 1865, p. 1251.

17. *John Bull*, Jan. 20, 1866, pp. 43–44.

18. *The Athenaeum*, Dec. 16, 1865, p. 844.

19. *The Illustrated Times*, Dec. 16, 1865, p. 379.

20. *The Scotsman*, Dec. 22, 1866, p. 5.

21. *The Spectator*, Aug. 1869.

22. *The Diaries of Lewis Carroll*, p. 309; *Alice's Adventures* sold 500 copies in the month after publication (ibid., p. 237).

23. *The Spectator*, Dec. 30, 1871, pp. 1607–09.

24. *The Athenaeum*, Dec. 16, 1871, pp. 787–88.

25. *Illustrated London News*, Dec. 16, 1871, p. 599.

26. *The Manchester Guardian*, Dec. 27, 1871, p. 3.

27. *The Spectator*, Dec. 30, 1871, pp. 1607–09.

28. *Illustrated London News*, Dec. 16, 1871, p. 599.

29. *The Times*, Dec. 20, 1871, p. 4.

30. *The Examiner*, Dec. 16, 1871, p. 1250.

31. George MacDonald, *George MacDonald and his Wife* (London: George Allen & Unwin, 1924), p. 342.

32. Amy Cruse, *The Victorians and their Books* (London: George Allen & Unwin, 1935), pp. 302–04.

33. Quoted by Derek Hudson, *Lewis Carroll* (London: Constable, 1954), p. 182.

34. *Pall Mall Gazette*, July 1, 1898, pp. 1–2.

35. Ibid.

36. Catalogue of the Centenary Exhibition "After Alice" (London: Library Association, 1977), p. 9.

37. F. J. H. Darton, *Children's Books in England: Five Centuries of Social Life* (1932; rpt. Cambridge: At the University Press, 1960), p. 268.

38. Gillian Avery, *Nineteenth Century Children: Heroes and Heroines in English Children's Stories 1780–1900* (London: Hodder & Stoughton, 1965), pp. 41–45, 121–24., 227. The chapters on fairy tales (2 and 6) were written by coauthor Angela Bull.

39. Quoted by Darton, p. 227.

40. Quoted by Darton, pp. 240–41.

41. Darton, p. 257.

42. Quoted by Elias Bredsdorff, *Hans Christian Andersen—the Story of his Life and Work 1805–75* (London: Phaidon, 1975), p. 358.

43. *The Athenaeum*, Dec. 16, 1865, p. 844.

44. *The Manchester Guardian*, Dec. 13, 1865, p. 1251.

45. *The London Review*, Dec. 23, 1865, p. 674.

46. *The Illustrated Times*, Dec. 16, 1865, p. 379.

Vastness and Contraction of Space in
Little House on the Prairie

Hamida Bosmajian

> To make a prairie it takes a clover and one bee.
> One clover, and a bee
> And reverie
> And reverie alone will do
> If bees are few.
>
> —Emily Dickinson

Although she lived in circumscribed territory, Emily Dickinson realized that sheer reverie allows an expansion of the imagination independent of the particularity of the images. Such images can either whirl the imagination into an open-ended reverie or particularize it within the concreteness of the text, from which the creative reader generates yet another reverie. Laura Ingalls Wilder writes in *Little House on the Prairie,* "The vast prairie was dark and still. Only the wind moved stealthily through the grass, and the large, low stars hung glittering from the sky. The campfire was cozy in the big dark stillness. . . ."[1] Her depiction of Laura in house and prairie is an indissoluble interrelation of memory and imagination, which, to use Gaston Bachelard's words, "give us back the images which pertain to our lives."[2] Bachelard finds the origin of reverie and oneiric images in childhood. "When the human world leaves him in peace, the child feels like a son of the cosmos. And thus, in his solitudes, from the moment he is master of his reveries, the child knows the happiness of dreaming which will later be the happiness of the poets" (*PR*, p. 99).

When we as adult readers of children's literature encounter a certain image, we become suddenly aware that the image has "touched the depth before it stirs the surface."[3] Intentionality, reason, and consciousness of specifics are slackened as our eyes wander off the page and "stare into the blue." Children's literature, especially fairy tales, often projects such singular images seemingly free of traditional meanings, but rather of such luminousness that they are retained in the memory as a kind of concrete metaphysics. The authenticity of such images attracts the phenomenologist. Furthermore, the double audience of children's literature, child and adult, urges the critic toward a phenomenological perception of the text and at the same time reveals the problems intrinsic to that kind of interpretation. As a phenomenon, the image appears to the child-perceiver with an autonomy that the adult reader rediscovers rarely, for the adult reader perceives the image with presuppositions and existential projections and can return to the being of the image only after laborious sublimation of knowledge. The adult reader is inclined to perceive the image as a symptom that transmits the values of culture and civilization. Such a reader *extracts* meaning from the image, robs it of its value, and relegates the creative imagination to a secondary position by assuming that the poet's imagination simply hides personal and cultural problems in the material of the image.

There is thus an inherent contradiction in critical analysis from a phenomenological perspective, for criticism traditionally claims objectivity whereas the phenomenological critic attempts to communicate a subjective response to the text. Therefore, we often find that when the phenomenological critic is most phenomenological, he or she becomes poetic, Bachelard being a prime example. It cannot really be otherwise, for the phenomenological critic who applies the concepts of phenomenology must overcome the subject-object dichotomy by describing and explaining the image in such a way that the image is constituted only in its intentional relationship with the perceiving subject.

The question of the objective reality of the image, its historical, cultural, or psychological validity, is usually bracketed by the phenomenologist. Phenomenological criticism, in contrast, presents illuminating descriptions of the correlative relation between the perceiving subject and the phenomenon of the text. In this way, as Wolfgang Iser argues, the images of a text are not used up in a kind of literary consumerism, for the vital feature of a text is retained: it does not lose the ability to communicate even after overt messages are decoded.[4]

I agree with Iser that all interpretation, including phenomeno-logical interpretation, involves a frame of reference; in addition, each frame deepens the text. Therefore, *Little House on the Prairie* gains dimension as it is seen in terms of the creative process that went into its shaping, its "unflinching assessment of repressive gentility and racial superiority," its autobiographical and fictionaliz-ing memory, and its projection of the American pioneer spirit.[5] A phenomenological perception of the book involves a sophisticated primitiveness that both approximates the child's perception and recognizes the absorption of the oneiric value of images as they are perceived in reverie.

Bachelard attempts to communicate that value and yet his critical theory and practice reveal also the problems inherent in the phenomenological approach. He synthesizes C. G. Jung's concepts of the active imagination, which creates images as a sublimation of unconscious content, with phenomenology, which accepts the liter-ary sign-image as a linguistic sublimation appearing autonomously to the experiential actuality of the reader, who then must complete the meaning of the image. While Bachelard, especially in *The Poetics of Space,* insists on the autonomy of the image and attempts to sublimate his vast learning in order to be "perceptive to the image the moment it appears" (*PS,* p. xi), his discussions demon-strate that he is unable to maintain such an authentic and sheer response. Only a child would be able to do this, but then ironically the child would not be able to discourse about it.

Given the origin of truly oneiric images in childhood and the fact that reverie, unlike the nightdream, is always desirable, Bachelard intends to focus on the spaces that we love, on "simple images of *felicitous* space" (*PS,* p. xxxi). But the reader soon becomes aware, as does Bachelard, that felicitous space can metamorphose into sinister, threatening, and even demonic space. There is irony beneath and within happy space, and with irony we move from oneiric existence to knowledge of the fallen world. It is with these ambiguities in mind that I have approached the depth and dimen-sion of *Little House on the Prairie,* a book that reveals an awareness of historical and cultural discontents and at the same time reverber-ates with the contentment of felicitous space where one's being is housed and with the excitement of vast space wherein one's being expands.

The storyteller begins with an expansion of memory, "A long time ago," and closes with a lyrical anticipation of future possibilities, "Daily and nightly I wander with thee." The book is a daughter's fictionalized memory of her father's anticipations expressed through a phenomenology of the spaces of vastness and contraction: the prairie and the little house. Anticipation, future time, urges towards happy space, but memory knows that both the vast and the intimately contracted space have been precarious and ambiguous as values of human experience in the world. With great subtlety *Little House on the Prairie* introduces the child to the ironies of American life and history, including the American dream and the temporal and spatial horizon of the mythology of Manifest Destiny. The dreamer about the West is unaware that moving toward the westward horizon is traditionally a move toward the end of a time. The narrator, however, knows it: "That long line of Indians slowly pulled itself over the Western edge of the world. And nothing was left but silence and emptiness. All the world seemed lonely and quiet" (p. 311).

The most radical expression of vastness and contraction occurs in the chapter "Fever 'N' Ague," when the Ingalls family suffers from malaria. Laura hallucinates in her fever: "Something dwindled slowly, smaller and smaller, till it was tinier than the tiniest thing. Then it slowly swelled up again till it was larger than anything could be" (pp. 186–87). We have here what Bachelard calls a "phenomenology without phenomena" that refers us directly to "our imagining consciousness" (*PS*, p. 184). The minuscule intimate point that contracts into itself is a defensive energy of such density that it would collapse of its own weight unless it expanded again aggressively. Both, extreme constriction and all-filling vastness, suck in or swallow the fragile ego. These phenomena, experienced here in their sheerness, apply also to the topography of the little house and the prairie as well as to the tensions within and between characters.

Vastness and contraction have a positive and negative end on a spectrum of values. The vastness of the prairie resonates with desire and the need for expansion as these are felt by the human heart, the wandering spirit. But the sublime vastness of the prairie consumes the exploring wanderer and, since the prairie is not really level, threatens with condensed pockets of danger. To keep intact, the ego must clear a containing space, a round shelter in the vastness: the circle of the camp, the shelter of the "hut-dream" (Bachelard) which becomes the little house. The house is the most positive image of civilization in the book, although its contracted space is always endangered from without and within. The image in transit between prairie and little house is the covered wagon with Ma and Pa in front anticipating the future and Laura shaping her memories by looking back at the abandoned house through the circle of the drawn canvas cover (p. 324).

Vast and contracted space and their values become correlatives for the three character groups in the book. The Indians have their camps, but they are really housed in the vastness of the prairie. Ma and Mary desire the contracted space of the house and its civilization. Pa Ingalls and Laura hover between the values of the open prairie and the values of the house. Ma, Pa, and Laura each has a personal image that condenses these values. Laura has the word *papoose,* Ma has the small china shepherdess, and Pa has his fiddle. Vast and contracted space as well as these personal images reveal the meaning of human experience in *Little House on the Prairie.*

The value of the prairie's vastness changes throughout the book. In the big woods of Wisconsin, a daydreaming Ingalls expands his horizon: "He liked a country where the wild animals lived without being afraid. . . . In the West the land was level . . . [and] stretched much farther than man could see, and there were no settlers" (p. 2). Certainly the deep dark woods are a primordial space for losing one's self, but not for Ingalls when he can hear the thud of an ax or the shot of a gun not his own. Since Ma does not respond to his daydream, he interprets her silence as consent: "Seeing that you don't object, I have decided to go West" (p. 3). Her reply about the snugness of their house in winter has no effect on him.

The irony of Pa's daydream of vastness is that it will always lead to contraction, if not constriction. He, the wandering ego—the sailor over waves of prairie grasses—will tame the space in which he would be lost, the animals will flee him, and settlers with similar daydreams will be his neighbors. The too-muchness of the prairie's freedom becomes imprisoning as the Ingallses travel through Kansas. "In a perfect circle the sky curved down to the level land, and the wagon was in the circle's exact middle . . . [but] they couldn't get out of the middle of that circle" (p. 13). The wagon is centered no matter how much Ingalls strives to reach the circumference. More intimate circles are needed for centers of refuge. The camp on the high prairie is such a cleared ground where fire can burn without becoming a conflagration, where coffee is ground, clothes are washed and ironed, and where Ma admonishes Laura: "You must mind your manners, even if we are a hundred miles from nowhere" (p. 40). She is right, for the rituals of civilization sustain the ego in its clearing in the wilderness. The circle is a horizon that organizes time as well, the days and the year during which this human experience takes place.

The prairie is not only experienced horizontally; it also beckons with upward and downward extension. The line of the horizon connects the eye with the vast space of the cosmos and suggests a concrete metaphysics in a story that makes no religious references. The following passage shows the images of that metaphysics as they move from the perception of phenomena to a phenomenology without phenomena and then back to the perception of phenomena:

> The prairie looked as if no human eye had ever seen it before. Only the tall grasses covered the empty land and a great empty sky arched over it. Far away the sun's edge ran a pale pink glow, and above the pink was yellow, and above that blue. Above the blue color was no color at all. Purple shadows were gathering over the land, and the wind was mourning. [pp. 26–27]

An example of the vertically downward line and its connection with sky and prairie is the well Ingalls builds after the house is finished. It is a convenience for Caroline so that she will not have to go to the creek when he is absent, but building that convenience seriously endangers a helpful neighbor's life, and Ingalls himself is threatened when he finds that he is sinking into quicksand the moment water rushes into the well. It is a dangerous human-made vertical whose depth excites Laura: "Mary preferred to stay in the house and work on her patchwork quilt. But Laura liked the fierce sun and wind, and she couldn't stay away from the well. But she was not allowed to go near its edge" (p. 158). To test oxygen presence and the possibility of gas at the bottom, Ingalls places a candle in the deep: "All the way down in the dark hole the little candle kept on burning like a star" (p. 158). This meaningful point of light is like the cosmic stars above the prairie, a beckoning assurance to the ego that it will not be enveloped by the depths above or below. At the end of the chapter, the author projects an image of wholeness: "In a little while the well was almost full of water. A circle of blue sky lay not far down in the ground and when Laura looked at it, a little girl's head looked up at her. When she waved her hand, a hand on the water's surface waved, too" (p. 160). The author creates an unusual image of the sky lying in the ground, but it is not buried—the depth will not extinguish the light in whose circle Laura sees a human face. The small child (she seems younger than Laura is) does not yet identify herself with the reflection; instead, she, who also experiences much inner solitude, relates with kindliness towards the other image. She is no alienated Narcissus! The water remains a gift from the depth that must be squared by a stout platform and a heavy cover.

Horizontally the prairie is not really level. It has depths that envelop and depths from which the unexpected can emerge. Both disappearance and emergence tend to be sudden and connote a vaguely comprehended threat. When Pa goes hunting, he disappears into the prairie (p. 42). Since her father fills her life, it always seems to Laura that "the outdoors was too large and empty to play in" (p. 208) when he is gone. Wolves, fire, and Indians can suddenly emerge as real dangers, but more ominous still, the prairie generates a feeling of anxiety: "She had a queer feeling about the prairie. It didn't feel safe. It seemed to be hiding something. Sometimes Laura had a feeling that something was creeping up behind her. She turned around quickly, and nothing was there" (p. 288).

Indians are housed and at home in the vastness: "No one knew how many Indians were hidden in the prairie which seemed so level but wasn't" (p. 275). Their tragedy is the inexorable contraction of that space by the settlers. A neighbor of the Ingallses argues: "Land knows, they'd never do anything with this country themselves. All they do is roam around it like wild animals. Treaties or no treaties, the land belongs to folks that farm it" (p. 211). Such farmers assert that "the only good Indian is a dead Indian" (pp. 211 and 284), a radical constriction that Ingalls meliorates by supporting the continued westward drive of the Indians by the government, though he admits that this must make the Indians hate the settlers.

Ingalls himself feels intensely aggressive and frustrated when the government determines that the land on which he has settled will remain Indian territory. He decides to leave immediately because he cannot tolerate being ordered off the land. Laura, too, can feel deeply aggressive, mainly toward her sister, who has already internalized all the value society associates with a "proper young lady." But the fiercest expression of aggression is in the tribal war cry of the Indians. The immensity of their wrath is restricted to the circumscribed space of their camp from which the cry rises, filling the vastness of the prairie and the intimacy of the little house. Laura does not know that the Indians have their own restrictive ritual for aggression. It seems to her that their anger is everywhere: "She couldn't hold on to anything; there was nothing solid anywhere. It seemed a long time before she could think or speak . . . [for] the drums seemed to beat deep inside her" (pp. 291–92). The nightmare of history "was real and Laura could not wake up. She could not get away from it" (p. 293). As her own aggressions against the pressures of civilization are absorbed in that cry, the immensity of aggressive feelings becomes her own intimate immensity and shapes her dreaming and waking consciousness.

Inaccessible as human beings to the Ingallses, the Indians become images of potential danger or of dreams of freedom, impossible for the settler's mentality. Pa communicates silently with them. He stands in awe of Soldat du Chêne, who supports the settlers and leads his contingent of Osages westward. In the chapter entitled "The Indians Ride Away," the family watches spellbound for a whole day as the Indians "went by as if the house and the stable and Pa and Ma and Mary and Laura were not there at all." Their expressions are the last option of dignity for the defeated. Laura perceives the leader's "proud still face" (p. 305) and she envies the freedom of the Indian children riding naked on the bare backs of their ponies. Discontent with civilization overwhelms her: "She had a naughty wish to be a little Indian girl. Of course she did not really mean it. She only wanted to be bare and naked in the wind and the sunshine, riding one of those gay little ponies" (p. 307). Her preconscious knows that that can never be. At this point, without using the word and thereby defining what she sees, she notices the papoose that Pa promised she would see in Indian country.

Though Pa defined *papoose* for her (p. 6), it is the word as word that fascinates her, a magical and reverie-provoking word freed from what it defines. When she does see the papoose she is unaware that the word has realized itself. The Indian baby is tucked into the basket that hangs on the side of the mother's pony and, as Laura makes significant eye contact with the baby's black eyes, she demands of her all-powerful father: "Pa, . . . get me that little Indian baby" (p. 308). Shocked, Ma responds: " 'Why on earth do you want an Indian baby of all things!' 'Its eyes are so black,' Laura sobbed. She could not say what she meant" (p. 309). The eye contact momentarily joins for Laura two horizons of experience: civilization will forever prevent her from riding naked on a pony. She feels a double aggression: toward the strictures that prevent her from the fulfillment of the desire for unhampered freedom and toward that which she desires so. Because she cannot have the freedom, she wants to possess that which is destined to be free and thereby destroy an elusive dream. Laura already shares the settler's fantasy in which the impulse toward freedom is exchanged for possession and control of the vastness of the prairie. In her childlike desire she is unaware of the paradox that this Indian baby is not *unhampered* but confined in the strictures of tribal customs. Similarly, the settler refuses to be aware that the Indians' disappearance over the horizon is a movement toward increasing limitation, not freedom.

When the family sets out again into the prairie, vastness domi-

nates once more until a new space will be cleared. Ingalls concludes: "It's a great country, Caroline. . . . But there will be wild
Indians and wolves here for many a day" (p. 325). The contraction
of vastness, however, is only a matter of time. When Ma complains
that a whole year's labor has been wasted, Pa replies: "What's a year
amount to? We shall have all the time there is." But the destiny of
the settler, too, will be manifested in its space and time.

The child-reader responds preconsciously, of course, to the
fictionalized memories of Laura Ingalls Wilder. The complexities
of personal, familial, and national life are communicated in such a
way as never to gain dominance over the image of the nurturing
mother, the protective father, the shared meals and special occasions, and, most of all, the little house. The memory of the
experience of reading this book leaves the contracting space of the
sheltering house intact, though the text actually gives to the house
as many ambiguities as it gives to the prairie. The child-reader
absorbs the images projected by the author's distillation of memory
and imagination and perceives them without antecedents, but at
the same time the images will become antecedents to future and
less oneiric perceptions. Nevertheless, as adult and child read
about the little house, they prefer to live in their own hut dream.

Charles Ingalls builds the house to put Caroline and the girls into
it. It is he who decides where the contracted space will be (p. 52).
For five chapters the reader follows the coming into being of the
house, from foundation to roof to hearth. Ma proves incapable of
working with Pa after she injures herself. Building the house is a
masculine activity, but Laura is the observer who takes in every
detail so that the house can again be constructed in memory. She
helps her father secure the house with a stout door, a process
described so precisely that it becomes a model of how to build a
door in order to keep nature out. Building the house means
struggling with the elements, as exemplified in the image of the
house as a ship at sea in the prairie, an image reinforced by Garth
Williams's drawing. Pa pulls the canvas wagon top as a temporary
roof over the skeleton structure: "The canvas billowed in the wind,
Pa's beard blew wildly and his hair stood up as if it were trying to
pull itself out. He held onto the canvas and fought it. Once it jerked

"He held onto the canvas and fought it." From *Little House on the Prairie*, by Laura Ingalls Wilder, illustrated by Garth Williams. Copyright 1953 by Harper & Row, Inc. Reproduced by permission of the publisher.

so hard that Laura thought he must let go and sail into the air like a bird" (pp. 72–73). Prairie, sea, and air synthesize and project Ingalls's image in a state of tension between settlement and the desire for flight.

After the hearth is finished, Ma places her little china shepherdess on the mantel shelf (p. 117). An emblem of continuity, the china figure takes on a special symbolic value for Caroline in *Little House on the Prairie*. The fragile lady, dressed with pretensions for rustic work, is for Ma a signature to the house, the family lar, the little household god of civilization carried from homestead to homestead. The figure projects the yearning of civilized humans for an

idyllic if not edenic setting and is at the same time Caroline's token
of affluence, of conspicuous consumption where a lady's function is
"to sit pretty." Ma loved and married "the wild man" Ingalls, and
she may be a hard-working pioneer woman, but she has internalized civilized proprieties. She resolutely refuses to adopt "Indian
ways" such as washing the clothes in the creek, even if that is more
practical. Drying the clothes on the prairie is already a concession;
she wants a clothesline (p. 76). The inside of the house is hers.
When the red-checked tablecloth is spread, she knows that "now we
are living like civilized folk again" (p. 129). After Pa built the bed
and helped her to carry in the prairie-grass tick, "she set up the
goose feather pillows, and spread the pillow shams against them.
On each pillow sham two little birds were outlined in red thread"
(p. 148). As an intensification of intimate space, the image cluster
of bedframe, tick, pillow, and pillow sham with birds parallels the
images of house, mantel, and china shepherdess, images of civilization that are as illusive and sustaining as Ingalls's dream of the
wide-open spaces.

The house is not a perfect refuge. It is threatened from without
and within. Indians enter, demand food, or try to steal Pa's furs.
The family's very life is endangered during the malaria attack. Fire
breaks out in the chimney and only Laura's courage and resourcefulness keep Mary, who sits terrified in the rocker with Baby
Carrie, from being burnt. Mary's helplessness as the most civilized
and ladylike character in the family comes here to the fore (p. 203).
Before the stout door is built, wolves that followed Ingalls home
encircle the house and howl at the moon. In spite of her fear,
Laura is fascinated by the leader of the pack—"she looked and
looked at that wolf." As her father circled inside from window to
window, Laura "lay and listened to the breathing of the wolves on
the other side of the log wall" (p. 98). Danger is alive here,
impinges on the intimate space, and reduces the hut dream to a
wish.

Charles Ingalls is a skilled builder of intimate space, but he never
once expresses the deep satisfaction of Caroline or Laura in having
a house. The day it is finished, he plans to buy window glass, which
will give him the connection with the expanse of the prairie. Ingalls

has a childlike joy in building the house, but afterward he does not really know what to do with it. The house is female space, and he prefers to go to town to get supplies or to sit in his favorite place—the threshold—and play his fiddle: "Pa sat for a long time in the doorway and played his fiddle and sang to Ma and Mary and Laura *in the house* and to the *starry night outside*" (p. 129, my italics). He is a man whose life Bachelard would see as governed by the dialectic of inside and outside.

The fiddle is his image of intimacy: "He laid the fiddle box carefully between the pillows, where jolting would not hurt the fiddle" (p. 5). The image is contracted potential and when he activates it, it swells with melodies and provokes the words that express his desires: carefree attitudes, joy in life, tenderness in love, romance, and the vastness of his yearning. His songs often assuage Caroline. After Indians came to the house and made her feel threatened, Pa plays the fiddle while she sings the lyrics to "Wild roved the Indian maid," a song about a woman questing for her lover, a romantic vision that expresses her own attraction to the "wild man" Ingalls and displaces pioneer reality into the romantic projection of the noble savage (p. 235). For Laura, Pa sets the world and cosmos into beckoning motion as he fiddles: "The night was full of music, and Laura was sure that part of it came from the great bright stars swinging so low above the prairie" (p. 51).

After they have been notified that they have settled on Indian territory, Pa lights out for the territory ahead like Huck Finn, leaving the civilizing house readily open for anyone who might need shelter. Laura assures herself that the house is not affected by their leaving: "The snug log house looked just as it always had. It did not seem to know they were going away" (p. 324). When they had left Wisconsin a year earlier, "the shutters were over the window, so the little house could not see them go" (p. 6). Laura learns to consign houses to objects that can readily be discarded as "once more the covered wagon was home" under the wide sky (p. 335), the pioneer's wheels over yet untracked land. Although they are in transit, there is the steady and beloved companionship of Pa, who with his music carries Laura into a sleep-dream of vastness wherein the prairie becomes the sea:

She felt her eyelids closing. She began to drift over the endless
waves of prairie grasses, and Pa's voice went with her singing:

> "Row away, row o'er the waters so blue,
> Like a feather we sail in our gum-tree canoe.
> Row the boat lightly, love, over the sea:
> Daily and nightly I'll wander with thee."

Little House on the Prairie abounds with images of immensity and
intimacy that evoke in the adult reader the feelings aligned with the
sublime. But the experience of the sublime is an oceanic feeling in
which the ego loses its boundaries. The growing child cannot
afford such ego loss, even while falling asleep, and needs assurance
and soothing from a familiar voice. Laura Ingalls Wilder's style
always anchors the child-reader's and Laura's egos in reassuring
specificity: "All around the wagon there was nothing but empty
silent space. Laura did not like it. But Pa was on the wagon and
Jack [their dog] was under the wagon; she knew that nothing could
hurt her while Pa and Jack were there" (p. 7). As she drifts over
endless prairie grasses into sleep, she is steadied by Pa's voice
evoking the boat image, the boat in which the fragile ego can row
lightly over the potentially enveloping element. In her ultimately
civilizing work, Ingalls Wilder prepares the child-reader for transi-
toriness, for separation, for the need to control the id, for the
necessity of civilizations, for historical guilt, and for the constant
urgency of dreams that drives us westward. But, as she re-collects
the images of childhood, her active imagination also expands with
reverie and enables the creative reader, caught in the spaces of
civilization, to realize that reverie alone will do to make a prairie.

Notes

1. Laura Ingalls Wilder, *Little House on the Prairie,* illus. by Garth Williams
(revised ed. 1953; rpt. New York: Harper and Row, 1971), p. 31. All references are
from this edition and hereafter are cited parenthetically.

2. *The Poetics of Reverie,* trans. Daniel Russell (Boston: Beacon Press, 1969), p.
105. See especially chapter 3, "Reveries Toward Childhood." Hereafter cited parenthetically in the text as *PR.*

3. Gaston Bachelard, *The Poetics of Space,* trans. Maria Jolas (Boston: Beacon
Press, 1969), p. xix. The first two chapters about the house—chapter 8, "Intimate

Immensity," and chapter 9, "The Dialectics of Inside and Outside"—have been especially valuable for my discussion. Hereafter cited parenthetically in the text as *PS*.

4. Wolfgang Iser, *The Act of Reading* (Baltimore: Johns Hopkins University Press, 1980), p. 4.

5. For a discussion of the creative process see the following essays by Rose Ann Moore: "Laura Ingalls Wilder's Orange Notebooks and the Art of the Little House Books," *Children's Literature*, 4 (1975), 105–19; "The Little House Books: Rose-Colored Glasses," *Children's Literature*, 7 (1978), 7–16; "Laura Ingalls Wilder and Rose Wilder Lane: The Chemistry of Collaboration," *Children's Literature in Education*, 11 (Autumn, 1980), 101–09. For a discussion of stereotyping see Elizabeth Segel, "Laura Ingalls Wilder's America: "An Unflinching Assessment," *Children's Literature in Education*, 8 (Summer, 1977), 63–70; for biographical data see Donald Zochert, *Laura: The Life of Laura Ingalls Wilder* (Chicago: Contemporary Books, 1976); for the pioneer theme see Anne Thompson Lee, " 'It's better farther on': Laura Ingalls Wilder and the Pioneer Spirit," *The Lion and the Unicorn*, 3 (Spring, 1979), 74–88.

Death and Rebirth in Pinocchio

Thomas J. Morrissey and Richard Wunderlich

What epic hero worth the title does not undergo some form of death and resurrection? This primal motif manifests itself in a number of ways in mythology and literature. Gods can die and be reborn, or rise from the dead. Such mythological events probably imitate the annual cycle of vegetative birth, death, and renascence, and they often serve as paradigms for the frequent symbolic deaths and rebirths encountered in literature. Two such symbolic renderings are most prominent: re-emergence from a journey to hell and rebirth through metamorphosis. Journeys to the underworld are a common feature of Western literary epics: Gilgamesh, Odysseus, Aeneas, and Dante all benefit from the knowledge and power they put on after such descents. Rebirth through metamorphosis, on the other hand, is a motif generally consigned to fantasy or speculative literature. Philomela, the Frog-Prince (in his many incarnations), the Beast of *Beauty and the Beast,* and Frost of Zelazny's "For a Breath I Tarry" are a few individuals who undergo such changes. These two figurative manifestations of the death-rebirth trope are rarely combined; however, Carlo Collodi's great fantasy-epic, *The Adventures of Pinocchio,* is a work in which a hero experiences symbolic death and rebirth through both infernal descent and metamorphosis. Pinocchio is truly a fantasy hero of epic proportions.

At first glance, American readers are likely to scoff at the greatness and symbolic importance of Pinocchio, for Collodi's masterpiece has suffered considerable deformation at the hands of adaptors and publishers.[1] To most of us *Pinocchio* is a light-hearted, light-headed tale of youthful mischief. Walt Disney's film capitalized on what was already, in 1939, a well-established tradition of simplification and misinterpretation. A few American critics, such as Glauco Cambon and James Heisig, have resisted the trend, and so have many American families; faithful translations of *Pinocchio* are readily available, even after ninety years of desecration. Our bibliographic research shows that, counting abridgements and adaptations, an average of two or more new *Pinocchio*s have appeared annually since the first U.S. printing in 1892. In Italy, moreover, *Pinocchio* has long been held a national treasure. Its author (born Carlo Lorenzini in 1826) was an often satirical journalist and a veteran of the military and political campaign for Italian reunification. He was both a man of letters and a man of the world whose social criticism did not always escape the censors. The period from 1981 to 1983 marks the *Pinocchio* centennial, and the Fondazione nazionale Carlo Collodi, a serious literary society, has tried to make sure that the world remembers the real *Pinocchio*.

Pinocchio is a fast-moving novel with engaging characters and crisp dialog. Much of the humor is ironic, usually at the expense of the heedless puppet. Furthermore, as a hero of what is, in the classic sense, a comedy, Pinocchio is protected from ultimate catastrophe, although he suffers quite a few moderate calamities. Collodi never lets the reader forget that disaster is always a possibility; in fact, that is just what Pinocchio's mentors—Gepetto, the Talking Cricket, and the Fairy—repeatedly tell him. Although they are part of a comedy, Pinocchio's adventures are not always funny. Indeed, they are sometimes sinister. The book's fictive world does not exclude injury, pain, or even death—they are stylized but not absent. How could Collodi write a true picaresque novel without accommodating the harsher facts of mortal existence? Accommodate them he does, by using the archetypal birth-death-rebirth motif as a means of structuring his hero's growth to responsible boyhood. Of course, the success of the puppet's growth is rendered in terms of his metamorphic rebirth as a flesh-and-blood human. On the road to rebirth, Pinocchio suffers setbacks that are themselves symbolic deaths and resurrections. Furthermore, along the way he joins the ranks of Odysseus, Aeneas, and Hamlet by obtaining information and advice from the world beyond. Beneath the book's comic-fantasy texture—but not far beneath—lies a symbolic journey to the underworld, from which Pinocchio emerges whole.

Pinocchio is one of those fortunate souls who does not always get what he wants but most assuredly gets what he needs. His behavior, or rather misbehavior, in the book's early episodes signals his need of correction, but the correction must come in the right form: experience tempered with a little good fortune. The puppet's misfortunes are the logical consequences of his folly, but they are also lucky opportunities for personal growth. What Pinocchio lacks at the beginning of the novel are the rudiments of self-control and civilized behavior—patience and concern for others. In the first eight chapters he has a chance to learn these virtues from Gepetto and the Talking Cricket, yet his failure to do so results in his exile from home and some symbolic lessons that foreshadow his encounters with the other world and its emissaries.

The disregard for his well-being and that of others that Pinocchio displays in the first four chapters is justly rewarded in the second four chapters, thus establishing the stimulus-response format that informs his quest throughout the book. The piece of wood that will become the hero is a bundle of amoral energy. It frightens Master Antonio with its insolence, then insults and strikes Gepetto, causing the two old men to come to blows. The carving of the puppet is like a nuclear chain-reaction in slow motion. As Gepetto liberates Pinocchio from the raw wood, he quickly learns with whom he is dealing. When the eyes are formed, they stare at the carpenter, who calls them "wicked,"[2] the nose grows faster than the old man can cut, the mouth derides him with laughter, and the hands grab the poor man's wig. Gepetto begins to regret having begun Pinocchio even before he has carved the feet; when they are finished, the puppet promptly runs away, the most immediate result of which is Gepetto's arrest for puppet abuse. Left temporarily fatherless, the puppet encounters the first non-parent significant other of his young life—the venerable Talking Cricket, whose warnings about the consequences of disobedience and sloth cause Pinocchio to "lose patience" (p. 27) and splatter him on the wall with a hammer.

These acts of unbridled passion are answered specifically in chapters 5–8 with symbolic and corporeal suffering. After killing the hundred-year-old cricket, the puppet receives a lesson in the value of revering life as his intended breakfast flies out the window when he cracks open its shell. Pinocchio is an agent of death who inadvertently becomes an agent of life; he also becomes very

Blind to the value of life, Pinocchio hurls a hammer at the Cricket. From *Pinocchio,*
adapted by Allen Chaffee, illustrated by Lois Lensky. Copyright 1946 by Random
House, Inc. Reproduced by permission of the publisher.

hungry. Searching for food, he gets his first taste of hell. He goes
out into the "infernal night" (p. 35) to wander alone in what
appears to be the "land of the dead" (p. 31). A man douses him with
a chamber pot and he returns home "a wet chicken" (p. 32), thus
resembling his fugitive breakfast, surely a humbling experience. In
the morning he awakens to find that the offending feet which have
caused such mischief have burned in Gepetto's purgatorial brazier.
Pinocchio's feet are restored, but at a heavy price. First, he must
endure a lecture by Gepetto; then he receives a gently symbolic

lesson when the carpenter uses the ubiquitous empty eggshell to mix the glue with which he repairs the puppet. These events do not turn Pinocchio into a model of patience, filial piety, and respect for life, but from them he does learn to love Gepetto and even vows to go to school. Yet his promises prove hard to keep when he leaves home and is tempted by the bigger world; hence, he must experience with greater ferocity more hells of his own making, and he must be helped by increasingly more mysterious agents.

Pinocchio undergoes a series of adventures that draw on the descent-to-the-underworld motif hinted at in the earlier chapters. Some involve traditional images of hellfire, one is gothic, and another classical. Fires are abundant. He is nearly used as fuel to cook the Fire-Eater's mutton; he is almost incinerated in a tree by the assassins; he eludes a disgruntled peasant who wants to sell him for firewood; and he barely escapes frying at the hands of the Green Fisherman. It takes a good scare to make Pinocchio admit the reality of death. Killing the Cricket and refusing to believe in the existence of assassins demonstrate his initial ignorance about the fragility of life, but this unrealistic attitude gives way when the possibility of his own death offers him an unforgettable object lesson in mortality. He laughs at the assassins' vain attempt to stab him, but then the hooded figures manage to hang him. Collodi makes no effort to hide the puppet's agony: "His breath failed him and he could say no more. He shut his eyes, opened his mouth, stretched his legs, gave a long shudder, and hung stiff and insensible" (p. 74). Incredibly, even hanging is not enough to impress Pinocchio, but things change when Collodi employs delightful gothic farce. Although he lies near death at the Fairy's cottage, he will not take her medicine. At first he boasts that he does not fear death, saying, "I would rather die than drink that bitter medicine," but when four ink-black rabbits carrying a bier tell him, "We are come to take you" (p. 82), he begs for the tumbler. Later, the journey to the land of Cocagne features images of Hades. The ominous Coachman is a Charon-like figure who drives a silent black coach in the dark of night. He bites off the ears of one of the boys-turned-donkeys and utters the book's only remotely ribald joke, when he says of the injured beast, "Let him cry; he will laugh

when he is a bridegroom" (p. 171). Collodi gives a tantalizing hint
of the Coachman's unearthly status in the fragment of song:

> During the night all sleep.
> But I sleep never . . . [p. 170]

Of course, Pinocchio and Candlewick pay no heed to imagery and
must literally turn into donkeys before they see their folly, but
Collodi deftly shares the truth with his readers.

Pinocchio would have survived none of these ordeals without
help from his friends, especially super- or preternatural ones. Like
Dante, he needs his Virgil; like Odysseus, he needs his Athene. The
Talking Cricket's ghost and the Fairy are the prime benefactors
who guide him in learning to follow the dictates of his basically
good heart. The Cricket is master of the *bon mot*. Just before
Pinocchio squashes him, the insect warns him that loafers inevitably end up in jail or in the hospital: Pinocchio loafs and ends up in
both places (the gorilla judge's prison and the Fairy's miraculous
clinic). If Pinocchio is impetuous, the Cricket is a very patient soul
who holds no grudge against the puppet for hammering him, for
he returns to the world three times to help the wayward hero. First,
he appears in ghostly form to warn Pinocchio about the assassins,
to no avail. Second, he turns up as one of the Fairy's council of
physicians. He is the only doctor who knows when to keep his
mouth shut, but when he does speak, he utters the stark truth that
awakens Pinocchio from his coma: "That puppet there is a disobe-
dient son who will make his poor father die of a broken heart!" (p.
78). Finally, he serves as the Fairy's go-between when Pinocchio has
finally proven himself worthy in the last chapter. The Talking
Cricket is throughout the book a reliable ghostly counselor.

The Fairy is the pivotal influence on Pinocchio's development.
Gepetto's self-sacrifice and the Cricket's good advice are important,
but the Fairy's enduring patience and magical powers are the
puppet's greatest assets. She has been called Kalypso[3] and the
archetype of the lost mother:[4] these she is and more. She is a vital
link in the merger of the death-resurrection and metamorphosis
motifs. Not only does she facilitate Pinocchio's resurrections and
final conversion to boyhood, but she too undergoes ritual deaths,

resurrections, and transmutations—all on behalf of her adopted brother-son. She is, first and foremost, a wielder of magical power. She can clap her hands three times and command a raven to fetch Pinocchio from the oak tree. This is a significant point in a book in which three is a special number. In chapter 16 the Fairy summons three doctors and forgives Pinocchio three lies. The puppet is threatened by three fires, and three times he is choked—once by a rope, once by a dog collar, and once by a donkey's halter. Gepetto searches for his son for three months and the pigeon who takes Pinocchio to him has not seen the old man for three days (p. 114). The ghost of the Cricket appears to Pinocchio three times, and the Fairy feeds the puppet a three-course meal in the Land of Industrious Bees. Also, Pinocchio has three great mentors, Gepetto, the Cricket, and the Fairy. Perhaps the frequent use of the number three is an echo of Dante; more likely, it is designed to approximate a formula or incantation reinforcing the magical quality of the fictive world personified in the Fairy-sorceress.

Although the Fairy has lived in the woods for a thousand years, she chooses to undergo death and metamorphosis in order to help Pinocchio to a better understanding of the meaning of life and love. She passes through the stages of life from child to old woman, thus serving as the puppet's only role model who undergoes the maturation process. The device is also useful because, at the time Pinocchio first sees her, he has already rejected a father's guidance and would be unlikely to heed a mother-figure. She appears first at the window as a ghostly apparition who speaks without moving her lips, in "a voice that seemed to come from the other world" (p. 74). She makes no effort to save the fleeing marionette from the assassins; instead she presents him with an image of death that should intensify his appreciation of the preciousness of life. It does not do so, of course, so that later she must summon the rabbit undertakers to amplify the image. After Pinocchio's medicinal care, he breaks his promise to return at nightfall to his would-be Fairy-sister and, as a result, loses his money, does a stint as a watchdog, and goes to prison for four months. But these lessons are not as powerful as the sight of the Fairy's grave. (A number of commentators have questioned how he could read the stone when he never had opened a book, but no matter.) Given that the Fairy has taught Pinocchio the meaning of death, it is a profoundly significant mark of his spiritual growth that he freely expresses his willingness to die that she might live (p. 112). From this point on, the Fairy plays the role of mother in Pinocchio's life, for once he has learned some semblance of filial piety, he is ready to accept guidance—although he manages to disobey his new mother by running off with Candlewick.

On a more symbolic level, however, both the Cricket and the Fairy are also emblems of death and resurrection. The Cricket dies but returns as a ghost. Whether he really remains a ghost or whether he actually returns to life in chapters 17 and 36 is not really clear. The Fairy dies twice. First, she is the dead child at the window, but she returns in child form to minister to the hanged puppet. Then she lies buried before her transformation into an old woman and mother. Whether she really dies on either of these occasions is unimportant: what matters is that Pinocchio believes she is dead. He sees, then, three striking images of victory over death, which, taken together, strengthen his courage to perform the ultimate heroic deeds—the rescue and subsequent care taking of Gepetto. Furthermore, these events help to establish for the reader the dominance of the death-resurrection motif as the paramount structural and symbolic device of the novel.

It is Pinocchio, the hero of the fantasy *bildungsroman,* who does the most dying and growing. Although he has a number of close calls with fires, the Serpent, and the Green Fisherman, his three major confrontations with death and the underworld involve his hanging, his descent to and escape from donkey-hood, and his rescue of Gepetto. The great resurrection is his metamorphosis in chapter 36. As mentioned earlier, Pinocchio's triumph over death by hanging is none of his own doing, but it strengthens his bond with the Fairy and his willingness to sacrifice on behalf of loved ones.

The events surrounding Pinocchio's adventures in Cocagne are of truly mythic significance. Both literally and figuratively they prepare him for his triumphant fate. The journey to Cocagne is an echo of classic descents into Hades. Once the boys arrive in

Cocagne the hellish torture begins. Although they are too ignorant to realize it, the absence of schools and masters is the start of their punishment, but Pinocchio and his comrades do not face damnation until they are converted into donkeys. The punishment fits the crime in a way reminiscent of the *Aeneid* and the *Inferno*. Their dehumanization is not complete, however, for it is the nature of their torture that they be aware of what they have lost in their metamorphosis. Pinocchio has already suffered symbolic loss of his humanoid status in the episode in which he becomes a watchdog. In that instance, though, he is playing a role; in Cocagne the change is real. His failure to heed the warning implicit in the earlier chapter results in his being demoted a few links on the great chain of being.

Pinocchio was released from the kennel for his honesty—all it required was removal of the collar. The escape from donkey-hood is a more complicated matter. In an event analogous to the appearance of the dead Fairy at the window before his hanging, Pinocchio sees the Fairy in the circus audience just before he lames himself and is sold for his hide. After his preternatural reminder of the Fairy's unfailing concern, he is put in a weighted sack and submerged. The devouring of his flesh by the fish, which liberates the puppet from donkey form, is a miracle second only to his metamorphosis to boyhood. It is a sea-change akin to Ferdinand's escape from drowning in *The Tempest* or to Aphrodite's rise from the sea. Having proven through his admittedly ill-expressed love for Gepetto and the Fairy that his heart is basically good, Pinocchio is redeemed in this singularly symbolic fashion by his loving mother. Like a soul emerging triumphant from a dying body, or like Dionysus or Jesus who are victoriously rended and consumed, the puppet comes to the surface with irrepressible joy and enthusiasm. Exultation is a valuable emotion for him to experience, for it gives him a glimpse of what life can be like for a heroic personality just before he himself embarks on his greatest adventure. There are two crucial points to consider in this episode. First, Pinocchio is helped both because he is lucky and because he deserves it by virtue of his having learned to love. His friend Candlewick, who is unaided and unschooled in matters of the heart, dies a spent

Pinocchio faces life and death in the form of the Dolphin and the Dogfish, *il pesce cano.*
From *Le avventure di Pinocchio,* illustrated by Roland Topor. Copyright 1972 by
Olivetti, Milan. Reproduced by permission of the publisher.

donkey. Second, although Pinocchio reassumes marionette form, he is no longer merely a puppet pulled hither and yon by good and bad influences. He emerges with a new sense of self-determination, ready to be a hero.

Pinocchio's rescue of Gepetto from the terrible shark, *il pesce cane*, is a voluntary heroic act which, unlike anything he has done before, he undertakes with forethought and single-mindedness. Entering the fish's cavernous mouth is yet another ritual descent, but it is no accident. The Tunny and Gepetto languish hopelessly in the fish's belly; it is Pinocchio who gives them the hope and will to escape. He addresses his father in the imperative mood, saying, "Get on my shoulders and put your arms tight around my neck. I will take care of the rest" (p. 209). He is Aeneas to Gepetto's Anchises, the model of filial piety and self-sacrifice.

Heroism is not enough to earn Pinocchio human form: he must shed indolence and learn to work for his bread. This he does in the final chapter, where he labors ceaselessly on behalf of the invalid Gepetto. His transformation to boyhood is as quiet and solemn as his birth to puppet-hood was raucous and disrespectful; he is changed in his sleep by the Fairy's kiss. From undisciplined puppet, hanged victim, watchdog, and donkey, Pinocchio comes to heroism and human form. Each of the deaths and resurrections in the novel is a symbolic reminder of this overall pattern. To underscore the motif, Collodi shows us Pinocchio looking at himself in a mirror "as happy and joyful as if it were the Easter holidays" (p. 221); surely this is the risen puppet's Easter.

To be reborn is not just to live again; it is to change and to grow as the Fairy does. Thus Pinocchio's picaresque journey leads him to a new status: boyhood. And what is boyhood to Collodi? It is a state of proto-adulthood, for Collodi's concept of childhood is similar to that of the medieval cultures depicted in Philippe Ariès's *Centuries of Childhood*. It is central to this concept that children have the same emotions, needs, and, to some extent, responsibilities, as their parents. They are not fragile ornaments to be sheltered but rather adults-in-becoming who must face, with parental guidance, the trials of the world so that they can function in it as responsible adults. Collodi does not show us Pinocchio as an adult, but he does, through epic symbolism, show us his potential to be one. The puppet-turned-boy is that hero that every loved and loving child can be. It is Collodi's tribute to children that he chooses to depict their very real trials and triumphs in terms of mythic patterns ordinarily reserved for adults.

Notes

1. Richard Wunderlich and Thomas J. Morrissey, "The Desecration of *Pinocchio* in the United States," *Horn Book,* 58 (April 1982), 205–11.

2. *The Adventures of Pinocchio,* trans. M. A. Murray (1892; rpt. New York: Lancer Books, 1968), p. 20. All citations are taken from this edition and hereafter are cited parenthetically in the text. Although the 1892 translation has become a little dated, it is a faithful rendition of Collodi's descriptive words and phrases.

3. Mark Van Doren, introduction to *Pinocchio* (New York: Limited Editions Club, 1937), p. vii.

4. James W. Heisig, "Pinocchio: Archetype of the Motherless Child," *Children's Literature,* 3 (1974), 31.

Jean de Brunhoff's Advice to Youth: The Babar Books as Books of Courtesy

Ann M. Hildebrand

The *Babar* books by Jean de Brunhoff have been enjoyed by children and acclaimed and purchased by adults for fifty years. They have been translated into many languages, changed in size and typeface, and reprinted in varying editions.[1] They have inspired clothes, dolls, games, television shows, ballets, and musical compositions of distinction. And on both sides of the Atlantic, they have been commended for their "fine dose of foolishness," "distinguished nonsense," "le charm naïf" and examined for their sophistication and wit, Freudian overtones, political didacticism, and subtle satire on human life.[2]

The books may indeed possess all these qualities, but that fact alone does not account for the permanent claim they have as superior children's literature. Underlying their pure delight, adventurous plots, lively characters, evocative settings, and whimsical style is their essentially serious theme: the earnest concern of a father for how his young family should be brought up, a concern for their morals and their manners. Failure to perceive this concern and the traditional mode in which it is expressed has led one critic to suggest that the books lack "a narrative proposition to guide or offer power" and to imply that they have no unifying principle, "the task not being to get somewhere in particular."[3] In fact, their "narrative proposition," their structure—and so their power—becomes evident only when their kinship with that old genre, the book of courtesy, is recognized.

At the end of *Babar and His Children*, the elephant-king sighs, "Truly it is not easy to bring up a family." As if acknowledging this, Jean de Brunhoff has written books of parental advice, the oldest type of courtesy literature, in which the clear task is to guide his own sons into honorable manhood, providing at the same time a courtesy ideal for other children, and all the while captivating an ageless audience.

I do not imply that Brunhoff set out deliberately to modernize the traditional book of parental advice and so merely adapted that genre, point by point, to his purposes. But the similarities between the *Babars* and the old courtesies are more than passing or occasional. The systematic attention to morals and manners that structures the early books also shapes Brunhoff's series. His style is not didactic like that of the traditional courtesies nor his purpose only to instill worthwhile behavior, yet his narrative and form, words and pictures, are balanced to delight *and* shape young personalities. The books' critical worth, the series' unity, and perhaps the universal and lasting appeal of the *Babars* are illuminated if seen as the thoughtful, solicitous wisdom of a father speaking to his own children.

The ideals reflect Brunhoff's own Gallic tradition, central to which is the family group *(le foyer)*, the ambience of "familyness" *(en famille)*, and the interrelation of distinct roles. Mother-father interaction is crucially influential on children and must be loving and constant; mother-child relationships are different from father-child bonds; sibling relationships are equally delineated. Children are taught to behave within a controlled structure of expectations and not to question parents' authority or discipline within the *foyer*. This insistence on control at the earliest age leads the child to exercise self-control when his world expands beyond the *foyer*. That world also has special behavioral expectations, and so French children learn to model the rules of correct social conduct. Freedom and true individuality, say French parents, are but the development of new variations on culturally accepted designs. They still love and indulge their children and understand childhood's unique charms, but they insist that

> childhood [be] a long apprenticeship in becoming a person. Through training, the child gradually is transformed from a small being into an individual, an adult with an awakened spirit, a developed imagination, and a critical intelligence, who knows the behavior appropriate to a man and a woman, and who has acquired the skills and control necessary for well-being. . . . The experiences of childhood are conceived as necessary preparations to achieve *bonheur*.[4]

This regimen implies continuing support from the entire *foyer*, but Jean de Brunhoff was often not physically present to fulfill his parental role. Born in 1899, he grew up in Paris, graduated from the *lycée*, went to war, and became a professional artist when he returned. In 1924, he married Cécile Sabourand, a Parisian physician's daughter and a pianist; shortly after, the Brunhoff *foyer* expanded to include sons Laurent and Matthieu. The family moved in cultured, courteous circles with, no doubt, the customary loving expectations of French parents for their children. Babar first appeared in bedtime stories told by mama; the boys retold the tales to papa, who caught their delight and began to draw the huge, gentle hero. But as Bettina Hürlimann points out, "the young father had soon to leave his family, compelled by a disease of the lungs to spend much of the rest of his life in a mountain resort in distant Switzerland" (p. 197). Hürlimann stresses Brunhoff's long stay at the sanitarium from which he wrote *Histoire de Babar, Le Petit Elephant*, implying that if there had been no illness, no absence, no heavy time, and no need to write to his sons rather than be with them, there would have been no Babar books. Certainly the enforced fresh-air therapy kept him away from an active, day-to-day paternal role. But the books, begun in happier times when the family was together, provide more than an absent father's daily link with his sons; they present a vision of civilized life, an ideal of loving, courteous maturity. And the determined urgency of a man who knew he might not live long marks their regular production— almost one a year from 1931 to 1937—and comprehensive subject matter: all that could happen to a family, from birth to death, does happen. In 1937, before his third son, Thierry, was two, Jean de Brunhoff died of tuberculosis, leaving his wife with three small sons—and seven books filled with objects and events dear to the Brunhoff family as the background for a father's affectionate counsel.[5]

The counsel was clear and thorough: Brunhoff wanted his children to acquire the experiences and develop the control necessary for *bonheur*. He could not be an enduring model, but he could make one from his own fatherly dreams and hopes. And so, the elegantly gallant Babar is the loving, guiding, ideal French father; he is also the *gallant et honnête homme*, the Parfit Knight, the

Compleat Gentleman of courtesy literature—the ultimate courtier in elephant's skin.

It was toward the making of these ideal types that all traditional courtesy literature was directed. The book of courtesy, *la civilité,* was more than a volume on etiquette. In his exhaustive study of the genre, John E. Mason defines *courtesy* broadly as "a code of ethics, esthetics, or peculiar information for any class-conscious group, and a courtesy book is a book which sets down such a code."[6] Generally, courtesy implied a moral philosophy and an apprecia- tion of refinement; specifically, it indicated how to achieve *noblesse* within a particular social structure. At its ideal best—and an ideal it was, for real life usually lagged far behind—courtesy rested on regard for and service to others before self. But "consideration for others is not inborn. It is instilled,"[7] that is, "introduce[d] little by little into the mind, soul, heart, . . . infuse[d] slowly or gradually."[8] For centuries courtesy books persevered in this task.

They were regarded as necessary adjuncts to education, what- ever the kind (though most were not actually schoolbooks, the earliest predating the custom of formal schooling). They were studied, practiced, and memorized, and their frequent admoni- tion, "Lerne or be lewde,"[9] was taken seriously by people with aspirations to gentility. They touched on every facet of behavior: religion and morality, the origin of true nobility, principles of leadership and diplomacy, domestic management, sexual ethics and the treatment of women, the nurture and education of chil- dren, travel, personal behavior, bodily care and dress, conversa- tion, and the diversions appropriate for gentlefolk.[10] In short, they were comprehensive manuals for living in the upper classes of society and set the standards for the ideal, cultivated gentleman in both inward and outward demeanor, according to the lights of each period.

The roots of European courtesy probably lie in chivalry, which, blended with medieval Christianity and Renaissance humanism, produced the ideal gentleman of courtesy literature. Whether the French of Provence or the Italians and Spanish of the early Renaissance initiated the genre is not certain; nevertheless it moved northwards, and courtesy treatises translated from earlier European sources began to appear in England around 1430, proliferating after Caxton. Those extant have been gathered into *The Babees Book,* a curious but fascinating compendium of types and periods, reflecting feudal structure and the reciprocity between French and English culture; many early English courtesies were direct translations from the "Frenssche" of books like *Avis aus Rois* (c. 1360) and *Contenance de Table* (fifteenth century).[11] The mutual influence continued until the seventeenth century, when the roads to chivalry began to diverge. The French continued to stress the *gallant homme* and "courtliness, refinement, elegance, careful consideration of conduct in the light of social authority," which peaked in the reign of Louis XIV. The English, on the other hand, emphasized the *honnête homme* and "frankness, sweetness, kindliness, subordination of self in deference to . . . principle."[12]

The audience of the early courtesies, as for most medieval writing, was well-born and homogeneous, ranging from "pueritia" to "senies," as Philippe Ariès documents.[13] The books, monotonously similar, were addressed to sons, daughters, wives, and highborn "henchmen" or "enfaunts"; many volumes gave advice on how to develop specific skills such as hawking, carving at table, or managing a house and servants. Later, when childhood emerged as distinct from adulthood, the courtesy audience was differentiated, and separate books contained advice ostensibly for children. But even then, "Most preceptual . . . [writers] were content to write as if they were addressing adults. And very often they would in effect be writing for adults."[14] Perhaps the very intent of traditional courtesies was antithetical to our modern conception of childhood, for writers "seldom considered the nature of the child as a child. Treated as a small adult, the child was to be trained out of his childish ways into the moral and rational perfection of regulated manhood."[15]

The style and tone of the old courtesy books was unrelievedly didactic; they did not aim to delight but to instruct. However, their form did vary. Some courtesy writers used an allegorical framework, others a dialogue or epistolary one. Some merely presented lists of flat dos and don'ts; others couched rules in solemn similes. Some courtesies were in prose; some were in verse designed to make memorization easier (not more pleasant!). The earliest, in manuscript, variously profited or suffered from a formal change when they were set in print. Continental courtesy literature was in Italian, Spanish, French, or Latin; when it was translated into English, form and style were often altered again at the pleasure of the translator. All this really didn't matter, though, for medieval editors agreed that their literary value was negligible. With later writers like Erasmus and eventually Chesterfield, personal wit and charm alleviated the didactic tone. But traditional courtesy writers operated on no educational theory of luring the child into correct behavior by masking moral and social advice in sprightly style or story.

All courtesy literature reflected its social milieu and attitudes toward youth. The earliest books resound with the status of medieval children, who were harshly treated and bartered like commodities for lucrative marriages.[16] The Renaissance was not much gentler toward the young, but humanist courtesies did at least stress individuality and education. Courtesy books of the seventeenth century, in proliferating number and variety, began to acknowledge childhood's unique characteristics and needs. And when Locke distinguished separate child and adult natures, recommending that children's "blank slates" be imprinted in the best way for their limited mental resources and experience, courtesies reflected his insistence on instruction with pleasure. Rousseau, less bent on imprinting than on freeing children's minds, fully "exposed" childhood as innately good, curious, open to experiential learning—and significantly different from miniature adulthood. His thinking hastened the demise of traditional courtesy books, which were supplanted by the "moral stories" of his didactic literary disciples; and it also stimulated the increased sensitivity toward children that marks social, educational, scientific, and artistic advances in the nineteenth and twentieth centuries. Whatever their form or period, the books which spurred or goaded young folk to genteel behavior were barometers of childhood's place in society.

In form and style, the Babars bear the imprint of the twentieth century with their delightful blend of pictures and words, fancy and seriousness. But in theme they echo an ideal of behavior that is structured traditionally. Of the four main types of courtesy books, the *Babars* are most like the practical, informal-intimate books of parental advice, directed by a particular father toward, usually, his

own children and exemplified by Lord Chesterfield's famous letters to his son. But they are also books of polite conduct, for their
theory of behavior is coherent, drawn from traditional authority,
and intended for a much less personal audience, like Erasmus's *De
Civilitate de Morum Puerilium*. They are books of policy as well, for
King Babar is careful to equip his royal children with principles for
governing, much like James I in *Basilikon Doron* and Elyot in *The
Governor*. And they are definitely books of civility like della Casa's *Il
Galateo,* guides to personal behavior in society, reflecting not only
the personal values and cultural ideals of their French creator but
also the best virtues of all courtly traditions—tolerance, gentleness,
fairness, respectfulness, and consideration—that lead to both self-
control and self-expression. In short, they are traditional and
modern, personal and universal, instructive and pleasurable, for
children and adults alike.

And in this they are unique. Children's stories concerned with
morals and manners appeared in the eighteenth century, as the
unitary function of traditional courtesies gave way to the separate
genres of moral story and etiquette book. The French Berquin and
de Genlis and the relentless English moralists such as Hannah
More and Mrs. Barbauld dressed moral-social preachments in
story—but thinly. Maria Edgeworth, probably the best writer of the
lady didactics, often shows a wry wit, though a scorn for Society
and etiquette, in stories like "Forester," who "was frank, brave, and
generous, but he had been taught to dislike politeness;"[17] even her
narratives had the inevitable lesson. Tales bursting forth in the
nineteenth century contained varying doses of morals and manners. Some writers were whimsically ironic, like Lear and Kipling,
but not clearly systematic; others, such as MacDonald, Alcott, and
the school story writers, were seriously concerned with morals,
manners, story, and even pleasure, but their focus was not a system
for behavior either. Social effectiveness was addressed in etiquette
books but usually not morality; even picturebook behavior models
like the Goops (or today's wry *What Do You Do, Dear?*) only imply
the importance of consideration, stressing mainly politeness. Systematic but negative attention is given manners in books like
Struwwelpater and others of the Grobianus tradition; even *Tom
Sawyer* teaches morals and manners by reverse precept. But there

are no stories that wed the systematic content and instructive intent of traditional courtesy books with the narrative and visual organization and delight of modern children's books—until the *Babars* accomplish the task so naturally.

Though all six storybooks contain Jean de Brunhoff's prescriptions for upbringing, the highest concentration of advice occurs in those which develop Babar's *foyer: The Story of Babar, The Travels of Babar, Babar the King,* and *Babar and His Children.*[18] In these stories, Babar is Brunhoff's chief persona, the *foyer* includes close friends and relatives, and the situations encountered are those of the real world. In *Babar and Zephir,* both the personae and the world change; it is Zephir the monkey's *foyer* and, though the book begins in the "real world" of Monkeyville, it soon moves into a fairyland of mermaids, monsters, and mythic-heroic rescues. The ideals implicit in the other books remain but added is a note of romance, a dose of fancy, and a distinct affirmation of love and imagination. *Babar and Father Christmas,* drafted in 1936 but unpublished until four years after Brunhoff's death, lacks both the sweet magic of *Zephir* and the serious wisdom of the other books; the author understandably seems to have run out of important advice, fresh dimensions to his characters, and indeed, energy for his art or his life. Still, taken as a whole, Père Brunhoff's stories address the same concerns that fill centuries of courtesy writings: *inward grace, outward grace, work, recreation, personal relations,* and *the nurture of children.*

The achievement of inward grace was a major focus of the earliest courtesy writings, such as Ramon Lull's *Le Libre del Ordre de Cavayleria* (c. 1200). Religious piety and virtue were the cornerstones of that grace: "Thenne yf thou wylt fynde noblesse of courage / demaunde it of faythe / hope Charyte / Iustyce / strengthe / attemperaunce loyalte / & of other noble vertues / For in them is noblesse of courage."[19] In his courtesy books, Jean de Brunhoff makes no reference in either words or pictures to a specific religion; there are no churches, priests, or nuns in the panoramas; Babar makes no provision for formal religion in his ideal city, Celesteville. But though not religion-based, Babar's philosophy of morality-in-optimism is clear: "Do you see how in this life one must never be discouraged? . . . Let's work hard and cheerfully and we'll continue to be happy" (3, p. 47). Brunhoff illustrates and further underlines his philosophy at one of the high points of the series: the elephant angels of love, health, happiness, hope, work, learning, joy, goodness, intelligence, patience, perseverance, and courage drive away the demons of fear, despair, indolence, ignorance, laziness, cowardice, misfortune, sickness, discouragement, stupidity, and anger (3, pp. 44–45). And Babar's insistence that virtue is accessible to all permeates the series. For, unlike the traditional courteous gentleman's Babar's ancestry is not noble; his wealth is no greater than anyone else's; his education is exceptional only because it is rare. But his nobility is undeniable, and it is by innate worth that he gains esteem. Right from birth, "he is a very good little elephant" (1, p. 4) and is chosen as ruler because of the personal attributes which inform his experience in the city: "He has learned so much living among men, let us crown him King" (1, p. 38). Brunhoff's gospel of optimism and his model of intrinsic, virtue-based morality offer a modern counterpart to Lull's noble goals and undeniable moral direction to youth's behavior.

Outward grace as a manifestation of the inward quality became central to the Renaissance concept of gentility. The new code is elaborated in Baldassarre Castiglione's *Book of the Courtier* (1528) and further codified in Giovanni della Casa's *Il Galateo* (1558) which, in its French translation, *La Galatée*, guided genteel French behavior for centuries. Essential to Castiglione's urbane, graceful courtier was an appropriate sense of dress: clothing should fit one's station and not be foppish or ostentatious. Brunhoff delights in dressing his elephant-king; for Babar, clothes literally make the man, and the little elephant can hardly wait: "I would like to have some fine clothes, too! I wonder how I can get them?" (1, p. 10). From the first matched outfit he buys through costumes for each occasion, suitable dress vividly separates Babar the civilized from the unclothed masses. And so Babar's greatest gift to those he loves—Celeste, Arthur, Cornelius, and his own subjects—is identity-giving clothes. Sometimes they are both splendid and appropriate, such as "beautiful rich clothes for holidays" (3, p. 14), but often just comfortably utilitarian, "serviceable clothes suitable for

OPPOSITE: The Gospel of Optimism. From *Babar the King,* by Jean de Brunhoff, translated by Merle S. Haas. Copyright 1935 and renewed by Random House, Inc. Reproduced by permission of the publisher.

... graceful winged elephants who chase Misfortune away from Celesteville and bring back Happiness. At this point he awakes, and feels ever so much better.

work-days" (3, p. 14). The most important item of clothing, though, is the hat, for it confers job identity and thus adulthood. When Babar loses his hat of office, the crown, he forfeits identity both as king and person: "No one will believe that they are actually King and Queen of the elephants," and "We are fed hay, as though we were donkeys!" (2, pp. 22–23), says Babar. There are many examples of hats as badges of maturity and position, all drawn with delicious inventiveness befitting the important item of clothing that traditionally makes a man hold his head high.

Conversation as a grace, an art with its own guidelines, was cultivated by Castiglione's courtier; yet even the earliest courtesy literature stressed decorum and tact in speech for overall gentility. In the *Babar* books, polished conversation is often wondrously civilized. The picture of Babar, casually graceful at the Old Lady's mantel, captures perfectly the poised elegance of a gentleman at his conversational best: "In the evening, after dinner, he tells the Old Lady's friends all about his life in the great forest" (1, p. 23). And Babar is scrupulously polite: "Babar says to her politely: 'Thank you, Madam' " (1, p. 11); "You must be tired, gentlemen. Won't you rest under the shade of the palm trees?" (3, p. 6). His introductions are impeccable: "Good morning, Mrs. Whale, I am Babar, King of the elephants, and here is my wife Celeste" (2, p. 14). Brunhoff's other characters are equally civil and the children pattern their conversation after these excellent examples, absorbing the etiquette and spirit of conversational art.

Correct behavior in all social situations was important to courtesy writers even though standards of correctness varied with the times. And Babar learned well his *Galatée;* excellent manners seem to come naturally to him. He never puts his elbows on the table; he removes his hat when appropriate; he walks on the outside of the street when escorting ladies; he keeps himself limber by exercising and clean by bathing; he gets proper rest. In addition to manners and hygiene, courtesy writers were concerned with graceful carriage, as the outer evidence of inner poise. Babar is a king and never slumps, slouches, or appears unconfident. He is able to remain composed in the face of others' bad manners and does not lose his equanimity when cannibals try to eat him, the ultimate *faux pas,* or when a giddy whale leaves him stranded (2). Brunhoff

Courtesy at meals, circa 1930. From *The Story of Babar, the Little Elephant,* by Jean de Brunhoff, translated by Merle S. Haas. Copyright 1933 and renewed by Random House, Inc. Reproduced by permission of the publisher.

shows children that gracious social behavior is indeed the outward mark of inward gentility and that it helps one handle most situations with élan.

Honorable, ennobling work, serving fellowman rather than self, is an important theme to Lull, Castiglione, and succeeding courtesy writers. In the *Basilikon Doron* (1599), James I of England speaks in considerable detail to his son Henry on the nobility and necessity of work and service. Traditionally, the worthiest job was that of advisor to the king, and most courtesy literature contained advice on statesmanship and administering a kingdom. Babar *is* king, but he still adheres to sound principles on choosing advisors, observing ceremonies, waging war, and making peace. He announces, "I am going to try to rule my kingdom wisely" (2, p. 48). He chooses his advisors prudently: Cornelius, his chief aide, is the oldest of the elephants and has the wisdom and stability of age and "good ideas"

(1, p. 40), and the Old Lady is a proven ally, experienced in life, and faithful. Babar loves and executes with great style all the ceremonies of statecraft: coronation-weddings (1); anniversary parades (3); cannonades announcing royal births (4). But he uses his military powers reluctantly, preferring to settle disputes with intelligence rather than force. Babar knows that "real war is not a joke" (2, p. 41) and rejoices unabashedly when peace is made, riding on an elephant's back and joining the cry, "Victory! Victory! The war is over! How perfectly splendid!" (2, p. 46).[20]

In early courtesy literature, law, medicine, philosophy, and other clearly established professions were also honorable outlets for gentlemen's capabilities. In Babar's thoroughly structured but classless monarchy, he is the king and of course very important; Cornelius his chief statesman, the Old Lady the teacher, Capoulosse the doctor, and Fandago the learned man are important. But so are Olur the mechanic, Tapitor the cobbler, and Hatchibombotar the street cleaner. Obviously, in Babar's kingdom, there is no hierarchy of occupations but rather a mutual recognition of each job's potential value to all: "If Capoulosse has holes in his shoes, he brings them to Tapitor, and, if Tapitor is sick, Capoulosse takes care of him" (3, p. 24). Celesteville is founded on the interdependence of honorable work of any kind, and the only disgrace is *not* working, because this leads to boredom, mischief, and unhappy consequences; the Gogottes, after all, "are not savage. But they are bored" (5, p. 25). In his courtesy books, Brunhoff extends the forms of honorable work but retains the ideal of service to one's fellowman that is implicit in traditional courtesy writing.[21]

Recreations suitable for a gentleman were catalogued unfailingly by courtesy writers. Among the many diversions of the eighteenth century, for example, the famous *Letters of Lord Chesterfield to His Son* (1774) suggest travel, sports, dancing, and theater. Babar embraces all of these—and more. His whole life is laced with travel, with its joys and hazards: frequent journeys between the great forest and the city, a honeymoon trip, work with a traveling circus, holiday excursions. And he travels by every means imaginable: on foot, by red motorcar, balloon, boat, bicycle, train, helicopter, and even on skis. He visits foreign ports, sees deserts and mountains;

Hürlimann says that he is "mad for civilization" (p. 195) and embraces it eagerly in as many places as possible.

Babar's enthusiastic endorsement of recreation is a founding principle of Celesteville, where "the Bureau of Industry is next door to the Amusement Hall which will be very practical and convenient" (3, p. 13); in this imposing, ornate building are separate facilities for "musique, circus, theatre, movies, danse" and an amusement park behind. Barbar himself does sports such as tennis, skiing, bicycling, and fishing, and dances at his own wedding. "From time to time Babar plays on his trumpet; he is fond of music" (3, p. 9), as are all residents of Celesteville. They are also avid theatregoers; one of the most fascinating drawings of the series shows the elephant citizens, dressed—of course—appropriately, spellbound by French classical theatre. And just pure play is an essential recreation: digging with shells in the sand (1, pp. 2–3), swinging, bouncing, watching parades, daydreaming (3). But there are clear limits to play, too, for when Babar "rides all the way up ten times and all the way down ten times," the elevator boy must admonish him, "This is not a toy" (1, p. 12). Babar makes sure that life is balanced. "At Celesteville, all the elephants work in the morning, and in the afternoon they can do as they please. They play, go for walks, read and dream . . ." (3, p. 26), that highest and most essential form of recreation. So too, Brunhoff's delighted readers participate in play as they absorb his quiet insistence on it.

Personal relationships, the day-to-day arenas for practicing virtuous, courteous behavior, were a major concern of traditional writers. The *caritas* that always motivated a true gentleman was manifested in all his dealings with people. He did not, either in public or in private, antagonize, gossip, or offend, but rather conducted himself with gracious civility. Writers like Sir Francis Osborn in *Advice to a Son* (1656) speak urgently to the need for personal diplomacy and friendship, even though in Osborn's case overtones of crass expediency creep in occasionally. But Babar's public demeanor is always commendable, motivated by a genuine love of his fellowman. He is careful to resolve quarrels; after winning the war, he signs a treaty with the rhinoceroses (3, p. 1); he forgives the troublesome dwarfs, holds no grudge (6, p. 27), and is always tactful. He exemplifies the prudent moderation in financial matters advised by many courtesy writers, avoiding both stinginess and extravagance. Babar is fair to his subjects, dispensing equally not only his honeymoon gifts—"He gives a gift to each elephant" (3, p. 14)—but also making sure that their homes, pictured in orderly tiers around Lake Celeste, are modestly equal: "Each elephant had his own house" (3, p. 12).

In his private, *foyer* life, friendship is important to Babar. As a baby, he plays with his peer-friends; as a youth, he treasures the friendship of the Old Lady, "who has always been fond of little elephants" and "gives him whatever he wants" (1, pp. 11 and 21); before marriage, he is Celeste's friend; and when he knows Cornelius better, Babar loves him enough to include him in the *foyer,* saying fondly, "Old Friend, you who have been my constant companion through good times and bad" (4, p. 1). Babar is courteous and agreeable to all but, like traditional gentlemen, chooses his closest friends from his social equals, in this case Celesteville's professionals. And so, although Celesteville is a classless Utopia, "Babar and Celeste like to play tennis with Mr. and Mrs. Philophage" (3, p. 26), the officer and his wife. One should note that Brunhoff is not perpetuating class distinctions based on snobbishness here but rather, as Mead notes, the French tendency to choose friends from a circle close to the *foyer* (pp. 31–33).

A traditional viewpoint, exemplified both in courtesy literature and in French social mores of the time, is seen in Brunhoff's depiction of women. Like the ideal courtesy gentleman, Babar was always gracious to ladies, as a sign of respect for their own gentle sakes and for their potential as mothers. And so he names his city after Queen Celeste and rules equally with her; he rewards the Old Lady, his first friend and patroness, for her brave war service and entrusts the children to her teaching. But the roles women play in the Babar books remain traditional ones: wife, mother, teacher, nurse, helper, quiet daughter, or lost princess. The potentially dynamic Crustadele, sibyl of the grotto, and Eléonore the mermaid seem passive compared to "that daredevil, Zephir" (5) and the other boys who do adventurous mischief. Care in choosing a wife, usually prominent in most courtesy books, is also implicit in the

Babars: Celeste is an equal, Babar's childhood friend who has all the potential for becoming a good mother. Though Brunhoff's perspective on women may be neither current nor popular, his perceptions are entirely consistent with his age, cultural background, and personal ideals. His attitudes should not be airily dismissed as chauvinistic but should be viewed, rather, as traditional; it is a subtle but valid distinction that must be made even for children today. And belief in abstract ideologies never causes Babar to be cruel or insensitive in his concrete relationships with people.

Nurturing children was a concern that engaged all courtesy writers. Erasmus devoted an entire Latin primer for schoolboys, *De Civilitate de Morum Puerilium* (1531), to the subject of the moral, educational, physical, and social upbringing of nonaristocratic youth. And in *De Pueris Statim ac Liberaliter Instituendis* (1529), he urged parents to "bestow especial pains upon [the child's] tenderest years."[22] Brunhoff "bestows pains" from page 1 of *The Story of Babar* throughout the series. Baby Babar himself is loved, rocked, sung to, and played with; Babar's own children are longed for—"Oh, how hard it is to wait for one's heart's desire!" (4)—and adoringly nurtured by their own parents. In fact, *Babar and His Children* becomes almost a manual on how to hold, feed, cradle, and dress babies, and on how to keep them from choking, catching cold, or falling out of trees. The environment is full of gentility, love, and warmth, as Erasmus advises; the parents are openly affectionate— Babar "embraces his wife tenderly" (4)—and provide unfailing models of behavior. Yet discipline is administered, not harshly as most courtesy writers advised but firmly and consistently, with explanations. Arthur and Celeste's mothers "are very happy to have them back but they scold them just the same because they ran away" (1, p. 30).

Education is an important aspect of nurture; what, where, how, and from whom children learned were matters of concern to courtesy writers. Babar's own schooling is private, quite traditional in method and subject: "A learned professor gives him lessons. Babar pays attention and does well in his work. He is a good pupil and makes rapid progress" (1, p. 22). His children have more progressive schooling under the ideal tutelage of the Old Lady:

"Lessons are never tiresome when she teaches" (3, p. 22). Although they learn in a progressive classroom with plenty of "discovery" experiences available, they still master traditional sums and letters, "for, that's what we study for," says Zephir (3, p. 23). A school is just part of the Bureau of Industry, one of Celesteville's two main public buildings; the rest is devoted to the library and the workshops. For Brunhoff, as for Erasmus and most other courtesy writers, the physical and educational nurture of children merits careful concern.

Jean de Brunhoff's parental advice echoes that of earlier courtesy writers with two major exceptions: his empathy for childhood and his regard for emotions.[23] More than the distanced awareness of childhood found in other courtesy writers, his is the participatory zest of one who is still part child himself. As if recalling the spirit of his own boyhood, he relives the motor sprinkler incident: "When Arthur and Zephir meet him, they quickly take off their shoes, and run after the car, barefoot. 'Oh, what a fine shower!' they say laughingly" (3, p. 30). When sweet-toothed Zephir falls into the vanilla creme, Brunhoff dwells with childlike delight on the moment (3, p. 18). Babar punishes both excesses but understands that "Arthur and Zephir are mischievous, as are all little boys" (3, p. 31). And when Arthur, distracted by a passing parade, forgets his babysitting responsibilities, Brunhoff lives Arthur's point of view: "Arthur is very glad to be trusted," but "Arthur is frightened and runs after them," and finally, when all is safe again, "Arthur is ever so pleased" (4). Brunhoff's obvious empathy with children's prankishness and thoughtlessness, but also with their curiosity and bravery, gives his fatherly advice the weight of still-fresh experience.

Courtesy books almost uniformly urge restraint of emotions—do not laugh too much or too loudly; do not cry; do not show fear—making the gentlemanly ideal seem impossibly far from a child's realization. But Babar displays all the honest emotions that arise from life. He often shows or speaks words of affection, a tender instance being when he bids farewell to the Old Lady and envelops her frailness in his great bulk: "He will never forget her" (1, p. 32). He is anxious before the birth of the children: "Babar is trying to read but finds it difficult to concentrate; his thoughts are elsewhere. He tries to write, but again his thoughts wander." But when the babies arrive, "he dashes headlong up the stairs, joyfully rushes into Celeste's bedchamber," and "embraces his wife tenderly" (4). Babar cries, too, not only when he is young and loses his mother but when he is older and sad. "He often stands at the window, thinking sadly of his childhood, and cries when he remembers his mother" (1, p. 24). And he acknowledges anguish and near-despair when he is a mature king: "What a dreadful day. . . . It began so well. Why did it have to end so badly? . . . We had forgotten that misfortune existed! . . . Oh! How long this night seems, and how worried I am!" (3). Through Babar's heartfelt, natural displays of emotion, Brunhoff tells children that feelings are a part of living and of dying.

Bettina Hürlimann calls Babar "something of an anachronism in our world-weary time," and yet at the same time "a wonderfully inspiring example," seeing him as "an enterprising elephant" partaking "in the evolution of an ideal society" (p. 195). Babar is, undeniably, enterprising, which according to our zeitgeist is good; he is also anachronistic and, according to the same zeitgeist, that is not so good. Yet it is Babar's sturdy out-of-timeness that makes him impervious to superficial values and thus inspiring to children. Jean de Brunhoff knew, just as the old courtesy writers did, that the *beau idéal* was backward-looking in attempting to recapture the best values of a time gone by; he also knew that it was future-oriented in its possible attainment. But above all, he realized that it had to be introduced in the present, for his own *foyer* a present fraught with absence, illness, and threats of impending war. The best ideal that Brunhoff could offer his own children had to blend anachronistic tradition and Utopian dream in a modern continuum of advice and enchantment. And so, just as early courtesy writers had done by their letters of parental advice, Jean de Brunhoff, through the delightful adventures of a noble, gallant, and courteous elephant-king, systematically instilled his ideals of manhood in his own three sons—and in whatever other children care to draw from his precepts.

Notes

1. The first three were published by Le Jardin des Modes: *Histoire de Babar* (1931), *Le Voyage de Babar* (1932), and *Le Roi Babar* (1933); Hachette published the last four: *A B C de Babar* (1936), *Les Vacances de Zéphir* (1936), *Babar en famille* (1938), and *Babar et le père Noël* (1940). The English-language editions were published by Random House (Methuen in England) and translated by Merle Haas. Most editions did not retain the original, expensively large size (app. 11″ × 15″), and many changed from the original, more aesthetic script typeface to a standard font, a dubious improvement perpetuated in *Babar's Anniversary Album* (Random House, 1981).

2. The first two phrases are from Mary Margaret Mitchell, *"Histoire de Babar* and *Le Voyage de Babar,"* *Horn Book Magazine,* 9 (1933), 29–30; in order, the others are from: Jean de Trigon, *Histoire de la Littérature Enfantine* (Paris: Hachette, 1950), p. 203; Margery Fisher, *Who's Who in Children's Books* (New York: Holt, Rinehart, Winston, 1975), pp. 34–35; Marc Sorian, *Guide de Littérature pour la Jeunesse* (Paris: Flammarion, 1975), p. 90; Bettina Hürlimann, *Three Centuries of Children's Books in Europe* (Cleveland and New York: World, 1968), p. 195; Ann S. Haskell, "Babar at 50," *The New York Times Book Review,* November 15, 1981, pp. 49–50.

3. Roger Sale, *Fairy Tales and After: From Snow White to E. B. White* (Cambridge: Harvard University Press, 1978), p. 14.

4. Rhoda Metraux and Margaret Mead, *Themes in French Culture: A Preface to the Study of the French Community,* Hoover Institute Studies; Series D: Communities, no. 1 (Stanford University Press, 1954), pp. 36 and 27.

5. "Jean and Laurent de Brunhoff," *News From Random House* (New York: Random House, 1980), p. 1. This publisher's bio-sheet notes some personal touches: "Babar wears the Norwegian cap of Jean," and "Celeste is wearing Cécile de Brunhoff's bonnet"; Maurice Sendak notes more in his introduction to *Babar's Anniversary Album,* pp. 7–14.

6. *Gentlefolk in the Making* (Philadelphia: University of Pennsylvania Press, 1935), p. 4. Certainly not the most recent look at the meanings and substance of courtesy, this work is still the most encyclopedic, spanning all centuries and varieties of the genre.

7. Esther B. Aresty, *The Best Behavior* (New York: Simon and Schuster, 1970), p. 295.

8. *Oxford English Dictionary,* s.v. "instil." This definition, the second listed, is substantiated with quotes from six sources ranging from Thomas More's *Answer to Frith* (1533) to F. Hall's *Two Trifles* (1895).

9. The phrase was the title of an alliterative ABC courtesy poem and was found in the text of many other early courtesy works as an admonition to teachers and students. Stratman's *Middle English Dictionary* defines *lerne (laeren)* as both "teach" and "learn"; *lewde (laewed)* is simply "unlearned" or ignorant.

10. Mason, pp. 392–98.

11. *The Babees Book,* ed. Frederick J. Furnivall (1868; rpt. New York: Greenwood Press, 1969).

12. William Schofeld, *Chivalry in English Literature* (Cambridge: Harvard University Press, 1912), pp. 267–68.

13. Philippe Ariès, in *Centuries of Childhood: A Social History of Family Life* (New York: Alfred A. Knopf, 1962), pp. 15–133.

14. William Sloane, *Children's Books in England and America in the Seventeenth Century* (New York: Columbia University Press, 1955), pp. 39–40.

15. Peter Coveney, *Poor Monkey* (London: Rockliff, 1957), p. 4. Robert Pattison, *The Child Figure in English Literature* (Athens: University of Georgia Press, 1978), gives a theological point of view.

16. For a close look at medieval "childhood," see H. S. Bennett, *The Pastons and Their England* (Cambridge: At the University Press, 1968), pp. 71–86; despite the interesting studies of the Jambecks *(Children's Literature,* 3), McMunn *(Children's Literature,* 4), and Talbot *(Children's Literature,* 6), I find the Ariès thesis more persuasive. Sloane's book (cf. note 14 above) well documents the range of seventeenth-century books. Samuel F. Pickering, Jr.'s *John Locke and Children's Books in Eighteenth-Century England* (Knoxville: University of Tennessee Press, 1981) provides a comprehensive sampling of both Locke's and Rousseau's influence on courtesy writing. Lloyd deMause's *The History of Childhood* (New York: The Psychohistory Press, 1974) offers a perspective different from Ariès's.

17. Gina Luria, ed., *Moral Tales for Young People,* I (New York: Garland Publishing Inc., 1974), 5.

18. The books are cited in order of their family development: *Babar, 1; Travels,* 2; *King,* 3; *Children,* 4; *Zephir,* 5; *Father Christmas,* 6. I do not include the nonnarrative *A B C of Babar,* or, like *Babar's Anniversary Album,* any stories of Laurent de Brunhoff, as the latter add nothing fresh to the courtesy structure.

19. *The Book of the Ordre of Chyvalry,* translated and printed by William Caxton, from a French version of Ramon Lull's *Le Libre Del Orde de Cavayleria* (London: The Early English Text Society, Oxford University Press, 1926), pp. 55–56.

20. Brunhoff's most powerful antiwar statement is the picture of utter devastation that evokes newsreels of ravaged fields in France, and the heartbreaking words under it: "A few broken trees! Is that all that is left of the great forest? There are no more flowers, no more birds" (2, p. 39).

21. Both Harry C. Payne, in "The Reign of King Babar," *Children's Literature,* 11, 96–109, and Patrick Richardson, in "Teach your Baby to Rule," in *Suitable for Children? Controversies in Children's Literature,* ed. Nicholas Tucker (Berkeley: University of California Press, 1976), pp. 179-83, address from different perspectives the matter of Babar's (and others') work and its modern implications.

22. In W. H. Woodward, *Desiderius Erasmus concerning the Aim and Method of Education* (1904; rpt. New York: Burt Franklin, 1971), p. 187. Like *Babar and His Children,* this is more advice to parents (or prospective ones) than to children.

23. Whereas Ann Haskell calls this empathy "a literary pact, based on integrity between author and audience" and supports my notions of the *Babars'* order and universal appeal ("this is literature from which no age group is excluded"), she does not recognize the link between the series and courtesy writings.

The Reign of King Babar

Harry C. Payne

The reign of King Babar is one of the most successful political ventures of the twentieth century. Created by Jean de Brunhoff in seven books in the 1930s,[1] his world is fictional, but his hold on the minds of children and adults—and the market they command—is quite real. The success of the Babar books has been enormous, both in France and in the English-speaking world. Brunhoff clearly concocted a world of both immediate and enduring appeal. What then is the nature of that appeal? Surely it is in part psychological in the narrow sense. Contained in the simple yet suggestive pictures and the cool, clear narrative, one finds a world designed to please and absorb the child. Trouble is not at all absent from the kingdom of Babar. There are scenes calculated to induce anxiety: the shooting of Babar's mother; the accidental poisoning by mushroom of Babar's royal predecessor; abandonment on a tropical island and the subsequent attack of cannibals; war with the rhinoceroses; the snake that bites the Old Lady; the fire that injures Cornelius; the rattle that almost chokes Flora; and so on. But these troubles always seem to dissolve. The Old Lady replaces Babar's mother; Babar routs the cannibals; the war is won with elephants' derrières painted in monstrous fashion; the Old Lady and Cornelius survive; the monkey Zephir extracts the rattle. Moreover, as Roger Sale has pointed out, the incidents are brief and narrated with a peculiarly adult, reassuring, cool tone.[2] The pleasures of the land of the elephants are, though, much more ample than the troubles overcome. Many are the gratifications for the child to see: ample opportunity for play; the companionship of mischevious monkeys; the pleasures of a school that is never dull; and the authority of adults who sometimes scold but always forgive in pleasant ways.

This is probably enough. Still, Babar is about more than children's fears and wishes. It is adult in more than tone. The central character is not a child but a young adult elephant who goes to the city, gets married, has children, and, quite simply, works very hard.

Babar is the happy lord of the numerous fêtes which populate the pages of the books, but he also is the exhausted parent at the end of *Babar en famille,* the energetic master-builder of Celesteville in *Le Roi Babar,* and the weary traveler trudging through the snow to bring Christmas to the land of the elephants in *Babar et le Père Noël.* The Babar books are as much about adult responsibility as about childlike gratification.

The view of adult life offered in the books is, therefore, reassuring but complicated. It is also quite social and political. Unlike the central characters of many children's books, Babar himself creates much of the world in which he works and loves. In most classic children's books, the central character stumbles into a world ready-made for adventure, anxiety, gratification, and triumph: the river of Rat and Mole; the barn of Charlotte and Fern; the wonderland of Alice; the Oz of Dorothy; the Boston Common pond of Jack, Kack, Lack, Mack, Nack, Ouack, Pack, and Quack; and so on. The world of these books exists before the story starts, inviting and shaping the fantasy that follows.

But Babar builds and nurtures a world before our eyes, especially in the central book, *Le Roi Babar,* which gives us the style of his reign. Paradoxically, he seems to create an adult world out of a more childish one. Our glimpse into the world of the elephants before Babar is brief. We know that they had a king. We know that they had a distant history and a folklore, since Cornelius teaches a song to the children that dated back to the time of the mammoths. We also know that Babar brings many innovations. Indeed, his major qualification for kingship is his experience in the city of humans and the knowledge he brings back. In the course of his reign, therefore, he introduces many of the ways of the cities: tools, houses, games, fêtes, libraries, schools, crafts and professions, clothes, theater, balloons, automobiles, sailboats, grand theater, formal gardens, and much more. Here again, the world of Babar seems to move against the grain of the logic of fantasy of most children's literature. Not only does he create a world instead of stumbling on one, he also creates a sophisticated, somewhat urban world where once there had reigned apparent rural simplicity. The assumption seems to be that the primitive stage of the elephants was a naive urdummheit, a pleasant stage not to be regretted but to be overcome by the work of a benevolent legislator. Babar is a gentle Lycurgus, though he does not disappear once his work is done.[3]

What, then, are the elements that make up the social and political world of Babar? First, hierarchy and deference. The king functions benevolently in a world that respects his authority and trusts his wisdom. Age is venerated. Honor goes to General Cornelius—the oldest and wisest of elephants—and to the Old Lady—nurse, governess, teacher, and storyteller. The children are occasionally mischievous, but they know their place and respond to authority.

The family is also central. The pleasures and duties of family life work through the various stories. *Babar en famille* depicts this side of life most fully, but the value of family prevails throughout. For in spite of newfound royalty, Babar is actually the perfect bourgeois, a citizen-king in a derby hat and green suit. Like his kingdom, his family is created before our eyes. We begin with radical desolation, the shooting of Babar's mother by the hunter, but the family is then gradually reconstructed. Babar finds an almost perfect substitute for his mother in the Old Lady, who, though she cannot replace his mother, brings with her the wisdom and resources of the city. Courtship and marriage to cousin Celeste culminate the first book. Cornelius rapidly becomes a wise and aged grandfather who, though not related by blood, is always present on family occasions. Then comes the birth of the triplets—Pom, Flora, and Alexander. With these children Babar does everything the ideal father should do: he plays in the nursery, goes on picnics, celebrates Christmas, rescues Alexander from trouble. "'Truly it is not easy to bring up a family,' sighs Babar. . . . 'But how nice the babies are! I would not know how to get along without them anymore.' "[4]

Turning from the family to Celesteville as a whole, one is struck by the balance of work, play, and festivity. Our first view of the new city, the symbol of Babar's civilization, shows a world of play beneath a hill on which are perched four buildings. On the far right is Babar's house, larger than the rest but still modest, symbol of the nature of his rule. On the far left is that of the Old Lady, symbol of age, continuity, urbanity. At center-right is the *palais du travail*, the Bureau of Industry, exactly counterpoised at center-left by the *palais des fêtes*, the Amusement Hall. The world of play is not new; indeed our first view of Babar among other elephants in *Histoire de Babar* shows children at play much as they are in the world of Celesteville. But Babar adds more structured play, work, and fêtes to this world.

The "work" of Babar's world is real enough but, as one would expect, quite pleasant. The *palais du travail,* dominated by school and library, has at one end the *ateliers,* the workshops.[5] We are, in fact, present at the creation of civilized work in Babar's society. It begins with the tools brought by the camels laden with goods from Babar's honeymoon. The tools are first used in an enterprise of cooperative building, as the elephants build Celesteville to the accompaniment of the Old Lady's phonograph and Babar's trumpet. With the opening of the city come the various crafts. Children naturally go to school, but their elders each choose a métier: shoemaker, soldier, painter, clown, street-washer, farmer, and so on. Babar creates a nicely harmonious craft society. The elephants serve one another in a serene world of mutual service, a Panglossian republic of work: "When Capoulosse had holes in his shoes, he took them to Tapitor, and when Tapitor was ill, Capoulosse attended him. If Barbacol wanted to put a statuette on his mantelpiece, he told Podular, and when Podular's jacket was worn out, Barbacol measured him for a new one."[6] This world of mutuality is further circumscribed by those who serve all: Hatchibombatar washes the streets, Olur fixes cars, and Doulamur plays music. All the elephants eat Fandago's fruit and laugh at Coco's clownish antics. We soon learn that elephants work only in the mornings; in the afternoons "they play, go for walks, read, dream."[7] We have then a world of perfect leisure that balances a world of ideal work.

Celesteville has many occasions to celebrate the values of the kingdom. Babar orchestrates numerous public fêtes, and he single-handedly imports the modern Christmas—replete with trees and presents—into his kingdom.[8] Whether it is at Babar's wedding feast or at Christmas in the family or just at a Sunday party, the land of elephants comes to enjoy civilized festivity. King Babar may not

The grand fête. From *Babar the King,* by Jean de Brunhoff, translated by Merle S. Haas. Copyright 1935 and renewed by Random House, Inc. Reproduced by permission of the publisher.

have had some of the perverse motives of his royal predecessor Louis XIV (whose gardens and theater he imitated),[9] but he surely saw the value to social solidarity of keeping people dancing and parading in each other's company. Most splendid, perhaps, is the grand fête near the end of *Le Roi Babar*. Babar reviews the great parade perched atop a wooden horse, which was, appropriately, shaped by Podular the sculptor, painted by Justinian, and mechanized by Olur. Beneath the reviewing stand are Celeste and the Old Lady. Lining the streets are the crowd, the king's guards, and young elephants dutifully aligned in scout uniforms (another of Babar's imports). The parade is colorful and resembles nothing so much as an oldfashioned parade of guilds, grouped according to trades: soldiers, farmers, bakers, sculptors and painters, sailors and fishermen, mechanics and drivers, and so on down the line. Dapper musketeers march in the middle, with their motto (and surely that of Celesteville), "One for all, all for one." We have, in other words, a perfect fête of solidarity. To be sure, near-tragedy strikes soon after: a snake bites the Old Lady and fire ravages the home of Cornelius. The two symbols of age and experience are endangered. The skill of firemen and doctors save them, but behind that skill are very oldfashioned values. After the two mishaps, and before he knows all will be well, Babar dreams. Unlike Pharaoh's dreams, his is transparent in meaning, as the forces of misfortune (fear, despair, indolence, ignorance, cowardice, laziness, sickness, misfortune, anger, stupidity) are routed by the forces of happiness (love, health, joy, hope, work, learning, patience, perseverance, courage, intelligence, goodness).

Such then is Brunhoff's world that he creates for his king. Even when he drew his Babar characters in a situation outside the land of the elephants—as he did in his *A B C de Babar*—the tone and values remain the same. Here he paints elephants in places and situations unrelated to Babar's land of elephants, in order to squeeze in as many objects that begin with the relevant letter. The signals, though, are all the same: scenes of idyllic bourgeois domesticity *(G,L,T)*; social rites that emphasize deference and solidarity *(D,E,M);* easy coexistence of old things such as carriages, farms, and monasteries with new-fangled factories, steamboats, and cars

(U,V). There is still trouble even in the land of the alphabet. We see an elephant with a wooden leg in *I-J*; quarreling bowlers in Q; an injured skier in S. But here, as in the land of Babar proper, troubles seem to melt away in a world that is curiously realistic, yet always caring and ultimately benign.[10]

So inviting, so real in its way, it is hard and perhaps disconcerting to remember that Celesteville was ultimately created not by Babar but by Jean de Brunhoff, not a mythical elephant but a French artist of the 1930s. Brunhoff created Babar during a period of long and ultimately terminal illness, largely absent from his family and his native France while he tried to recuperate in Switzerland.[11] The tales, then, are in part a father's way of talking to his children about the world, its anxieties, and its powers of restoration. It is, no doubt, in part the work of someone who instinctively knew not to hide trouble from children but, in the end, wanted to reassure and amuse them. Hence the Babar stories are childish fantasies for children and those adults who become like children again as they read. They are in part personal fantasies of a separated father. Hence the knowing tales of fatherhood and domesticity and the concern for the domestic side of life grew in the later books. But they are also social tales, very adult fantasies for other adults.

For the Babar tales are also about personal and social integration. The period of the late 1920s and 1930s was especially trying for French society and politics. Depression came slower to France than to England or America, because it was a less-advanced economy, more embedded in the residues of the economic old régime. But depression did come, and with it the inevitable social disruption, violence, and political volatility. France oscillated among a variety of unstable Third-Republic options, and most notably plunged from an experiment in left-wing socialism (1936–38) to right-wing fascism (1940–44) in short order. Those economic and political troubles only aggravated longer-standing difficulties associated with the transition to modernity: rebellious youth; the transition from craft to factory labor; the growth of cities and abandonment of the countryside; the disappearance of old traditions and the failure of new ones to command affection and loyalty, and so on.[12] A world like Babar's would appeal to the adult buyer

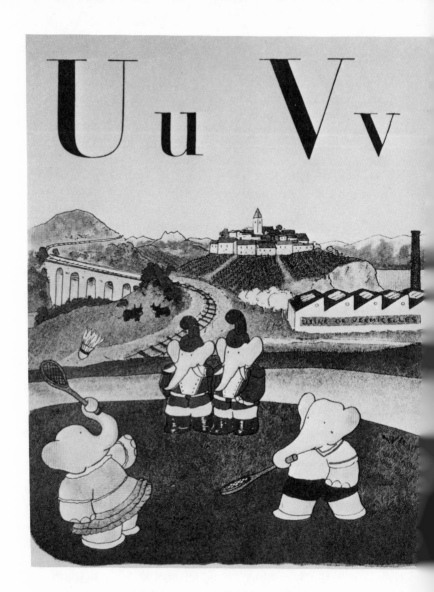

The dwelling together of old and new in the elephant world. From *A B C de Babar*, by Jean de Brunhoff, first published in 1936 by Hachette. Reproduced by permission of the publisher and Laurent de Brunhoff.

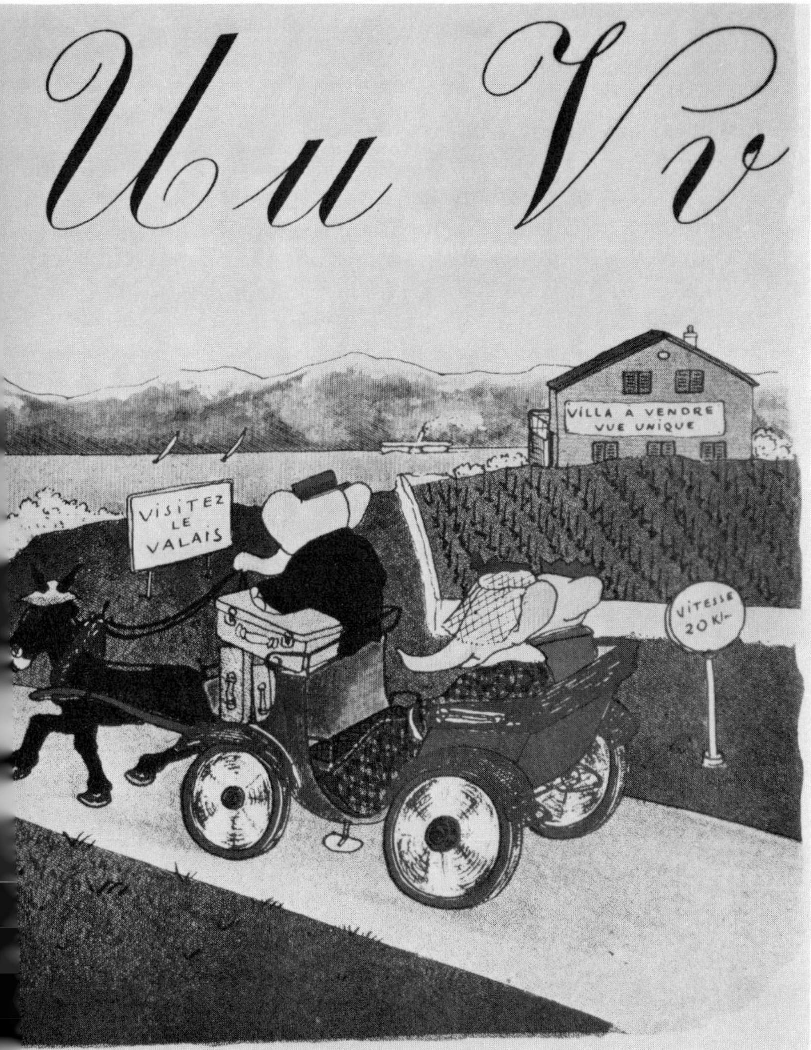
Uu Vv
VILLA A VENDRE
VUE UNIQUE
VISITEZ
LE
VALAIS
VITESSE

and reader, therefore, in an adult way. It is a sort of French Utopia. It has much specific reference to France—the gardens and theater of Versailles; the enemy rhinoceroses who look suspiciously like German soldiers of World War I; the guild parades that resemble those processions of craft groups (*compagnonnages*) that still endured into the twentieth century; bicycles, balloons, and sports popular since the 1890s; the scout troops; and the domestic Christmas scenes, among others. Though Babar's kingdom is nowhere in particular—a dreamworld—Brunhoff keeps in close symbolic touch with the realities and anxieties of his own France.

Indeed Babar's kingdom seems, in many ways, an incarnation of a popular French social concept of that time—solidarism. "Solidarism" had become an official creed of French politics in the 1890s under the leadership of the radical politician Léon Bourgeois.[13] As a style of politics, though, it infiltrated much political thinking before and after. The yearning for solidarity was essentially a petit-bourgeois ideal, a way to have the fruits of modernity but some of the imagined comforts of an older régime. Solidarist thinkers looked for a world in which individual initiative would be rewarded and the fruits of modern technology might be harvested, but also where individuals and groups recognized the need for organic interdependence. Hierarchy would remain, but it would be a hierarchy suffused with a sense of social responsibility and mutual care. In other words, solidarists wanted to overcome a world of competition and class conflict with a world of voluntary interdependence. Such a vision of society was not the exclusive property of either right or left. It could inform the radical politics of a Georges Clemenceau as well as the Vichyite politics of Philippe Pétain. The 1930s, the age of Babar, gave these dreams a special poignancy.

Babar's solidarism is itself just one incarnation of the worries about modernity in a more general sense. The first volume of Brunhoff's utopia appeared not long after that modern anti-utopia, Sigmund Freud's *Civilization and Its Discontents* (1930). They are both, in very different ways, about the same thing—the pressures of modernity and the barriers to personal and social satisfaction in a modernizing world. Freud's work is concerned with why that dream must remain largely only a dream; Brunhoff's with how we might still at least dream it with our children. Freud's successors in the world of ego-psychology, of whom Erik Erikson is the most prominent, have continued to worry through this difficulty. A world of class conflict, loose parental and social authority, and rapidly changing conditions is a difficult one in which to construct an identity. While social dislocation may not cause personal anxiety, a disordered world is a difficult one in which to work out the problems inherited from childhood. Babar's kingdom is a good place to be a child *and*, unlike the world of most children's books, a good place to be an adult. With its deferential politics, clear patterns of work, ample provision for play, and substantial doses of care and love, the problem of identity and adaptation are easily resolved.[14] Babar grows up in this world, and when he brings some modernity to it, he does so in ways that are both personally and socially satisfying.

Insofar as we burden children's books with interpretation—and we do so gingerly and perhaps at some risk—we tend to look for hidden agendas. The most popular and easy to find are the folkloric roots of tales in earlier times, the didactic attempts to socialize children, and the psychological appeal of tales to the most atavistic of childhood fantasies.[15] The uniqueness and depth of the appeal of the Babar tales rests, though, in this other agenda, immersed creatively in adult concerns of personal integrity and social harmony. But the division between the child's fantasies and the adult's is only one of convenience. Brunhoff offers a vision of an elephant-child who grows up, in spite of obstacles, with ease, trust, and initiative, and who nurtures a society that makes it easy for others to do the same. In that sense the delight of children and the affection of adults are not so much different "levels" of reading as two versions of what has become a perennial modern dream.

Notes

1. *Histoire de Babar* (1931); *Le Voyage de Babar* (1932); *Le Roi Babar* (1933); *Les Vacances de Zéphir* (1936); *A B C de Babar* (1936); *Babar en famille* (1938); *Babar et le père Noël* (1940). Quotations will be from paginated English editions; French editions are unpaginated.

2. Roger Sale, *Fairy Tales and After* (Cambridge: Harvard University Press,

108   HARRY C. PAYNE

1978), pp. 12–13. The Babar tales are briefly mentioned in several works on children's literature but, curiously, never really dwelled upon. Sale's brief remarks, scattered through his book, are the shrewdest we have. The essay by Ann Hildebrand in this volume adds, like this essay, a perspective on the place of the Babar books in wider French social traditions.

3. In this sense, he resembles (albeit in a childish way) the Legislator envisaged by Jean-Jacques Rousseau in *Du Contrat social* (1762), Book II, chapter 7, who enters a crude, uncultured world and sets it going. The Babar tales, in their concern for personal identity and social integrity, are, as we will show below, Rousseauian in a larger sense.

4. *Babar and His Family* (New York: Random House, 1966), p. 40.

5. *Atelier* implies the craft "workshop," as opposed to *usine*, or "factory."

6. *King Babar* (London: Methuen, 1976), p. 24.

7. Ibid., p. 26.

8. Here, as elsewhere, Babar's values are largely of the modern bourgeois. See François Isambert, "Du Religieux au merveilleux dans la fête de Noël," *Archives de sociologie de religion*, 15 (Jan.–June 1963), 63–70.

9. On the power of music and fête in Louis XIV's scheme of life and monarchy, see Robert Isherwood, *Music in Service of the King* (Ithaca: Cornell University Press, 1973).

10. In another community created by Brunhoff in *Les Vacances de Zéphir*, values of playfulness and simple home life prevail, set off against the picaresque world which Zephir must traverse in his rescue of Isabelle.

11. Bettina Hürlimann, *Three Centuries of Children's Books in Europe* (London: Oxford University Press, 1967), pp. 195–200.

12. The literature on decadence in modern life in France is quite wide. See especially K. W. Swart, *The Sense of Decadence in Nineteenth Century France* (The Hague: Nijhoff, 1964). On the crisis in festivals see Rosemonde Sanson, *Les 14 juillet; Fête et conscience nationale, 1789–1975* (Paris: Flammarion, 1976) and Roger Caillois, *L'homme et le sacré* (Paris, 1939), chapter 4. On the problem of youth, see Eugen Weber, "Pierre de Coubertin and the Introduction of Organized Sport in France," *Journal of Contemporary History*, 5, no. 2 (1970), 3–26. Scouting—of which Brunhoff seems to have been fond—was also a response to the problem of discipline for youth. Baden-Powell's invention found much support on the continent.

13. See J. E. S. Hayward, "Solidarity: The Social History of an Idea in Nineteenth-Century France," *International Review of Social History*, 4 (1959), 261–84. On its continuation in various forms in the twentieth century, see Robert Paxton, *Vichy France: Old Guard and New Order 1940–1944* (New York: Norton, 1975), pp. 211 and 232.

14. Babar's society seems to contain in itself an almost perfect depiction of the social world envisaged by Erik Erikson as ideal for human growth and identity, providing amply for stages of trust, autonomy, initiative, industry, identity, intimacy, and solidarity, generativity, and integrity. See Erik Erikson, *Identity and the Life Cycle* (New York: Norton, 1979), pp. 108–76.

15. For examples of the last two, see Isaac Kramnick, "Children's Literature and Bourgeois Ideology: Observations on Culture and Industrial Capitalism in the Later Nineteenth Century," in Perez Zagonin, ed., *Culture and Politics from Puritanism to the Enlightenment* (Berkeley: University of California Press, 1980), pp. 203–40 and Bruno Bettelheim, *The Uses of Enchantment* (New York: Knopf, 1976).

Eliot's Cats: Serious Play behind the Playful Seriousness

Paul Douglass

> I have received from whom I do not know
> These letters. Show me, light, if they make sense.
> —James Merrill

In an essay in *Children's Literature,* Marion C. Hodge charges T. S. Eliot with the offense of moralizing: "In *Prufrock,* in *The Waste Land,* in *Four Quartets,* he preaches to adults. In *Old Possum's Book of Practical Cats* he preaches to children (and adults)."[1] Hodge contends that these lines from "The Ad-dressing of Cats" invite us to see the book as didactic:

> You now have learned enough to see
> That Cats are much like you and me
> And other people whom we find
> Possessed of various types of mind.
> For some are sane and some are mad
> And some are good and some are bad . . .[2]

Hodge treats the cats as object lessons. The Old Gumbie Cat, for example, is "damned . . . because she does not realize the depth of man's depravity." *Practical Cats* testifies, then, to Eliot's "conviction that catkind/mankind is prone to crudity, cruelty, and violence, and is beyond reformation"; secondarily, it is a "quest for order."[3] I wish to defend *Practical Cats* against such overseriousness, and yet suggest that it is one of Eliot's serious undertakings, a book that makes sense in terms of his career as a poet.

Very few students of *Prufrock* and *The Waste Land* would argue that those poems moralize; in any case, the charge cannot be successfully prosecuted against *Practical Cats* with the lines that Hodge quotes, as the *subsequent* lines make clear: "some are better, some are worse—/ *But all may be described in verse*" (*CPP,* p. 169; my italics). Old Possum here clearly disavows any intention to praise or condemn; he has not judged but merely catalogued and marveled. We feel, moreover, no surprise when, in the book's last poem, Possum acknowledges the obvious resemblances of his cats to humans with more and less serious failings. But *Practical Cats'* "lesson" is *spiritual*, not *moral*. Cats live; this is the deepest impulse behind Eliot's writing. Vital, sassy, perseverant, wrongheaded, perverse, magical, and mysterious they are—but never indifferent, mundane, or mediocre. Their conformity to any laws religious or social is clearly irrelevant to Eliot, who seems to have chosen his genre with escape from such adult baggage specifically in mind.[4]

Eliot's cognomen, "Old Possum," which was given to him by Ezra Pound, emphasizes his desire to escape the adult responsibility to be sensible. On closer examination, *Practical Cats* comes more to look like a side of Eliot's character and poetic practice that we do not often see, but which runs deep—namely, a fascination with children's voices, "chantant dans la coupole!" (*CPP*, p. 43). Neither a sermon nor an aberration, the book expresses Eliot's love for dog-, cat-, and mankind, and his desire to keep alive in himself the irreverent child.

Eliot the reactionary, it is known, began as Eliot the rebellious son. He married against his parents' wishes and even dressed the dandy. He rehearsed at Harvard the bitter ironies of Laforguian verse. Manuscripts in the New York Public Library's Berg Collection make it clear that he excised and left unpublished much poetry dealing explicitly with sex. He guarded his privacy; there are many letters that will not be available until well into the next century. The nickname of "Old Possum" seems to fit especially well that quizzical yet flaunting attitude that Eliot took toward the somewhat dour mask he showed the world, a mask he apparently loved to remove in friendly company. He was not anxious to please those who wished to canonize him for literary posterity, and he no doubt took delight in the puzzlement with which some readers received *Practical Cats* in 1939. John Holmes, reviewer for the *Boston Evening Transcript*, thought *Practical Cats* an indiscretion: "It should have been prevented," huffed Holmes.[5]

Eliot had long been interested in children's rhymes; they played a role in *The Waste Land* ("London Bridge is falling down") and

"The Hollow Men" ("Here we go round the prickly pear") (*CPP*, pp. 50, 58). Drafts of the Sweeney play also struck such notes: "Under the bam / Under the boo / Under the bamboo tree" (*CPP*, p. 81). Eliot never leaves the child's voice far behind; it seems to call to us like Marina through the fog.[6] And the child's fascination with nonsense is Eliot's, too. In the 1930s, he began to work seriously on nonsense themes. "Five Finger Exercises," first published in *The Criterion* in January 1933, sounded muted notes that were to become the Jellicle Ball:

> Pollicle dogs and cats all must
> Jellicle cats and dogs all must
> Like undertakers, come to dust.
> Here a little dog I pause
> Heaving up my prior paws,
> Pause and sleep endlessly. [*CPP*, pp. 91–92]

The "Exercises" bow to Conan Doyle, Dodgson, and Lear, whose wistful "How Pleasant to Know Mr. Lear" becomes, in Eliot's hands, the wry and self-deprecating "How Unpleasant to Know Mr. Eliot."

Real children's voices haunted Eliot, as well. He visited Burnt Norton, Gloucester, in the late summer of 1934. The house was vacant; its gardens attracted him, and he strolled there. Robert Sencourt tells us that "although he thought he was alone, some children had hidden themselves in the shrubberies; finally, they burst out laughing, so he was in pleasant company."[7] A year later, Eliot reworked discarded lines from *Murder in the Cathedral* (published in May 1935) and finished "Burnt Norton" in time for its inclusion in *Collected Poems, 1909–1935* (published in April 1936). The experience framing "Burnt Norton," and ultimately the whole of *Four Quartets,* is of children in the leaves, "hidden excitedly, containing laughter" (*CPP*, p. 118). The genesis of "Burnt Norton" coincides with that of *Practical Cats.*

Faber and Faber announced in its winter 1935–36 book advertisement that by Easter 1936 Eliot would have his book of "children's verses" ready: "several of the poems, illustrated by the author, have been given in private circulation in the Publishers' various families" already, the notice said.[8] The book would be called "Mr. Eliot's Book of Pollicle Dogs and Jellicle Cats as Recited to Him by the Man in White Spats." Three years after the intended publication date, Old Possum stepped forward with a text that had gone to the cats, for only one dog poem was included: "Of the Awefull Battle of the Pekes and the Pollicles." A few poems that might have fit the original project were published elsewhere. Two appeared in a book intended to raise funds for medical care in the war effort, *The Queen's Book of the Red Cross:* "Billy McCaw: The Remarkable Parrot" and "The Marching Song of the Pollicle Dogs."[9] As late as 1952, Eliot contributed to the *Animals' Magazine* (a husbandry publication) "Cat Morgan's Apology," memorializing Faber and Faber's deceased mascot, reprinted in subsequent editions of *Practical Cats* as "Cat Morgan Introduces Himself."[10]

Unpublished spinoffs from *Practical Cats* exist as well. Eliot had been in the habit of meeting with friends at John ("the man in white spats") Hayward's flat in Bina Gardens. When the group appeared to be disbanding they pooled efforts and brought out a privately printed pamphlet, *Noctes Binianae,* in the summer of 1939. Eliot contributed a third of the poems, including "The O'Possum Strikes Back" and "Ode to a Roman Coot." He also left an unfinished poem, "Grizabella, The Glamour Cat," and a poem written to a little girl who had sent him a lavender bag, "The Practical Possum."[11]

This interest in children's rhymes and nonsense literature is a wide vein in Eliot's work. But is it a rich one? Only if we resist the temptation to view it from the adult side of the looking-glass. Felix Clowder, for example, claims that elaborate punning conceals "the fact that an apparently humorous book is actually a serious one." Clowder suggests, only half-facetiously, that we read the title, "Old Parson's Book of Practical Catachumens," a reading that is, though less condemnatory, still in line with Hodge's.[12] Taking a cue from "Five Finger Exercises," Clowder demonstrates Eliot's delight in the ambiguity of the "Prior's Paws" and makes a not unconvincing case for reading "Jellicle" as a foreshortening of "evangelical." Many have recognized the theological touches in the book, like the cats' trinity of names (*CPP,* p. 149). Yet Eliot is *not* writing from serious theological intentions; rather, he is having a little adult fun (perhaps occasionally a little too much) as he writes in all seriousness for children. Rather than use the unwieldy crowbar of his adult verse on *Practical Cats*, we ought to let the children's book shed its light on the larger canon. To begin we ought to ask, What are Old Possum's operative principles?

Above all, there is that dualism with which the book began, now obscured by the insubordinate cats, who overran the ship. The inscrutable cats were to stand opposite those "simple souled" dogs (*CPP*, p. 170). What clues are left us? The dogs we glimpse in *Practical Cats* are "dour Yorkshire tykes" spoiling for a fight, or else police dogs who slip into the local pub for a drink (*CPP*, p. 159). Pugnacious he may be ("my name it is Little Tom Pollicle; / And WHA MAUN MEDDLE WI' ME?"),[13] but the dog is essentially an innocent:

> He's very easily taken in—
> Just chuck him underneath the chin . . .

> Again I must remind you that
> A Dog's a Dog—A CAT's A CAT. [*CPP*, p. 170]

Dogs are innocent with an adult's sort of innocence (ask any child about this!). They symbolize an established order, a routine, though not fatally dull, approach to life. No wonder Eliot found the cats more interesting! They have their "sensible everyday names" (*CPP*, p. 149). They can assert order, as the Old Gumbie Cat does in teaching mice to crochet and cockroaches to act like boy scouts. But they also have their "peculiar . . . more dignified" names—private identities and special qualities, like endurance, independence, sophistication; they can feel disdain and even exercise magical powers.

Practical Cats does not try to avoid the cliché of the cat's mysterious longevity. Old Deuteronomy is this typical indestructible cat who has lived "many lives in succession." He has, Possum tells us with pun in cheek, "buried nine wives / And more—I am tempted to say ninety-nine" (*CPP*, p. 157). The cat's prepotent powers awe local humans. If Deuteronomy falls asleep in the road, they close it. No dog could command such respect. No dog could possess such dignity.

And no dog has the sophistication to know that he is more than one individual, that the self is hetero-, not homogeneous. The cat, in contrast, requires a trinity of names: one public, one private, and one sacred. The cat never discloses the mystery of his self; he never confesses the "deep and inscrutable singular Name" upon which he meditates. One must never hope, according to Possum, to know this name. To "ad-dress" a cat, begin with the public identity and hope to earn the right to call the cat by its private name. Unlike the simple dog, the cat "resents familiarity" (*CPP*, p. 170). So proceed carefully. While the dog will answer "any hail or shout," the cat must be approached with reverence.

Practical Cats describes many cats, of course, and few are actually to be revered. Some assert social order: the Old Gumbie Cat is a do-gooder. Skimbleshanks keeps the mail on time. The Great Rumpuscat puts the fear of God in the Peks and the Pollicles. Some cats harm no one in particular: Gus, the garrulous theatre cat, is obsessed with his past. Bustopher Jones, white spats and all, gourmandizes at the garbage heaps of fashionable clubs. But then there are the magical characters, like Mr. Mistoffelees, who alters gender at will. The majority of Possum's cats seem to have "practical" ends in view that do not conduce much to social stability; they can be difficult, devious, and even dangerous. There is the Terror of the Thames, Growltiger, who intimidates the world, albeit less effectively than Rumpuscat; and those spiritual Siamese twins, Mungojerrie and Rumpelteazer, who exploit their "plausibility" to disrupt and plunder the households they invade. They feed themselves on the "Argentine joint" the family expected for Sunday dinner. They demolish without compunction the vase in the library "said to be Ming" (*CPP*, pp. 156–57). The darker side of feline magic is epitomized by Macavity, "the Napoleon of Crime," whose agents all other nimblewitted and footed cats are said to be: "He's outwardly respectable. (They say he cheats at cards.) / And his footprints are not found in any file of Scotland Yard's" (*CPP*, p. 163).[14]

The mystery seems not so impenetrable, after all. It's a simple, if delightful, exercise to fantasize through cats those things we children, of whatever age, are forbidden. Capable of anything, we become, like Macavity, responsible for nothing. We can afford perversity like the Rum Tum Tugger's: "When you let him in, then he wants to be out; / He's always on the wrong side of every door" (*CPP*, p. 153). With a Rumpuscat glare, we scatter our foes; we steal from the larder with impunity. The parent, unable to *prove* which one of us has smashed the vase, bites his tongue in frustration. Remarkably, Eliot's cats manage to serve as alter egos without losing catness. For adults who have internalized the parent-figure, harmonies between fantasy and reality offer lovely entertainment. "Where *did* Mr. Mistoffelees get those kittens?" asks the baffled child. The portliness of Bustopher, the intractability of the Rum Tum Tugger—these are unobtrusive adult touches. They make *Practical Cats* a book with which both adults and children can grow, a book, really, about what *Four Quartets* calls the "inner / And the outer compulsion," the battle between ego and social self.

But the "practical" value of *Cats* lies precisely in its openhanded play with these experiences, in the playground it affords for what some will misidentify as the "depravities" of human behavior. The poems may *evaluate*, but they are not monitory; indeed, they stress the value of daydreaming. The proof of this lies, I believe, in their apparent delight with themselves. Elizabeth Sewell rightly observes that one finds in them

> all the love and charity which cause Mr. Eliot, as Nonsense poet, so much trouble in the rest of his poetry, but released and reconciled. Here, too, sin is behovely ("I could mention Mungojerrie, I could mention Griddlebone") but all shall be well; and there is set moving in "The Song of the Jellicles," at long last and in spite of all impediments and far beyond any of the supposedly more poetic works, a dance so free and loving and joyful, yet quiet and half-secret, that it is a clear image of heaven and an invitation thither.[15]

Sewell sees Eliot as having worked throughout his career with classical nonsense techniques in order to dominate "potentially subversive material" without denying it ("one and one and one," as the Red Queen says).[16] I believe she is right that *Practical Cats* calmly accepts its own fascination with human imperfection, and further, that the book creates a joyful dance.

But how does it do so? We must assess the prosody of *Practical Cats*, if we are to answer this question. And we cannot really bring Old Possum's poetic practice to light unless we have dug a little way into Eliot's. The operative principle here is clearly *ritual*. "*All* art," Eliot wrote in 1923, "emulates the condition of ritual. That is what it comes from and *to that it must return for nourishment*."[17] Eliot's fascination with nonsense and children's verse began with the ritualized forms of children's rhymes and popular song. One thinks immediately of the songs in *The Waste Land:* "Goodnight ladies"; "O O O O that Shakespeherian Rag"; Mrs. Sweeney and her daughter, who "wash their feet in soda water"; and, of course, "London Bridge is falling down." These elements are relatively diverse, of course, and they function more as background than foreground music. But they are part of a larger pattern of refrain found in all Eliot's work.

"Prufrock" marks off time with recurrent phrases: "In the room the women come and go . . ." and "How should I presume?" In *The Waste Land* Eliot's attention turns more frankly to the infrangible syllables of onomatopoeia: "Twit twit twit / Jug jug jug jug jug"; "Drip drop drip drop drop drop drop"; "Weialala leia / Wallala leialala"; "Co co rico co co rico." The adult verse often makes a pastiche of voices—one might think of Eliot as a sort of sound-mixing technician merging the drone of barroom conversation quickly with prayer:

> ". . . humble people who expect
> Nothing."
>   la la
>   To Carthage then I came
>
>   Burning burning burning burning
> O Lord thou pluckest me out
> O Lord thou pluckest
>
>   burning

Effects pioneered in *The Waste Land* recur in "The Hollow Men" ("For Thine is / Life is / For Thine is the") and "Ash Wednesday" ("Because I do not hope to turn again / Because I do not hope")

(*CPP*, pp. 59, 60). In the Sweeney fragments they take a bitter edge ("And perhaps you're alive / And perhaps you're dead / Hoo ha ha / Hoo ha ha") (*CPP*, p. 85).

But the manic dance is soothed in *Practical Cats*, where refrains are allowed to grow naturally, unchopped and unsliced by the anxious mixer sweating over his tape. Eliot came to believe that a poem begins "first as a particular rhythm," which gives birth to "the idea and the image."[18] In order to continue to create voices out of the rhythms of the unconscious, a poet must guard his flow of voice jealously. *Practical Cats*, more than any other of Eliot's works, taps the child's fountain of voice and tries to get a sense of the verbal playground into its very structures.

After 1925, Helen Gardner notes, Eliot's verse constantly recurs to the "four-stress line, with strong medial pause."[19] Northrop Frye concurs, pointing out that this four-stress line is "the bedrock of English versification: it is the rhythm of alliterative verse, of nursery rhymes and of ballads, all rhythms close to Eliot."[20] *Practical Cats* works with this tetrameter at the heart of English verse. Of the fourteen poems in the 1939 edition, seven use the four-beat line. Eliot is fondest of dactyls and anapests. Dactylic tetrameter pops up in "The Naming of Cats":

> The Naming of Cats is a difficult matter
> It isn't just one of your holiday games [*CPP*, p. 149]

and in "Deuteronomy":

> Old Deuteronomy's lived a long time [*CPP*, p. 157]

and in "Gus: The Theatre Cat":

> Gus is the Cat at the Theatre Door. [*CPP*, p. 164]

The anapestic tetrameter of the last stanza of "Song of the Jellicles" is less common:

> They are resting and saving themselves to be right.
> For the Jellicle Moon and the Jellicle Ball. [*CPP*, p. 155]

Only one poem uses iambic tetrameter; that is "The Ad-dressing of Cats":

> You've read of several kinds of Cat
> And my opinion now is that . . . [*CPP*, p. 169]

Of course, Eliot teaches us how effortlessly the dactyl slips into the anapest, and vice versa, as in "The Naming of Cats":

> His mind is engaged in a rapt contemplation
>   Of the thought, of the thought, of the thought of his name:
>   His ineffable effable
>   Effanineffable
> Deep and inscrutable singular Name. [*CPP*, p. 149]

and in "The Pekes and the Pollicles":

> They will now and again join in to the fray
> And they
>   Bark bark bark bark
>   Bark bark BARK BARK
> Until you can hear them all over the Park. [*CPP*, p. 159]

These poems fairly waltz.

Several of the remaining seven poems, though they do not use a straight four-beat line, are nonetheless in four-beat rhythm. "The Old Gumbie Cat" is in octameter, but it rhymes across the lines at the fourth and eighth foot:

> I have a Gumbie Cat in mind, her name is Jennyanydots;
> Her coat is of the tabby kind, with tiger stripes and leopard
>   spots. [*CPP*, p. 150]

And the refrain reasserts the straight tetrameter structure:

> But when the day's hustle and bustle is done,
> Then the Gumbie Cat's work is but hardly begun . . .

The really noticeable change, from stanza to refrain, is the shift from a two- to a three-syllable foot, not from octameter to tetrameter. "Mungojerrie and Rumpelteazer" also uses octameter stanzas and tetrameter refrains. And the poem added in the 1950s, "Cat Morgan Introduces Himself," also employs a tetrameter line with a three-syllable foot, so that, by a final reckoning, ten of *Cats'* fifteen poems use four-stress lines almost exclusively.

Yet the favored foot is always three-beat, and the meters of cats owe a secondary allegiance, as well, to trimeter. In "Growltiger" and "Macavity" Eliot works with a line that might be scanned in several ways. Strictly speaking, it is iambic heptameter:

> Growltiger was a Bravo Cat who lived upon a barge:
> In fact he was the roughest cat who ever roamed at large.
>   [*CPP*, p. 151]

> Macavity's a Mystery Cat: he's called the Hidden Paw . . .
>   [*CPP*, p. 163)

But at least two other possibilities present themselves. We might claim to find four stresses in the line (admittedly a strain, but possible):

> Growltíger was a Brávo Cat who líved upon a bárge:

or even claim to find *five* stresses—surely there is a shift from two- to three-beat rhythm at the end of the line:

> Growltíger was a Brávo Cat who líved upón a bárge:

"Growltiger" and "Macavity" may really be in strict heptameter, but they often give the effect of using a four-syllable foot.

The mixing of fours and threes becomes a line-by-line matter in "Mr. Mistoffelees":

> You ought to know Mr. Mistoffelees
> The original conjuring cat [*CPP*, p. 161]

and in "Bustopher Jones":

> Bustopher Jones is *not* skin and bones
> In fact he's remarkably fat [*CPP*, p. 166]

and in "Skimbleshanks":

> He gives one flash of his glass-green eyes
> And the signal goes "All Clear!" [*CPP*, p. 167]

But this shifting and pressing *never* comes to the sort of studied withdrawal from the implied general cadence that characterizes most of Eliot's adult verse.[21] *Practical Cats* presses the limits of rhythm only to return to home ground with evident satisfaction. Even when the even- and odd-numbered rhythms coexist in a single line, the effect is harmonious, not schizophrenic:

> Jellicle Cats are black and white
> Jellicle Cats (as I said) are small. [*CPP*, p. 155]

The cadence varies; it does not play peek-a-boo.

Practical Cats, then, uses simple materials to make sometimes elaborate ritual dances. And while the dances are mostly very regular, they do have their moments of near-disintegration, when the cadence erodes, only to re-assert itself. Those moments come exclusively in the *refrains*. But before we examine these, we must glance briefly at another key element in the joy of the dance, one not strictly speaking a "metrical" matter.

The key to much nonsense appears to lie in names—that is, in the Boojums, Jabberwockies, Pobbles, and Jellicles the nonsense poet offers us. *Practical Cats* clearly states its thematic and strategic interest in "naming," as the first and last poems of the 1939 edition prove. Possum starts us off with "Munkustrap, Quaxo, . . . Coricopat, . . . Bombalurina," and "Jellylorum." Subsequently, the narrative poems, "The Old Gumbie Cat" and "Growltiger," seem to be taking stock of names, their application and manipulation ("I have a Gumbie Cat in mind, her name is Jennyanydots"). The trick, from the versifier's point of view, is never to allow the metrical slot to cancel the name's illusion of spontaneity. Possum uses plenty of "real" names that might as well be made up, and this makes the nonsense names perhaps even more remarkably convincing. Growltiger's demise starts a global festival, and the last stanza offers a festival of names: "Oh there was joy in Wapping . . . At Maidenhead and Henley . . . at Brentford, and at Victoria Dock, / And a day of celebration was commanded in Bangkok" (*CPP*, p. 153).

In *Practical Cats* names echo constantly. We hear "Rum Tum Tugger" eight times in three stanzas (*CPP*, pp. 153–54). "The Song of the Jellicles" hammers on the word *jellicle,* as if seeing just how far it can go before becoming an outrage. And Eliot's use of refrain is directly related to this strategy—this *naming.* At the most basic level, he works with set-phrases: "But when the day's hustle and bustle is done," in "The Old Gumbie Cat," for example; or *"Macavity's not there!"* in "Macavity"; or "Firefrorefiddle, the Fiend of the Fell," in "Gus: The Theatre Cat." But in several poems the recurrence to set-phrase becomes a much more complicated, and interesting, matter.

The Rum Tum Tugger, we learn in every single stanza, is a "Curious Cat," and the poet lets a phrase roll out that we know fascinated him once before; it is the locution of Podsnap in *Our Mutual Friend* (Bk. 1, ch. 11), which was to have stood as the title of *The Waste Land.* Speaking of Sloppy, Podsnap says, "He do the police in different voices." And the Rum Tum Tugger

> . . . will do
> As he do do
> And there's no doing anything about it! [*CPP,* p. 153]

The refrain from "Mr. Mistoffelees" is even more complex:

> Presto!
> Away we go!
> And we all say: OH!
> Well I never!
> Was there ever
> A Cat so clever
> As Magical Mr. Mistoffelees! [*CPP,* p. 161]

Eliot's refrains seem always to be exclamatory, always drawing attention to themselves. He finds a phrase and leans on it until it becomes a game, and sometimes until it seems the ritual has become a spasmodic dance:

> The Oldest Inhabitant croaks: "Well, of all . . .
> Things . . . Can it be . . . really! . . . No! . . . Yes! . . .
> Ho! hi!
> Oh, my eye!

> My mind may be wandering, but I confess
> I believe it is Old Deuteronomy!" [*CPP,* p. 158]

This staccato interjection, and its ultimate resolution back into tetrameter, does not just by chance happen to describe a moment of recognition, a *naming.*

To name something is to achieve a not altogether illusory power over it—just as a mastery of rhythms may help to bring out of the "order of speech . . . the beauty of incantation" [*CPP,* p. 111]. The nonsense poet at his best can achieve, I think, a sort of naming that does not accede to the illusion of a linguistic finality. As fast as the nonsense word gathers meaning to itself, it erodes that meaning, and so the "Jabberwocky" is a more or less hideous shape *always forming* in our minds, but never finally formed. And so, nonsense does specifically direct our attention to the shaping dance of the line.

That dance is also, I believe, what makes "The Song of the Jellicles" so appealing to Elizabeth Sewell and to others who have let the verbal play of *Practical Cats* have its way with them. "The Song of the Jellicles" is a ritual poem about ritual; and the Ball is a ritual dance of life, no *danse macabre,* that is so free and unpressured that its mere *anticipation* gives joy. In the relatively short space of thirty-six lines (counting the epigraph), the word "Jellicle" appears twenty-six times, nineteen times at the beginning of the line. Magically, the insistent recurrence of "Jellicle" does not seem, nor is it, redundant:

> Jellicle Cats have cheerful faces
> Jellicle Cats have bright black eyes
> They like to practise their airs and graces
> And wait for the Jellicle Moon to rise. [*CPP,* p. 155]

The poem offers us something very much like "London Bridge is falling down," but without the anxiety of *The Waste Land.* It accepts its own joy. What are the Jellicles? What is jellicle-ism? Jellicles live unreservedly and take pleasure in more than one kind of life. Perhaps they are soulful; they are certainly not interested in judgments, condemnatory or approving. Jellicles "wash behind their ears," "dry between their toes," and know how to be seen and not heard in the morning and afternoon. But they reserve a certain field of play for themselves. And the emphasis is on the here and now: "Jellicle Cats come out tonight" (*CPP*, p. 154). Shouldn't the child grow up knowing how to survive in the adult world of dignity and routine, yet never forget to dance by the light of a Jellicle Moon?

"The Song of the Jellicles" does not preach this gospel, however. It offers rather a lesson that seems a found quantity—the penny left on the sidewalk, the phrase running through one's mind in a moment of distraction. That is a most difficult sort of effect to achieve in verse. When James Merrill received some letters sent to him seemingly by mistake, he tried to bring to light some "sense" in the serendipity and finally wrote the beginning lines quoted as epigraph to this essay. In asking what sense the "letters" make, Merrill was also asking where poems come from. And *Practical Cats* tries to preserve as much as possible a sense of the free giving in which poetry originates. Paradoxically, it is through a simpler and more rigorous patterning that such freedom is best implied. Poetry here makes sense by laws having nothing directly to do with the common sense that parents so much want their children to display. To the poet who writes for children, the claims of these two readerships seem at first in conflict. Unless he wishes to join the Wilhelm Busch school, the artist must both remind the parent reading to his child that there is a deep practical value in free, uncensored play *and* bring the child to see that in order to control our impulses, we must recognize them, embrace them as part of us. With the gift of Old Possum and his cats, T. S. Eliot makes us see how consonant these goals truly are.

Notes

1. Marion C. Hodge, "The Sane, the Mad, the Good, the Bad: T. S. Eliot's *Old Possum's Book of Practical Cats*," *Children's Literature,* 7 (1978), 129.

2. T. S. Eliot, *The Complete Poems and Plays, 1909–1950* (New York: Harcourt, Brace & World, Inc., 1971), p. 169. Further references to this edition will appear in the text with the abbreviation *CPP*.

3. Hodge, pp. 131, 137.

4. In *The Use of Poetry and the Use of Criticism* (London: Faber and Faber, 1933), p. 139, Eliot asserts that "any theory which relates poetry very closely to a religious

or social scheme of things aims, probably, to *explain* poetry by discovering its natural laws. . . . Poetry can recognize no such laws." We ought to distinguish, then, between Eliot making social judgments in his prose and Eliot making poetry. He does.

5. John Holmes, "Eliot on Roistering Cats," *Boston Evening Transcript*, Nov. 15, 1939, p. 15. See Eliot's piercingly ironic poem on the *Transcript*, *CPP*, 16–17, which was first published in 1915.

6. *CPP*, 72–73. The figure of Marina, daughter of Pericles in Shakespeare's play of that title, whom he had thought dead, symbolizes a reawakening to life.

7. Robert Sencourt, *T. S. Eliot: A Memoir* (New York: Dodd, Mead & Co., 1971), p. 187.

8. Donald Gallup, *T. S. Eliot: A Bibliography* (London: Faber and Faber, 1969), p. 363.

9. *The Queen's Book of the Red Cross* (London: Hazel Watson, Viney, Ltd., 1939), pp. 51–54.

10. *The Animals' Magazine* 7 (n.s.), no. 9 (Sept. 1952), 4.

11. Only twenty-five copies of *Noctes Binianae* were printed. See Gallup, p. 124. Harvard has #10. The Bina Gardens group engaged in considerable joking about nicknames. "Grizabella" is apparently among papers Eliot left to Valerie, his widow. "The Practical Possum" is in Harvard's Eliot Collection.

12. Felix Clowder, "The Bestiary of T. S. Eliot," *Prairie Schooner*, 34 (Spring 1960), 37.

13. *The Queen's Book of the Red Cross*, p. 52.

14. A number of critics have commented on Eliot's borrowing from Conan Doyle. Priscilla Preston elucidates all the hard evidence in the case in her "A Note on T. S. Eliot and Sherlock Holmes," *Modern Language Review*, 54 (Oct. 1959), 398–99.

15. Elizabeth Sewell, "Lewis Carroll and T. S. Eliot as Nonsense Poets," in *T. S. Eliot: A Symposium for His Seventieth Birthday*, ed. Neville Braybrook (London: Hart-Davis, 1959), rpt. in Robert S. Phillips, ed., *Aspects of Alice* (New York: Vanguard Press, 1971), p. 126.

16. Ibid., p. 123.

17. T. S. Eliot, review of *Poems*, by Marianne Moore, *The Dial*, 75 (Dec. 1923), 597.

18. T. S. Eliot, *On Poetry and Poets* (New York: Farrar, Straus, and Cudahy, 1957), p. 32.

19. Helen Gardner, *The Art of T. S. Eliot* (London: E. P. Dutton & Co., 1950), p. 29.

20. Northrop Frye, *T. S. Eliot* (New York: Barnes & Noble, Inc., 1966), p. 37.

21. This is the conclusion reached by Sister Mary Martin Barry in her study of Eliot's prosody, *An Analysis of the Prosodic Structure of Selected Poems of T. S. Eliot* (Washington, D.C.: Catholic University of America Press, 1969).

Memory and Desire in Fly by Night

Thomas H. Getz

> A brilliant blue jay is springing up and down, up and down,
> On a branch.
> I laugh, as I see him abandon himself
> To entire delight, for he knows as well as I do
> That the branch will not break.
>
> —James Wright

At its best, a book written for a child is a narrative spoken by a mature adult who listens to his own voice and simultaneously anticipates how he might be overheard by his audience. The adult must remember what it was like to be a child and imagine possible paths that might lead the child-audience to maturity. The narrative itself is, of course, one of the paths the child takes; the author recognizes that different children will walk that path in a multitude of ways. Just as the author remembers his childhood, the child desires the mature sensibility of the author of the narrative. The interaction—of the author, the child in the author, the child, the author in the child—works against the notion that children are merely childish as they read and that authors must reduce themselves to childlike personae as they write for children. There must be no condescension.

Genuine fantasy, such as Randall Jarrell's *Fly by Night* (illustrated by Maurice Sendak),[1] is by its very nature an imaginative journey away from something: constraint, laws, normality. Like other fantasies, it contains the element of opposition: the quality imagined, wished for, fantasized is opposed and animated by what it rejects. As the naturalistic waking world at the beginning of the story opposes the night flight of fantasy, so Sendak's realistic illustrations (only those on the cover of the book and on pages 26 and 27 are fantastical) oppose the dreamlike quality of the text. In this way they present perfectly the quality of hallucination, which is only hallucination when we think it is real.

Fly by Night is a performance encouraging the participation of

125

the audience. Jarrell and Sendak give the child-reader a narrative through which to pursue possible combinations of haunted fantasy and mature self-conscious adult perceptions. The narrative moves with the perspective of the main character, David, through three different levels of imagination and sleep, from David's conscious, naturalistic reality through his night flight of dream or hallucination to his most subtle power to create a fictionalized parable from his most painful deprivations. At all three levels the narrative voice is coeval with David's imagination, but the voice cannot be David's because he cannot yet use a language which would integrate dream and reality.

The line that announces that *Fly by Night* is fantasy is "At night David can fly." Up to that point the perspective is matter-of-fact, the completely naturalistic description of David's home following a strictly ordinary set of directions:

> If you turn right at the last stoplight on New Garden Road and go north for a mile and a half, you come to a lake on a farm. Beyond, at the edge of the forest, there is a house with a window seat and a big willow. [p. 3]

With the statement "At night David can fly," the fantastical non sequitur, we have the abrupt jump to the extraordinary or dis-ordinary perspective. Most children blithely accept the non sequitur—the shift from one point of view to its opposite—by shifting their perspective. They have not yet been educated about the potential chaos of simply accepting a fantastical narrative as though it were "real." The non sequitur initiates their new, but still natural-istic, point of view. Adults, suspicious, trained to bifurcate fantastic and real, are confused and likely to remain so by the directness of the statement: Is it ingenuous? Is it meant ironically? Is it actually saying "At night David *dreams* that he can fly"? Narrative directions are harder for adults to follow because adults hear directions with more predispositions. The line indicates, basically, that participa-tion in the story, involving suspension of the reader's sense of natural law, is welcomed. In fact, children, remembering their own vividly experienced fantasies, and adults who can still summon up good faith in fantastic narrative, will yield readily to the authority

At night David floats through the house. From *Fly by Night,* by Randall Jarrell, illustrated by Maurice Sendak. Copyright 1976 by Farrar, Straus & Giroux. Reproduced by permission of the publisher.

of the sentence. David himself is not really surprised by his ability to fly, nor by anything else in the story except his discovery that owls catch fish.

Following the announcement of David's fantastical nighttime ability, David goes one whole step further than *the good dream,* often found in children's literature, for example, in Sendak's *Where the Wild Things Are* and *In the Night Kitchen.* Floating through the house—a kind of omniscient sleep-wanderer—David can see the good dreams of his father, mother, and dog. All are presented as stereotypes but with some element of childlike charm. The dreams are contained in glowing nimbuses and present David's wishful version of reality: his miniaturized father is giving full-size David a piggyback ride; his mother is preparing a stack of pancakes; Reddy (the dog) is chasing something furry. (Later, outside, he sees that the sheep are dreaming of eating or sleeping.) In contrast to the self-contained, stereotyped dreams, David's physical motion is expansive. Even though he has little control (he can use his feet like a rudder), he floats over the dreams, out of the house, into a mysterious black-and-white-striped world: part of David's bed was shadow, part was "white with moonlight"; outside, the garden is black-and-white-striped, as is one of the ponies; there are white limbs and black shadows, white and dark ducks, and crows "all black against the snow." All of the oppositions of dark and light culminate in the marvelous description of the owl:

> It looks at him with its big round brown eyes; each of them has a feathery white ring around it, and then a brown one, and then a white one till the rings come together and make big brown and white rings around its whole head. There are sharp brown stripes on its whitey-brown breast, and its brown wings and brown tail are all barred with white bars. [p. 17]

In this night world, itself a series of oppositions of light and dark, many other sorts of reversals seem plausible, as natural laws are dominated by the laws of imaginative perspective. The cat, the mice, and the rabbit (and later the owl) talk to David. The animals' manner of speaking is animated by some fundamental quality of "opposition." The cat, for example, in the style of incantation, says,

> Wake by night and fly by night,
> The wood is black, the wood is white,
> The mice are dancing in the moonlight. [p. 9]

As David's shadow touches the mice, one says, "What's that great big black thing in the sky?" (p. 10). The rabbit, which is the only animal without companions, seem to play at sharing with David. And as the rabbit speaks, the visual patterns of opposition seem to influence the rhythm:

> A squash for me, a beet for you,
> A beet for me, a squash for you . . . [p. 13]

The animals talk to David, but to a great degree David is enclosed in himself. He is an observer, a passive wanderer in the tradition of Huck Finn. Huck can be involved with people on shore and then reject them and return to the raft, but David has small effect on the world of "nature" which surrounds his flow of motion. His shadow interrupts the mice at play, but they still hide from the cat; and when David tries to talk to the cat and rabbit, he cannot. This explains to a large extent the quality of Sendak's visualization of David. David is always floating (as Huck lazes down the river) with eyes closed or nearly closed, hands and arms protectively near his head. In fact David is always in the various postures of a child sleeping, but there is no bed. David can't touch the cat or the pony; he can't talk to the cat or the rabbit; he frightens the mice and the ponies. Nature itself begins to look lonely:

> On one side of him the field stretches off white in the moonlight, cold and lonely, with nothing on it but the humps the sheep make. [p. 14]

There is, in fact, an element of sadness in *Fly by Night*. Frequently there is the suggestion that our deprivations—our lack of ease, our isolation, if not our fear and pain—are closely related to the movement of our imaginations. Our daydreams, our nightdreams, our nightmares, also our works of fiction are often our haunted responses to our memories and desires. Waking preoccupations occupy, intrude upon, our dreams. Immediately following the description of the desolate field, David is adopted—to be an owl till morning—by a mother owl, who speaks with the sound and rhythm of Blake's *Songs of Innocence.*

> My nest is in the hollow tree,
> My hungry nestlings wait for me.
> I've fished all night along the lake,
> And all for my white nestlings' sake.
> Come, little nestling, you shall be
> An owl till morning—you shall see
> The owl's white world, till you awake
> All warm in your warm bed, at daybreak. [p. 18]

At this point, on the verge of yet another fantasy world, David discovers that, in contrast to the animals, he is able to give shape to his perceptions by creating analogies, or, the equivalent at the level of language, similes and metaphors. Early in his night flight, his parents' images—as seen by David—are naive, pictorial, cartoonish. But as he flies further, deeper into the fantasy world of his subconscious, he develops much more subtle ways of shaping reality in terms of imagery. He learns that human beings can express feeling and idea as *image.* David begins to experience reality in terms of analogy before he explicitly and self-consciously realizes his power. He sees the sheep as "six woolly gray mounds the size of the mound his mother makes in the bed" (p. 14), and at the end of the description of the owl the narrative voice says, "the fish in its claws shines in the moonlight like a spoon" (p. 18). David's epiphany follows an extended description of the owlets, in which the similes subserve a general feeling of buoyancy and exuberance:

> They look as if somebody had poured handfuls of white woodshavings over them, or as if they had stayed outside all winter and had got covered with patches of wet snow. And when they have gobbled up the fish and sit by each other again, instead of looking beautiful, like puppies or kittens, they have a sad absurd look, as if they were sitting there waiting for their real feathers to come. *But when the big owl turns its head toward them its eyes look loving—David thinks, "It doesn't know the way they look."* [p. 19, my italics]

David perceives and figuratively *names* the way they look, and he realizes that the pure look of love of the mother owl indicates that the animal can immediately experience the elemental love between herself and the owlets, but she cannot mediately describe that love. For the mother it doesn't *matter* how they look.

The owl's bedtime story is the third narrative level within the book; it takes the form of a narrative-within-a-narrative. The mother owl is the ideal storyteller; she is ideal because it is David's own imagination which gives her shape, substance, style. She is David's projection, his character. When we are told "the owl floats along by David, and says to him in such a low deep voice it is almost like hearing it inside his head . . .," we realize that even if we aren't all our own mothers, at least we are all the mothers of our own dreams. At this deepest level of fantasy and sleep, David both creates the story and listens to it with total absorption. He translates his serious waking problem of loneliness into articulate narrative terms: character, action, language, plot, and so forth. David is unaware that the narrative elements express—in a sort of pure metaphor—the truths of his life. As David "listens" to the story, the more naive reader simply enters a different narrative world; his selfconsciousness is dominated by the authority of the voice presenting its own point of view. The more mature reader begins to recognize the deeper metaphorical parallels expressed through the story.

First, the owl narrator demonstrates sympathy for her audience. Even though the ostensible purpose of the narrative is a bedtime story for her children, she seems to tell the story directly to David, and lets the owlets listen in. The pain of the isolation of the owlet she describes in her story is perfectly congruent with David's loneliness and longing for a playmate in his waking world. The story begins with the utterly mundane fairy tale opening, and from then on sounds a good deal like a version of the opening of *Fly by Night* itself.

> There was once upon a time a little owl.
> He lived with his mother in a hollow tree.
> On winter nights he'd hear the foxes howl,
> He'd hear his mother call, and he would see

> The moonlight glittering upon the snow.
> How many times he wished for company
> As he sat there alone! [p. 20]

We remember the first picture of David sitting alone in his tree (he already has an owl's perch; the sparrows are used to him) and the isolation he faces in the naturalistic opening of the book. As the narrative continues, the owl addresses the needs of the listener—David himself and the child reading the book—in an imaginative manner, so that the listener can participate in the experience of fulfillment. First there is the challenge, the test of owl-hood or boyhood/manhood. The leap into the untried element must be made:

> The world outside was cold and hard and bare;
> But at last the owlet, flapping desperately,
> Flung himself out upon the naked air
> And lurched and staggered to the nearest limb
> Of the next tree. [p. 22]

The leap of faith and courage of the owlet into the naked air is a harsh revision of the naked David's flow through the gently mysterious air of his night. But soon comes the reassurance and the confidence which will provide the core for the rest of the adventure:

> How good it felt to him,
> That solid branch. [p. 22]

Having found the second owlet, discovered that she can be his sister-friend, evaded dogs, boys, crows, and played and eaten, the two owlets nestle to the mother's breast. At this point, as "the white of the moonlight and the black of the shadows are beginning to be gray," the fantasy experience of David's night, including as it does his fictionalization of his own feelings, must end. He has learned (albeit unconsciously) about his loneliness and discovered his urge to return home, to awaken to the loving reality of his mother.

The central premise of *Fly by Night,* that which gives it the feeling of a parable that can in its simplicity explain a good deal of our imaginative life, is this:

"Why do I always forget? I always forget. If I remembered in
the daytime I could fly in the daytime. All I have to do is
remember." [pp. 5, 6]

David cannot translate the experience, perceptions, or point of
view of his fantasy worlds into his naturalistic world. Jarrell, of
course, encompassing all perspectives in the world of his book,
could have his narrator make the translation, but he refuses to do
so. Perhaps the reason is that he wants to place the child-reader in
what I might call a position of potential awareness. In this position
the child is exposed to the variety of perspectives, and it is up to
him—a function of his mental sophistication—to make or not make
the connections implicit in Jarrell's act of shaping the whole book.
The child can remain totally naive or reach Jarrell's level of mature
selfconsciousness. A good deal of the appeal of the book is that the
character David is more naive than most of the child-readers of the
book, while expressing as much imaginative potential as any of
them. The vividness of his fantasy—the non sequitur is not at all a
non sequitur for him—is largely caused by his *inability* to remember
or articulate the deepest level of his fantasy when he returns to the
waking naturalistic world. When it comes time for him to reenter
that world, in other words, to wake up, David can't finish his
images:

> When they come to the house the owl sails up to David and
> tilts its wings so that it stops still in the air; then it looks at
> David with its shining eyes, almost the way it had looked at the
> owlets, and flies away. David thinks, "The owl looks at me
> like—"
> But he can't think. [p. 29]

His imagination continues to stutter: "I slept so late because I—
because I—"
Finally, his mother looks at him like—

> "Like—" thinks David, "like—"
> He can remember, he can almost remember; but the sun-
> light streams in through the windows, he holds his hand out
> for the orange juice, and his mother looks at him like his
> mother. [p. 30]

The naturalistic world—orange juice, pancakes, sunlight, a loving mother—overwhelms the pain and the benefit of the night fantasy. Jarrell's presentation of David's naiveté—David's ability to create and enter opposing perspectives on reality, but only one at a time—gives the reader the chance to translate, if he can, one world into the other. Thus the child hearing the last page of the book is likely to shout, with all the enthusiasm of making the important connection,

> "The owl looks at me like *my mother;*
> his mother looks at him like *the owl.*"

If David could remember, he could join his two worlds; he could be the mature author of his own life or, more modestly, he could write *Fly by Night* rather than be a character in it. As it is, his waking reality can intrude on his fantasy; his fantasy can actualize his preoccupations and longings; his waking reality will eventually be haunted by the intimations of the night world as he travels down the path of his fantasy toward maturity. It is in this sense that David's flying and consequent night-time world are both the consequence and source of imagination. Imagination is the combination of memory and desire expressed as metaphor. It is the power of metaphor, of one's personal ability to shape feeling into image, which provides the firmest confidence—"The branch will not break."

Notes

1. *Fly by Night* (New York: Farrar, Straus & Giroux, 1976). Further references are cited parenthetically in the text.

Annie M. G. Schmidt: Dutch Children's Poet

Henrietta Ten Harmsel

Windmills, tulips, canals, Rembrandt, Vermeer, Van Gogh: these are the words and names, all nonliterary, which many foreigners associate with Holland. For Dutchmen themselves there is another name that has become a household word: Annie M. G. Schmidt. Hollanders of all ages read, memorize, and sing the poems of this prolific and versatile prize-winning writer. Her twelve volumes of children's poetry are never out of print and continue—with her children's stories, other light verse, and recent long-running musicals—to captivate large audiences. Although Annie Schmidt has already been translated into German, French, Japanese, Swedish, Danish, and Finnish, her poems have only recently appeared in English (my own translations, in *Pink Lemonade* [Grand Rapids, Mich.: Eerdmans, 1981]). A brief introduction to her and her work is, thus, in order. It is based on interviews with her in her home, on comments furnished by her publisher in Amsterdam, and on glimpses and analyses of the poems themselves.

Annie Schmidt was born on an island off the coast of southern Holland in 1911. Her father was a minister in a small village in the province of Zeeland, where she led a rather lonesome existence, isolated from her schoolmates in their provincial costumes by her more modern clothing and literary background. But she had other companions: the books which she constantly read, beginning at age four. She read all the children's books and girls' stories she could find, read *Andersen's Fairy Tales* "to shreds," lived with *Alice in Wonderland* so much that its fantastic images still continue to amuse and inspire her, and raided her father's library whenever she ran out of books for children. She smilingly reports that she had there first selected Ibsen's *A Doll's House*, thinking that it must contain something for a girl of her age. All of this personal reading, the stories her mother told and read to her, and the generally literary atmosphere of her home laid the first foundations for the imaginative world in which Annie Schmidt's poetry began to develop.

Although she wrote for her own amusement even as a child,

Annie Schmidt's schooling, in the old, classical tradition, did very little to encourage her imaginative talents. Her love for books led her naturally to prepare for a library career, which gave her opportunities to work in various Dutch libraries, finally, for more than a decade, in the children's room of a library in Amsterdam. Since Dutch children's literature had been dominated by a highly didactic, moralistic tone, she was urged to use such literature—or at least highly "literary" materials—to edify the children who came to hear her read or tell stories on Wednesday afternoons. From this period Annie Schmidt reports an amusing incident which she says was much more instructive for her than for her young listeners.

One day when she was attempting to inspire them by reading something very "uplifting," they staged a noisy rebellion, demanded the return of the two cents apiece they had paid, and finally had to be dismissed by the concierge. When Annie Schmidt left the library that day, several children again accosted her for their two cents, for money was precious to them in that depression era. "They taught me a lesson I never forgot," she says. "After that I began to read and tell only stories and poems which would genuinely appeal to children, even including some of my own things, which I had then never considered publishing." Again Annie Schmidt's imaginative world was being formed: a genuine children's world containing no condescension but allowing plenty of room for stimulation, fantasy, and challenge. She learned that "something must happen" even in poems, which for her always contain narrative and dramatic as well as rhythmic and lyrical elements. She believes that any "edification" which occurs must be so subtle that it seems only to amuse and so natural that the poem could not exist without it. Children all over Holland, therefore, are now willing to pay far more than two cents to buy or hear the poems or stories of Annie Schmidt.

Extremely critical of her own writing and diffident about publishing it, Annie Schmidt was finally encouraged by friends to publish—first in newspapers and journals and later in the books of poetry that soon became best sellers. Her public career began late but led speedily from one success to another: many volumes of children's poems; children's stories; a radio series ("The Family

Cross-Section"), which kept most Hollanders at home on the nights it was broadcast; a popular television series; various outstanding prizes (including the first Dutch national award for children's literature and an Austrian national award); and, in recent years, several musicals that ran for two years in Amsterdam, and later all over Holland. Still Annie Schmidt agrees with the writer of this article that it is her writing for children, still constantly in progress, which will probably be her longest-lasting contribution. A few illustrations from the poems themselves may best show whether this is true.

Like all good children's poetry, Annie Schmidt's poems are full of fantasy. The Andersen influence is strong but appears in a uniquely Schmidtian form that always transcends mere imitation. In an elemental princess-in-a-tower poem, she presents the heroine as "the girl with nylon hair," who is rescued from her tower prison by a young fisherman only after her own tears cause the surrounding waters to ascend:

> Because so many big tears fell there,
> Up rose the water of Saint Koedelare.
> Up rose the boat to the window—fast!
> They were together at last.
>
> Off went the girl with the nylon hair,
> Off with the fisherman, with him to fare
> Over the waves and water, and then
> They never came back again.

The absurd but realistic "nylon hair" demonstrates how Schmidt transforms old fantasy by giving it a current touch, but how she still maintains its authenticity in a new era. The "nylon" appeals to Dutch children, who often have dolls with nylon hair, but also suggests that even in our synthetic age the traditional fairy-tale motifs persist.

The setting for another of Annie Schmidt's imaginative romances is not a far-away tower but rather a cozy hearth, where she has the poker marry the tong, thus charmingly domesticating the old theme of love and marriage. Just as in Andersen's "The Steadfast Tin Soldier" the toys come to life, begin to play, receive guests, and enjoy parties, so in Schmidt's poem "Miss Poker" the poker and the tong come to life and merrily dance together "a sarabande by the fire":

> "Miss Poker, Miss Poker," said Mr. Tong,
> "We're hanging here next to the fire.
> We've known each other for such a long time,
> I now can say, 'I think you're sublime,
> You're the one I love and admire.' "

> "Why my dear Mr. Tong, my dear Mr. Tong,
> I'll marry you right away,
> For I'm made of iron and you are, too.
> I'll go through smoke and fire with you!
> We'll belong to each other for aye!"

> Then they danced together, a merry round,
> A sarabande by the fire.
> The chorus of coals sang a happy song,
> And the hanging kettle went ding-a-ding-dong,
> And the flames burned higher and higher.

> So the Poker and Tong got married last week.
> Now they're hanging together, cheek to cheek.
> They cuddle each other in all kinds of weather,
> And whenever they glow, they glow together.

The ending of the poem reveals Annie Schmidt's penchant for happy endings, which she considers important for the creation of a secure world for children. In bringing inanimate objects to life and having them marry, like the poker and clout in Andersen's "Little Sandman," the poem stands in a long fairy-tale tradition but seems also realistically and humorously to affirm the warmth, gaiety, and charm of "love in the kitchen."

Like Andersen's tales, Annie Schmidt's poems often contrast the rather stuffy, logical adult world with the highly imaginative world of the child. In "Little Ida's Flowers" Andersen dramatizes something of the complexity of bringing the two worlds together: the jolly student who encourages Ida's dream visions; the tiresome old counselor who calls them "silly rubbish"; the vivid beauty of the flowers who dance for Ida at night; and the resonant amalgam of sorrow and hope in the morning "burial" of the poor dead flowers. In Annie Schmidt's poems, often more literally connected with everyday life, the child's imaginative world usually triumphs, sometimes rather amusingly, over the adult world. In "Henry John and Henry Joe," a poem with the comical tone of a Belloc or a Silverstein, the twin boys look so much alike that even their father can't tell them apart. Totally exasperated, he finally decides to clip one boy's head completely bald and force the other to wear braids. "All right, from now on I will know who's who," the father says. But with charming simplicity the boys' world still wins out:

> But look, the poor man still can't tell!
>   I'll be! I still don't know!
> The bald one, is that Henry John,
>   Or is it Henry Joe?
> And so the father still repeats—
>   Just as he used to do—
> Now which is which, and what is what,
>   And who is really who?

Although this situation is far removed from Andersen's dream visions, it coyly suggests the inability of some adults ever to comprehend or master the child's world.

In other Schmidt poems the gap between the child's world and the adult world is delightfully bridged. Sometimes her adults, like the student Andersen presents in "Little Ida's Flowers," naturally accept the child's dreams and fantasies. Such a merger occurs in one of Schmidt's dream poems, "The Little Bed That Can Ride." It contains a traditional dream journey, much more realistic than those that Andersen's "Sandman" inspires, but still in the same tradition. In Schmidt's poem the little boy who goes for a long ride in his bed every night—through tunnels, down streets, past flashing traffic lights, and finally to New York—finds his mother very understanding the next morning:

> Then back to his room—quick as a leap—
> For Johnny is tired
> And wants to sleep.

He says hello to the sheep on the wall
And falls asleep curled up like a ball.
Next morning Mom says, "Where have you been?"
"The same," says John, "to New York again."

Although here the radiant visions of Andersen's dancing flowers
are replaced by much more realistic street scenes growing out of
Johnny's everyday aspirations to drive off in a car, and although
the life-and-death imagery which brings "Little Ida's Flowers" to an
almost mystical conclusion is missing, still the reader senses that
childhood fantasy is beautifully affirmed in Schmidt's poem and
that the amusing and enigmatic aplomb evidenced by both John
and his mother establishes a rich and satisfying world which child
and adult can inhabit together.

In "The Time of Elves,"one of Annie Schmidt's finest poems, the
child-hero, whose dream visions take him to the fairy world every
night, is confident and adamant in his affirmation of the "never-
never land" about which is parents are trying to disillusion him:

> I always hear my father say,
> "The time of elves has gone away.
> They don't dart now, like long ago
> between the flowers along the row;
> not in the park, nor do they perch
> on flowering bushes by the church.
> Not under the willows, night or day;
> the time of elves has gone away."
> But one night as I lay awake,
> the moon shone bright on grass and lake.
> A little man under the apple tree
> brought a silver-white horse for me.
> Pooh, pooh, fiddle dee doo,
> nobody knows what's really true!
>
> I always hear my mother say,
> "No, elves do not exist today.
> Not in the garden, not under the moon,
> nor on the very highest dune.
> Perhaps in books about queens and kings,

but books can say soooo many things!"
But that same night, I saw his face,
him and his horse—the very same place.
But then he said he'd sell his horse—
for a dime and a copper button, of course.
Pooh, pooh, fiddle dee doo,
nobody knows what's really true!

My father and mother were fast asleep
when over the fence I took a leap.
Away on the silver-white horse I rode
over the bridge and down the road.
Nobody saw me swinging high
in a spider web right up to the sky.
Nobody knows what fun to play
magic tricks with a hawthorn spray,
to play toy soldier with an elf
or hopscotch with the king himself!
Pooh, pooh, fiddle dee doo,
nobody knows what's really true!

Here Annie Schmidt's eclectic style comes to a resonant poetic climax. As always in her poems, there is a plot—something happens. Here the happening, drawn from the long tradition in which Andersen's "Sandman" is a leading example, becomes dreamlike in spite of its realistic dialogue; psychologically authentic in spite of the parents' unqualified disagreement with the child; and, although not evidencing Andersen's frequently religious symbols and overtones, almost mystical in the credo it states in the closing refrain of each stanza. Here, too, the sharp conflict between the child and his parents centers on a world that is visionary—as, for instance, R. L. Stevenson's "The Little Land" charmingly affirms such a world—but it goes beyond mere charm to assert with dramatic power the inescapable conflict between the literal and the imaginative, concluding on the recklessly triumphant credo of the boy's indestructible dream vision.

Even in the detailed denials of the parents there lies a rich psychological affirmation of the very world they are trying to destroy. They admit that there once was (for them?) a "time of

elves," since it has "gone away." The colorful clarity with which the
detail that world—the darting of the elves, the park, the flowering
bushes, the moonlit garden, and the highest dune—belies their
disbelief and almost turns their protesting into bravado. At least
the fast sleep which blinds the parents to the boy's imaginative
flights may be more than literal, for it represents the adult darkness
in which the vivid denizens of his dreamworld disappear. But the
boy can still "see as a child" as he swoops from one exciting
experience to another, finally even playing "hopscotch with the
king himself," a delightfully absurd but triumphant climax. The
complex credo of the closing couplet allows the reader to believe
that fortunately neither the boy himself, nor the protesting parents, nor anyone who is human will ever be able to discover a neat
world in which everyone knows "what's really true."

And so, with unending variety, the poems go on, not all equally
good, of course. The title poem of the *Pink Lemonade* collection at
first seems simply charming, lightly comical, and playfully proper:

> In a beautiful garden in faraway France
>   Cool paths curve along in the shade
> And tulips and lilies and roses surround
>   A pond full of pink lemonade.
>
> The children go rowing around in a boat—
>   It's never against the law—
> And when they're not singing, they take a cool sip
>   Through a very long, elegant straw.
>
> The pond is bright pink, almost raspberry red,
>   And sometimes the children may wade
> With trousers and dresses pulled up very high
>   In the pond full of pink lemonade.
>
> If one of the children flops out of the boat,
>   They rescue him quick as a wink,
> And then they start licking so that he won't stay
>   So terribly sticky and pink!
>
> It really is charming, that garden in France—
>   The flowers, the paths in the shade—

>   But still you'll agree that the nicest of all
>   Is the pond full of pink lemonade.

Although the charming fairyland of "Pink Lemonade" might fit a collection of R. L. Stevenson's poems, here again there are hints of a more versatile and resonant vision supporting Schmidt's images. Delightfully comic touches give a desirable edge to the charm: sipping from the pond through the "very long, elegant straw" and licking the children who have flopped out of the boat. In fact, underneath the placid charm lies even a hint of fairy-tale horror, lightly suggested by the quick rescue of the children from the "terribly sticky and pink" pond on which they are so serenely sailing.

One concluding poem should serve to round off this introduction to Annie Schmidt and to encourage readers to get to know her better. "Late at Night" presents one of her imaginative, traditional visions of the dream world. In fact, it could be considered a direct descendant of Andersen's "The Little Sandman." However, Schmidt's poem takes on a more dreamlike tone, partly through the mesmeric quality of its music. It integrates the two stanzas into an organic psychological unity instead of presenting a dream for each night of the week, and it entirely omits Andersen's moralistic note that naughty children will receive no pleasant dreams.

>   As soon as it gets dark out, and the moon begins to shine,
>   The people in the houses draw their curtains and their blinds.
>   And then the big fat carpenter and Mrs. Taylor, too,
>   All go to sleep just like the cat and all her kittens do.
>   And all the colts fall fast asleep, each one beside his mother,
>   And all the little pigs, and Mr. Farmer and his brother.
>   The little calves, the little lambs, and even the big dog,
>   And all the little children lie there sleeping like a log.
>   And when the hens are sleeping, and the fishes in the
>   streams,
>   A little man comes running with his basket full of dreams.
>
>   As soon as they start dreaming, all the fishes think they're
>   whales;
>   The carpenter starts counting all his hammers and his nails.

And Mrs. Taylor dreams that she is taking cooking courses,
And all the little colts that they are finally big horses.
The children dream of ice cream, and the hens about their
   eggs,
And all the little calves that they have very sturdy legs.
Yes, just at ten, when all the fish are sleeping in their streams,
That little man comes running with his basket full of dreams.

He has just one left over, made of yellow, pink, and blue,
And when you fall asleep tonight, that dream will be for you.

The psychological connections between stanzas one and two
demonstrate Schmidt's constant desire to bring the worlds of
reality and imagination together. Although some of the dreams
that come to Andersen's little boy connect naturally with his
everyday life, most of them are pure fantasy—long sailing voyages
through fairy worlds to far-off countries. Each of Schmidt's
realistic situations in stanza one is soundly developed in the
corresponding dream version of stanza two: Mrs. Taylor takes
cooking courses, the colts finally become "big horses," and the little
calves finally attain "very sturdy legs." Thus fantasy in the fairytale
sense of the term is retained but also attains the realistic dimension
of the everyday fantasies of life as they appear in "dreams come
true."

In the poem's closing lines Schmidt demonstrates both com-
parisons and contrasts with Andersen's famous tale and his characteristic tendencies. Since her poems never convey an overtly
Christian vision, she does not introduce death, the ultimate
conveyor of beautiful or horrible dreams, as Andersen does at the
end of "The Little Sandman." But, like him, she does step from the
imaginative poem into real life as she ends with an invitation to the
reader to enter the wide-awake world of her colorful imagination:

He has just one left over, made of yellow, pink, and blue,
And when you fall asleep tonight, that dream will be for you.

Editors' note: For a review of *Pink Lemonade,* see pp. 188-90 below.

From Here to Eternity: Aspects of Pastoral in the Green Knowe Series

Jon C. Stott

On first reading, the six novels that make up L. M. Boston's Green Knowe series appear to follow the ironic conventions of pastoralism. A young boy finds a home at Green Knowe and discovers its timeless essence only to see it invaded by destructive forces, not the least of which are those of modern civilization. However, rereadings reveal important departures from the conventions: Boston allows her pastoral setting to survive the threats to its existence and provides her heroes with the means of maintaining their lives in it. Thus, whereas most pastorals show the impossibility of escaping the destructiveness of time, the Green Knowe books imply that those who have fully experienced and completely committed themselves to the pastoral world will always remain part of it. In studying this aspect of the Green Knowe series, we shall first examine the central setting, Green Knowe, and the children who most fully comprehend its timelessness, and then trace the overall structure of the six novels, showing both relationships to the pastoral tradition and significant departures from it.

A major aspect of the pastoral world is its difference from the area that surrounds it. It is a natural, pure, and calm setting in which truth, tranquility, contentment, and innocence dominate, a contrast to the sullied, artificial, complex world beyond its borders, a world in which the more evil aspects of progress—especially greed, anxiety, and ambition—are found. The pastoral setting is an oasis which, except for the recurrent rhythms of nature, seems eternal. These aspects and these contrasts are found in the central symbol of the Green Knowe series, the manor itself.

Built nine centuries ago, during the reign of William Rufus, its dominant characteristics are its antiquity, its continuity, and, most important, its essential timelessness.[1] Thinking about her home as she awaits Ping's arrival in *A Stranger at Green Knowe*, Mrs. Oldknow muses: "It was of such antiquity that its still being there was hardly believable. By all the rules of time and change it should long long ago have become a ruined heap of stone. . . . Somehow, century after century while much younger castles and houses rotted or were burnt down, or their owners grew tired of them and cleared them away to make room for new, Green Knowe stood quietly inside its moat and its belt of trees."[2] While it has been altered externally, its fundamental structure has remained the same. Chief of its features is the great fireplace, "the hearth [which] from all time was the center and heart of the family."[3] The words Boston used to describe her own home can be applied to Green Knowe: "Inside, partly because of the silence within the massive stone walls, partly because of the complexity of incurving shapes, you get a unique impression of time as a co-existent whole."[4]

The grounds of the manor are an extension of the manor itself. The garden, referred to by one visitor as a "wild paradise" (*Stranger*, p. 136), is a pleasant place. Hidden from the road, it contains Mrs. Oldknow's roses, "to her the clearest sign of the essential nature of life,"[5] and is watched over by the beneficent statue of St. Christopher, created from the same living stones as the house. At the edge of the garden flows the river, "sleepy and timeless,"[6] while bordering the property is Toseland Thicket, jealously guarded by Mrs. Oldknow as a bird sanctuary. As one of Mrs. Oldknow's guests notes, the area is a "real sanctuary. Nowadays everything is changing so quickly we all feel chased about and trapped. . . . Here, in the heart of industrial England, is this extraordinary place where you can draw an easy breath" (*Stranger*, p. 90).

Those who approach Green Knowe in the proper spirit can experience a timelessness which does not exist beyond its boundaries. They can come in contact with the "truth about being and knowing" (*Enemy*, p. 116) which emanates from the house, and which is absent from the modern world outside. The contrast between Green Knowe and the world beyond is most clearly presented in *The Stones of Green Knowe*, when Roger travels from the Norman period into the twentieth century. He first notices the "stale dead air" (*Stones*, p. 102) and the litter and is terrified by the noise and speed of automobiles and airplanes. Only when he enters the garden and sees the manor does he feel secure.

While many individuals enter into the pastoral world of Green

Knowe, not all can perceive its elemental timelessness or achieve what Hallett Smith describes as the sense of *otium*,[7] or contentment, which is central to the pastoral experience.[8] Adults cannot generally respond as fully as children, and not all children respond with equal success. Of the adults, Mrs. Oldknow, who had contacted the spirits of earlier children when she was a girl, remains closest to the pastoral world. Adults such as Susan's mother, who lives for the newest fashions, Dr. Maude Biggin, who cannot perceive the past existing in the present, or Melanie Powers, who hates the goodness of the house, are oblivious to the spirit of the place. Only those children who possess a will to believe can perceive the essences of Green Knowe. As Mrs. Oldknow notes, "I love to have children here, because to them nothing is ordinary" (*Stranger,* p. 70). As she tells Tolly, "I'm waiting . . . to see what happens now that you are here."[9] Only the children travel in time, meeting other children from earlier or later eras. Although the children may die young, as Toby, Alexander, and Linnet do in the plague, or may become adults as Susan does, they take the form of children when they become "others," spirits living in the timeless dimension of Green Knowe.

Tolly is told by his great-grandmother that Sefton, Susan's cruel brother, will not appear: "He thought nothing of the place" (*Chimneys,* p. 17). Oskar, Ping, and Ida, although they do meet beings from the past, never contact Roger, Toby, Linnet, Alexander, or Susan. Ping, a central character in three of the books, is not included in *The Stones of Green Knowe,* when "the others" gather under the Yew Tree. Jacob, Susan's black companion, is not present at the final reunion either; as Susan tells Roger, "He is slow about *the others.* I suppose it's because he wasn't born here" (*Stones,* p. 84).

The Children of Green Knowe and *The Chimneys of Green Knowe* (the latter published in the United States as *The Treasure of Green Knowe*) describe the steps by which a young child, Tolly, enters the pastoral world of Green Knowe and understands and becomes a part of it. Although at first he appears to be a lonely exile, he does, as Mrs. Oldknow recognizes, "belong here. . . . He has it all hidden in him somewhere."[10] He quickly becomes aware of the continuity of Green Knowe. He resembles his grandfather and his name, like

that of his great-grandmother, has been in the family for generations. Moreover, the house contains many objects from the past,
one of the most important of which is a large portrait of Tolly's
seventeenth-century ancestors, Toby, Alexander, and Linnet, who
had died during the plague. Tolly finds objects belonging to them
and hears from Mrs. Oldknow a number of legends about their
lives. He earnestly wishes to meet them, but to do so he must
exercise patience and must allow them to get to know him first.

At first, the spirit children tease Tolly, laughing, appearing in
mirrors, and clapping their hands over his eyes. Wandering in the
garden, which has been magically transformed by a snowfall, he
finally sees them and, on returning to the house, learns that he has
been accepted. The fullness of their acceptance of him is revealed
during their second meeting, when Alexander warns Tolly of the
dangers of Green Noah, a topiary figure that had been cursed
several generations before Tolly's time. Two nights before Christmas, while he is wandering in the garden during a violent electrical
storm, Tolly is attacked by the giant figure. In terror, the boy calls
out to Linnet for help and hears her voice and "Toby's and
Alexander's . . . and other unknown children's" (*Children,* p. 138)
imploring aid from the statue of St. Christopher.

Although at the end of *The Children of Green Knowe* Tolly has been
accepted by the spirits of the three children and feels secure in the
old house, his integration into the eternal world of Green Knowe is
not yet complete. In *The Chimneys of Green Knowe,* the process is
completed; he enters into the early nineteenth century and plays a
role in the history of Green Knowe.

Home for the Easter holidays, Tolly discovers a threat to the
security of the house: the portrait of Alexander, Linnet, and Toby
has been loaned to a museum and may have to be sold to finance
repairs to Green Knowe. Tolly objects, saying that with the picture
gone Toby, Linnet, and Alexander "would have nowhere to *be*"
(*Chimneys,* p. 11). His assumption is correct, for, exploring the
grounds, he cannot make contact with them: "He could feel that
they were gone quite out of reach" (*Chimneys,* p. 13). To restore his
friends, Tolly decides to find Maria Oldknow's lost jewels and thus
enable his grandmother to return the picture to its rightful place.

However, he first must learn more about the past. He hears n ore of Mrs. Oldknow's legends, meets Susan, his blind ancestor, and aids in a daring rescue in the past.

The stories are told in the evenings as Grand, as Tolly calls her, repairs a very old patchwork quilt. As had been the case for Kate and Mrs. May in Mary Norton's *The Borrowers*, the act of sorting out pieces of cloth and sewing the quilt serves as a metaphor for the restoration and recreation of the past. Tolly plays an active role in both processes: he finds a box containing patches of cloth from Susan's time and, in his contacts with Susan, learns about aspects of the past unknown to Mrs. Oldknow. His new knowledge helps him to discover the lost jewels and so to insure the security of Green Knowe.

Tolly must travel into the nineteenth century alone. While Mrs. Oldknow is visiting a friend, the boy, after exploring an abandoned tunnel, emerges above ground to find that "he had quite lost his sense of time" (*Chimneys,* p. 120) and that "everything seemed fixed in a trance of eternal sameness" (*Chimneys,* p. 120). Entering the house of a century and a half earlier, he learns that Fred Boggis is in danger of being transported for poaching, and Tolly courageously helps him. When he returns to his own time, he listens to Grand tell about the final rescue of Boggis before he recounts his own role in the events. Mrs. Oldknow then remarks in surprise: "I was going to tell you about the strange boy who came in the nick of time, and was never seen again. I always thought it was Alexander" (*Chimneys,* p. 132).

On the final day of his holidays, Tolly discovers the jewels, the picture is restored to its rightful place, and he once again sees Toby. The security of the house has been reestablished. Tolly has played a central role by recovering the jewels and, most significant, he has been integrated into the timeless present of Green Knowe.

Although the emphasis of the first two Green Knowe books has been on Tolly's discovery of and integration into the world of the manor, Boston has shown that the area has often been threatened. In *The Children of Green Knowe*, Petronella, the gypsy mother of a horse thief, places a curse on the topiary figure of Green Noah. In *The Chimneys of Green Knowe*, Sefton and his mother try to hide the original home beneath modern exteriors and Caxton the manservant tries to destroy it. In both books, the forces of the modern world surround Green Knowe, and Tolly must get up early in the morning so that he can enjoy an environment which seems pastoral: "He continued to get up very early in the morning when he could hear neither cars nor aeroplanes nor farm machines nor factory sirens, and the heron might be standing on the edge of the moat looking like one of the pterodactyl family" (*Chimneys*, p. 103). In *A Stranger at Green Knowe* and *An Enemy at Green Knowe*, the fourth and fifth books of the series,[11] threats to Green Knowe become more forceful. The pastoral world is seriously endangered.

In the Carnegie-Medal–winning *A Stranger at Green Knowe*, the forces come from modern, mechanized civilization. Hanno, the magnificent gorilla who escapes from his cage in a London zoo, finds a temporary refuge in the thicket bordering Green Knowe. However, his "three real days" (*Stranger*, p. 168) cannot last. In the garden, he is shot and killed by the big-game hunter who had first captured him eleven years earlier. To use Leo Marx's terminology, "the machine has entered the garden"—quite literally.[12]

Hanno had been born in the jungle, which was dominated "by the equatorial sun, the frier of the earth [where] the weight of silence in a thousand miles of forest, the ruthless interchange of life and death, are a millennium without time" (*Stranger*, p. 160). When he is captured, a life governed by the rhythms of nature is replaced by one of endless monotony endured in a world of concrete, which, as Ping recognizes, is "a kind of solid nothingness, it takes nothing in, it gives nothing back" (*Stranger*, p. 43). It is appropriate that Hanno should seek refuge at Green Knowe, for of all places in England it most closely resembles the timeless, elemental quality of his birthplace.

However, this refuge proves to be accessible to Hanno's trackers. As Mrs. Oldknow had recognized, his end was inevitable; the modern world had destroyed his elemental world: "Even if he covered twenty-five miles a night, he'd never find his Africa. He'd only find Birmingham" (*Stranger*, p. 114). Moments before his death she remarks: "There's no forest for Hanno, poor splendid thing. Only a tight little urban overbuilt England" (*Stranger*, p.

162). Crowds clamber over the rock wall, a large cut is made in the hedge, and Hanno lies dead in the garden, a victim of the modern world which had taken him from his rightful home.

Although peace is restored at the end of *A Stranger at Green Knowe,* and Ping, the Burmese exile, is offered a home with Mrs. Oldknow,[13] the conclusion of the book does not offer the sense of security found in the earlier books. The catastrophe has occurred too recently; the central figure has died. Even while alive, he was, at best, a stranger, as the title states, a temporary and threatened visitor. He did not find fulfillment at the manor. Once he had been taken from "his heritage, the elemental earth" (*Stranger,* pp. 35–36), there was no peace for him until death.

Early in *An Enemy at Green Knowe,* Mrs. Oldknow states that the house "has enemies and it needs guarding all the time" (*Enemy,* p. 30) and remarks, "The fact that it is different from anything else, with memories and standards of its own, makes quite a lot of people very angry indeed. . . . Over and above all the rest, it seems to me to have something I can't put a name to, which always has had enemies" (ibid.). Whereas in *A Stranger at Green Knowe* the threatening elements had been specifically presented as the forces of modern civilization, in *An Enemy at Green Knowe* they are more universal. Embodied in Melanie D. Powers, evil assaults the fundamental goodness of Green Knowe. Her evil is linked to the past and touches earlier occupants of the house, especially Susan, whom she temporarily bewitches.

Each of Melanie Powers's attacks on Green Knowe fails in large part because of Tolly and Ping. As in the earlier books, children play central roles, for they are most sensitive not only to the timeless essence of Green Knowe, but also to threats against it. Looking into the Persian mirror, they see an image of Melanie Powers and intuitively realize that she is dangerous. When she visits they perceive her evil character: "They watched her with the eyes of youth that see what they see and do not try to believe it is something different" (*Enemy,* pp. 48–49). When Mrs. Oldknow is under Powers's spell, they release her by placing the chain with the magic stone around her neck. Ping summons the spirit of Hanno to drive away the cats, and the two boys drive the snakes from the garden. Most important, they discover the ancient book that contains the spell which drives away the forces attacking the house, and they learn the secret name which they use to destroy the witch's evil powers.

In *An Enemy at Green Knowe,* the house, which had earlier survived and, indeed, been purified by a fire, faces its greatest threat as it comes close to being torn apart. Although it is safe at the end, its vulnerability has been clearly revealed. Up to this point, the series has followed the patterns of pastoralism: Tolly has entered and become part of the ideal place and forces from outside have attempted to destroy it. If the patterns of pastoralism are to be completed, the sixth book, *The Stones of Green Knowe,* should present the final destruction of this world and the return of the central character to the outside world, a wiser, sadder, more adult individual. However, instead of following the circular journey pattern of pastoralism, the final book transforms the series into a linear journey in which the characters complete their union with the world of Green Knowe. In this respect, *The Stones of Green Knowe* fulfills the series in a manner not unlike that of C. S. Lewis's *The Last Battle* in the Narnia books.

The central figure is Roger, son of the builder of Green Knowe. He has a reverence for old things: "He did not need to fear things for being old. It was rather a reason for loving them" (*Stones,* p. 37). Thus, when he first sees the magic stone seats, he relates them to his wish for the new house to have a future, to become, as it were, old: "He supposed all stone was the same age, all dating back to the day of the creation when God made the earth, so that really the windows of his house, though newly tooled, were as old as the stones. They could last as long into the future as those went back into the past. He passionately wanted the new house to be there forever" (*Stones,* p. 43).

Each of Roger's travels into the future is motivated by his wish to see if the house has survived, and in his trips he comprehends more fully the enduring essence of the house. After racing his horse against Toby's, he learns that his own name has been given to one of the islands in the river and thinks: *"It's my own house and I'm there all the time"* (*Stones,* p. 69). Walking toward the house in the early nineteenth century, he at first fears that it has been replaced by a Georgian edifice. On learning from Susan that it is only hiding behind a false exterior, "Roger's eyes filled with tears as he realized how dear these things were that had endured" (*Stones,* p. 83). Returning to his mother, he can confidently announce, "I'll always come home, always. . . . And this will always be here" (*Stones,* p. 100).

Roger's trip to the twentieth century fills him with the greatest misgivings. We are told that "far as he had gone into the future, except that each time more land was cultivated and new ways of dressing had come in, there had been nothing totally strange to him, nothing totally beyond his comprehension" (*Stones,* p. 101). In the modern world, he is appalled; he misses the sounds of animals and birds and is frightened by modern technology. Only in the garden at Green Knowe does he feel relief. He meets the children and Mrs. Oldknow who, transformed into a girl, pledges: "I'll keep this house for you, Roger the First, and Tolly will do so after me" (*Stones,* p. 112). She gives him a ring which, she notes, will return to her. In so doing, she creates an inviolable, endless circle of time. From her present, she gives a gift to the past; Roger in his present will pass the gift on to the future.

At twentieth-century Green Knowe, surrounded by the destructive elements of modern technology, children from five eras reaffirm their commitment to the manor. Through the ages, it has stood "to repel invaders, to receive heroes, to outlast perils, to withstand in its living stone walls the evils of witches and demons" (*Stones,* p. 23). Children are able to move backwards and forwards in time to aid its defense; after their death they become "others," spirits living in the eternal continuity of Green Knowe. Although, at the conclusion of the novel, the stones are moved to a museum, the final note is one of confidence. The love and reverence of the children, their services to the house, and their eventual translation into "others" all suggest that Green Knowe has the guardians that will insure its survival.

Viewed in relation to the pastoral tradition, the ending of *The Stones of Green Knowe* may strike some readers as escapist in the way that the conclusion of Virginia Lee Burton's *The Little House* is escapist. It might be argued that, given her anxieties about the future of her own house,[14] Boston is creating a happy ending by ignoring the course of twentieth-century life. However, considered in relation to the entire series, the conclusion is consistent with a major theme developed throughout: that within the physical boundaries of the area is embodied an eternal present that can be experienced by those who approach Green Knowe with the proper attitudes. Created out of living stone, Green Knowe has the power to create in those who love and reverence it an understanding of a timelessness superior to the passage of centuries. Thus the children's time at Green Knowe should not be seen as a temporary, pastoral period of retreat but rather as the initial step of a linear journey out of time. *The Stones of Green Knowe,* by moving from past to present rather than from present to past, emphasizes that direction is not so important as attitude. Mrs. Oldknow's passing of the ring to Roger makes time circular rather than linear—the journey that the main characters make is into that circle and then into eternity.

Notes

1. For a discussion of Boston's treatment of time see Eleanor Cameron, *The Green and Burning Tree: On the Writing and Enjoyment of Children's Books* (Boston: Little, Brown, 1969), pp. 107–18. *The Stones of Green Knowe,* written after the publication of this book, in many ways confirms the ideas Cameron has found in the earlier books.

2. L. M. Boston, *A Stranger at Green Knowe* (1961; rpt. Harmondsworth, England: Puffin Books, 1977), pp. 60–61. All subsequent references to this book, abbreviated hereafter as *Stranger,* are from this edition and are cited parenthetically in the text.

3. L. M. Boston, *The Stones of Green Knowe* (1976; rpt. Harmondsworth, England: Puffin Books, 1979), p. 19. All subsequent references to this book, abbreviated hereafter as *Stones,* are from this edition and are cited parenthetically in the text.

4. L. M. Boston, "A Message from Green Knowe," *Horn Book,* 39 (June 1963), 259.

5. L. M. Boston, *An Enemy at Green Knowe* (1964; rpt. Harmondsworth, England: Puffin Books, 1977), p. 52. All subsequent references to this book, abbreviated hereafter as *Enemy,* are from this edition and are cited parenthetically in the text.

6. L. M. Boston, *The River at Green Knowe* (1959; rpt. Harmondsworth, England: Puffin Books, 1976), p. 10. All subsequent references to this book, abbreviated hereafter as *River,* are from this edition and are cited parenthetically in the text.

7. Hallett Smith, "Elizabethan Pastoral," in *Pastoral and Romance,* ed. Eleanor Terry Lincoln (Englewood Cliffs, NJ: Prentice-Hall, 1969), p. 18.

8. Lynne Rosenthal, in "The Development of Consciousness in Lucy Boston's *The Children of Green Knowe," Children's Literature,* 8 (1980), 53–67, specifically refers to Green Knowe as a "non-pastoral world" (p. 64) and argues that Tolly learns to accept the positive and negative elements of both himself and Green Knowe, thereby developing an integrated, healthy consciousness. While agreeing with many points in this fine article, I cannot accept the definition of Green Knowe as a nonpastoral world. Boston's description of it throughout the six books clearly distinguishes it from the outside world and shows that its enemies are all forces from the outside.

9. L. M. Boston, *The Chimneys of Green Knowe* (1958; rpt. Harmondsworth, England: Puffin Books, 1976), p. 18. All subsequent references to this book, abbreviated hereafter as *Chimneys,* are from this edition and are cited parenthetically in the text.

10. L. M. Boston, *The Children of Green Knowe* (1958; rpt. Harmondsworth, England: Puffin Books, 1975), p. 30. All subsequent references to this book, abbreviated hereafter as *Children,* are from this edition and are cited parenthetically in the text.

11. I have not included *The River at Green Knowe,* the third book in the series, in my discussion as, in its presentation of characters and incidents, it is a somewhat tangential book. However, it does reinforce many of the themes of the first two novels, the chief of these being the contrast between children's and adult's ability to respond to Green Knowe. Oskar, Ida, and Ping, while only temporary visitors, are deeply sensitive to its power. Their guardian, Dr. Maud Biggin, an archeological scholar, is oblivious to the spell of the place. One of the adults the children meet offers a contrast to their approach to the river world. Exploring a hidden island, the children discover a hermit, a London busman who had rejected civilization many years before to live a Crusoelike existence. However, his eccentric life is pathetic and escapist. One must live fully and sympathetically in the present as the children do.

12. Leo Marx, *The Machine in the Garden: Technology and the Pastoral Ideal in America* (New York: Oxford University Press, 1964).

13. Note that although Ping is given a home at Green Knowe, he leaves the series at the end of the fifth book when his father arrives with Tolly's father. Green Knowe has been a refuge for the exile, not a final home.

14. See, for example, her comments in an interview included in Justin Wintle and Emma Fisher, *The Pied Pipers* (New York: Two Continents Publishing Group, 1975), pp. 277–84.

The Fresh-Air Kids, or Some Contemporary Versions of Pastoral

Lois R. Kuznets

Pastoral literature traditionally demonstrates the human need for the healing powers of the simple, rural, or rustic life, by contrasting that life with the complex, urban, or urbane one. Such traditional pastoral needs and contrasts can be seen not only in adult literature but also in children's literature, including contemporary books such as Jean George's *Julie of the Wolves* and Betsy Byars's *The Midnight Fox* and classics such as *At the Back of the North Wind, The Adventures of Tom Sawyer, The Wind in the Willows, The Secret Garden, Heidi,* and of course *Alice's Adventures in Wonderland,* seen by Empson as prototypically pastoral, with Alice as "swain."

Even the contemporary children's books that I examine here—Felice Holman's *Slake's Limbo* set in modern Manhattan and Paula Fox's *How Many Miles to Babylon?* set in modern Brooklyn—evoke pastoral contrasts within urban settings.[1] The two books manage to arouse and satisfy our need for pastoral reconciliations in different ways: the first through a story of primitive survival that reaches back to seasonal myths promising pastoral rebirth, and the second through a story of a dangerous journey that echoes pastoral romance. Both books treat Manhattan and Brooklyn realistically yet avoid the bitter irony that usually pervades adult books in which protagonists seek pastoral healing in an urbanized world.

These urban novels—whose protagonists perhaps will never have the opportunity to visit the country except as fresh-air kids, temporarily breathing, as Holman says of her hero, "someone else's fresh air"—initially seem to vary in important ways from those children's books that are set primarily in wilderness or country.[2] The two books considered here have buried the pastoral imagery deep within the psyches of the protagonists and similarly buried

A version of this paper was first delivered at a special section, "Versions of Pastoral for Children," at the MLA Convention, Houston, December 1980.

the pastoral plot of retreat and renewal deep within the structures of the novels themselves. When the pastoral imagery emerges from the individual psyche in dream and fantasy, it often does so in exaggerated and distorted forms. And it is the problem of the novel as a whole to bare the *essential* aspects of the pastoral plot itself, giving the protagonist an opportunity to turn pastoral dreams into an urban reality devoid of ironic overtones.

This process is clearest in *Slake's Limbo,* the strange and wonderful story of thirteen-year-old Aremis Slake, virtual orphan, who made his home for one hundred and twenty days of winter in a cave off the subway tracks under the Commodore Hotel, and who was there transformed from a "worthless lump" (p. 5) into a "vendor of papers, a custodian of a small thriving coffee shop and a discriminating scavenger. And he was also a hobbyist" (p. 73).

Slake's potentiality for transformation is first expressed in his propensity to dream, usually of "somewhere else. Anywhere else" (p. 4). But these dreams seem impotent and essentially debilitating in the context of tenement, street, and school: "Dreaming thus led him into lampposts, up to the ankles in puddles, up to the elbows in spilled things, sprawling down stairways while teachers scolded and classmates scoffed, pushing him down again as soon as he gained his feet" (p. 4). His fantasies are also distortions of pastoral images, turning natural, cyclical gardens into desperate illusions of eternal Gardens of Eden. So, though we may applaud, we also grimace at Slake's attempt to climb a tree in Central Park, to tie back on to it the last of the autumn leaves in order to fulfill "an old fantasy that this year the leaves would stay on the trees" (p. 10).

The ways in which well-meaning people have hoped to give him a brief taste of pastoral life are satirized in Slake's nightmare during his first night in his subway cave. He dreams that he is back as a terrified fresh-air child being chased by his "family's" pet pig (p. 22). Later, noticing a man helplessly caught in a subway rush, he is reminded of a trip to the beach, during which he first got sick in the bus and then was knocked over and nearly drowned by the surf (p. 78). A day at the shore, a fortnight in the country—neither was a healing experience.

Paralleling Slake's distorted pastoral fantasies and indicating their pervasive nature among urban dwellers are the distorted pastoral dreams of a subway driver, Willis Joe Whinny, who once saw a movie about Australian sheepherders and longed to become one, until he traded in his dream for the promise of a motorman's pension—in spite of the fact that Willis, unlike Slake, had country connections, a grandmother whom he used to visit in Iowa. She actually once had known a Montana sheepherder. By the time we met Willis, his dream has resumed but has been distorted into an image of his subway passengers as soulless sheep whom he herds from station to station.

Throughout the book, the middle-aged Willis and the young Slake are moving toward each other as inevitably as Bloom and Stephen Dedalus in Dublin, but we are most immediately aware of the contrast between the two. The first becomes more and more alienated from humanity in the distortion of his pastoral dream, becoming, as Holman says, not really the herder but simply the "lead sheep" (p. 88); the second becomes more human, more connected, more farsighted in establishing his underground home, changing from an "outlander in the city of his birth (and in the world)" (p. 4) to one who is "oddly in touch with the flow of the world" (p. 80).

The motif of renewal pervades the novel, but it is so realistically implemented, and renewal is so rarely elsewhere exclusively associated with the underground, that we may not initially recognize this motif as outlining a pastoral story of retreat and regrowth. It is not usual for us to accept a freshly cleaned public bathroom as an omen of a new life, nor are we accustomed to thinking of the recycling of urban waste as a basically pastoral image. Yet Slake's first business is the reselling of secondhand newspapers, and his first meal is the restaurant leftovers of a hurried businessman. By the time a cleaning woman to whom he talks daily gives him her son's old jacket, mended, and he makes for himself a pair of adequate glasses from among the many dropped lenses he has scavenged, we know that recycling applies to wasted human possibilities as well as to trash and garbage: we are witnessing an example of true urban renewal.

Holman continually pushes in the direction of the pastoral

discovery and settlement theme by her similes: "He began to know the signs of the subway as a woodsman knows the wilderness" (p. 44), and "surely as any explorer who had first set foot anywhere— the Arctic, the Moon—Slake was certainly at least one of the few and only settlers in this piece of dark continent" (p. 98). Slake thus takes his pastoral place among frontiersmen.

Holman also pushes underground imagery back to its origins in nature myths. We have tended recently to associate the underground with death, hell, or insanity from which modern heroes are rarely able to emerge. Holman disassociates the underground from its hellish finality and reassociates it with the cyclical wintering place of Persephone from which she is annually reborn, albeit with struggle, into the arms of her earth mother. In these terms, the one hundred and twenty days that Slake spends underground clearly constitute a period of germination. He experiences anxiety that makes him actually sick when he discovers that his cave will probably be covered over in much-needed subway repairs, but his being pushed out of his underground home in the spring is as cyclically inevitable as his going down into it in the fall. When Slake lies ill upon the tracks, holding a sign that says "Stop," it is also inevitable that Willis will be driving the train that screeches to a halt a few feet from the fallen Slake. Willis himself reconnects with humanity, holding Slake "as he once held his new son and daughter" (p. 110). Mothered by the cleaning woman, Slake, the orphan, is in his rebirth fathered by the motorman.

If we now think of *Slake's Limbo* in terms of its relationship to children's literature in general, we see that, although the urban reality depicted in the book in some ways serves to mask the pastoral allusions, the very detailed and circumstantial nature of that reality also links it with certain emphases characteristic of children's novels, particularly those with rural settings.

The emphasis on practical means of survival in a new environment is particularly evident in this context. We are fascinated by Slake's stratagems for survival, his transformation from ineffectual dreamer to effective actor. The practical survivalist aspect of *Robinson Crusoe* and *Swiss Family Robinson,* strong elements in their fascination for young and old alike, generally have been carried

over into books more specifically directed toward the child reader.[3]
There seems to be an understanding on the part of writers and
publishers of children's books, both classic and modern, that the
more urban becomes the experience of the child-reader, the more
fascinating become the details of feeding, clothing, and sheltering
oneself. The relative simplicity, directness, and recent novelty of
doing these things in a rural environment account for some part of
the enormous popularity of Wilder's *Little House in the Big Woods*,
with its detailed description of processes of meeting basic needs,
processes in which even the very young can participate in some
capacity.

For older children, the idea of being able to survive alone
becomes more attractive and tenable, although frighteningly for-
midable in modern times. Erik Erikson describes the seven-to-
twelve-year stage of development as a period in which "industry"
attempts to overcome "inferiority" and "the child becomes ready to
handle the utensils, tools, and weapons used by the big people."[4]
How attractively reassuring it is to read about Karana in *The Island
of the Blue Dolphins* and Julie-Miyax in *Julie of the Wolves* who, forced
to put into practice the ancient lore and skill of their peoples, are
able to survive through the use of relatively simple tools (in contrast
to the complex machinery of modern industrial society). Slake
makes it look relatively simple, too—recycling the waste of this
society in a way not unlike Mary Norton's Borrowers!

Over and over in children's books, we find practical details of
living in a simpler society emphasized and fulsomely described,
whether this society exists in rural fields, desert islands, or big
woods. Sometimes in this existence, direct experience and experimentation are specifically contrasted to booklearning. This is certainly true in Slake's case since the newly alert Slake is, of course,
playing hooky from school, in which he had wandered in a daze: he
is Wordsworth's "growing boy" on whom "Shades of the prison
house begin to close." Such a contrast also is surely part of the
pastoral element in *Alice's Adventures in Wonderland*. Alice, one
recalls, tries frantically to bring to mind some imperfectly mastered
booklearning that would serve her underground, but only reason-
ing from experience and experimentation will get her into the

garden she first glimpses. In *A Wild Thing*, a modern young-adult book that resembles *Slake's Limbo* in many interesting ways, Morag, a runaway who has been deemed retarded by the school system, is capable of learning to survive, at least temporarily, alone in the Highlands.

The simple order that Slake imposes on his daily life signifies an understanding and control of diurnal rhythm that is also characteristically emphasized in other children's books that partake of the pastoral. Eating, sleeping, and working begin to become meaningful activities—no longer imposed from above—once Mary Lennox gets into the secret garden. Morag, too, in *A Wild Thing*, experiences the need for meaningful orderly activity in her life, even if it is no longer dominated by the clock (or perhaps because it is not).

Moreover, we are not at all surprised in *Slake's Limbo* to discover, in keeping with a pastoral convention well honored in children's books, that Slake's growth underground includes the nurturing of an animal (that the creature should be a rat seems both inevitable and weirdly pastoral in the identification of child keepers with their animal charges). In adult traditional pastoral, of course, shepherds and shepherdesses do not engage in much practical care of sheep. Shepherding simply seems to provide a leisure for the composition of poetry. But animals and birds do have symbolic functions there, especially in pastoral romance, where they serve as guides into the gardens and forest groves where the hero will experience whatever epiphanies he is meant to experience. The robin for whom Mary Lennox feels the first glimmerings of positive emotion functions not only initially to stimulate her nurturing instincts, but also as the traditional pastoral guide into the garden. In children's pastoral, animals require nurturing and provide companionship, serving in both roles as guides into the essential pastoral experience. The use of animals is even more true of *How Many Miles to Babylon?*, which will be discussed below, than of *Slake's Limbo*. It is certainly true of Tom's midnight fox in Byars's novel, the wolves and bird in *Julie of the Wolves*, the wild dogs, birds, and otters of *The Island of the Blue Dolphins*, and the nanny goat and kid of *A Wild Thing*.

Linked still further with developmental ideas of children's literature is the *rite of passage* suggestion in Slake's age, thirteen. Slake

can be seen as having won his entrance into adulthood by the trial
of his underground independence. The pastoral experience in
children's books can often be seen as such a testing-ground for life
in the wider world, presaging a reentry into society and into a
larger maturity. As in Tom's return to the city after his experience
with the midnight fox in the country, the protagonist often
emerges not only wiser but often sadder. Some of this sadness
clearly is related to a loss of innocence that marks the return from a
pastoral world.

Be that as it may, Slake (who is not necessarily sadder, but
certainly wiser) has won his independence as well as his right to
society through his experience underground. After being briefly
cosseted in the hospital and having his existence in the minds of
others confirmed by the receipt of a card from Willis, Slake slips
away at the suggestion that the "juvenile authorities" will step in to
help him. We are once again reminded that, in literature if not in
life, when orphans finally find their parents they usually no longer
need them as *parents,* having found an identity that first incorpo-
rates and then transcends them. Indeed, the parents themselves
are often in need of the help of their children: Slake rescues Willis
as surely as Willis rescues Slake; James of *How Many Miles to
Babylon?* calls his mother back to real life from a mental institu-
tion—facts that certainly contribute to the theme of pastoral healing in these two books.

The experience of James, the ten-year-old black protagonist in
How Many Miles to Babylon?, shares these urban pastoral characteristics in a less pervasive and concentrated way, but the pattern of
distortion and transformation of the pastoral through urban experience is similar. Although the three aunts who take care of
virtually orphaned James are clearly more attentive and concerned
than Slake's vaguely present aunt, James's life prior to the main
experience of the book is just as fragmented, dream-dominated,
and haunted by failure.

He has Willis's nostalgia for a pastoral life known by his ancestors
and solicits stories from his aunt of country days gone by:

But James wanted to hear all about that—about the country store where you could buy everything from a pork chop to a hoe, about the long dirt roads where the soft dust slipped around your bare toes, about the black stove in the kitchen where pine wood burned all winter long.[p. 5]

His longing takes the form here of creation of imaginary "felicitous space," such as Slake finally creates for himself in the subway cave. The pastoral fantasy that he conjures up to make his tenement, street, and school existence tolerable is one in which we find fragments of traditional pastoral romances of the sort that Shakespeare used in *The Winter's Tale:* royal babies left to be brought up by rustics, their identity to be revealed only in the crisis of adolescence:

He was being guarded by those three old women so that no harm would come to him. His mother had gone across the ocean to their real country, and until she came back, no one was supposed to know who he really was. She had to fix everything. . . . He knew he was not the only prince. He knew there were others. When everything was all right, all the princes would come together in a great clearing, dressed in their long bright robes and their feathers, and after that everything would be different. [p. 25]

James's version of the pastoral romance is obviously derived from stories of African ancestry that James's mother had told him before his father left them and before she herself disappeared one night into a mental hospital. It is not much different from Geeder's fantasy about Zeely in Virginia Hamilton's *Zeely.* But James has started to act out his fantasies—when he finds a dime-store ring in the dirt, he is sure it is a sign from his mother that she will send for him soon. By the time we meet James, we can see that the fantasy has taken over even those parts of his life that are not particularly unpleasant. His teacher, though pastorally named Miss Meadowsweet and demonstrably concerned about him, is unable to reach him through his fog of daydreaming. He, like Slake, plays hooky, slipping away from the school to the basement of an old

condemned brownstone, where he has worked out an elaborate
ritual designed to bring home again his queenly mother. Urban
reality breaks into his dance in front of a cardboard figure of Santa
Claus left behind in the household debris; three young dognappers
find him, make fun of his ring and ritual, and put his innocence to
work for them in conning the dogowners.

James's experience is much more like the pastoral journey-
return plot than is Slake's four-month sojourn in the underground. (Comparing their titles—*Slake's Limbo* and *How Many Miles
to Babylon?*—confirms their respectively different emphases on
stasis and movement.)[5] After acquiring Gladys, a small white poo-
dle with a red bow, Stick, Gino, and Blue force James to accompany
them on their bicycles out to Coney Island, where they are already
hiding another expensive dog in the funhouse. James's growing
feeling of responsibility for Gladys, although he has hitherto been
afraid of dogs (just as Slake had hitherto been afraid of rats) is a
central part of his maturing experience, and, of course, a pastoral
convention of animal companionship. When they first pick her up,
he is annoyed by this responsibility—"With what he had on his
mind why should he fuss about a dog?" (p. 56)—but by the time
they arrive at Coney Island his concern about her overshadows his
own anxiety:

> James felt terrible about Gladys at the moment. She must be
> frightened and homesick. He felt he cared more about Gladys
> than anything in the world except his mother. The thought of
> his mother surprised him. He hadn't had a picture of her in his
> mind for awhile. Well, she couldn't help him now. He was
> completely alone. [pp. 80–81]

The projection of his own fear onto Gladys, his immediate association of Gladys with his own mother, his ensuing feeling of responsibility for his own fate are all neatly tied together in this paragraph.
Reality is overtaking fantasy.

Still another true pastoral image acts as a corrective to the old
one. Arriving at Coney Island in the evening, James experiences
the ocean for the first time; it is appropriately invigorating: "James
felt almost hopeful, smelling the water, listening to the sound of

the waves breaking" (p. 90). But he also learns something about the distorted nature of his fantasy: "No matter what he pretended, he knew she couldn't have gotten across the Atlantic Ocean" (p. 103).

Like Slake, James moves from dreaming incompetence to alert competence, and does it in a similarly incongruous place, not a subway cave but the Coney Island funhouse. Once upon a time, back in the classroom, James had been admonished by Miss Meadowsweet, who claimed that he was such a dreamer that he couldn't "find his way out of a paperbag" (p. 102). Yet, after they are locked in the funhouse by a passing security guard, it is James who, as a result of a previously aborted escape attempt, knows a possible way out behind the merry-go-round. When they crawl among the painted horses, Blue shouts, "Get those horses in the corral," reminding us of still another type of pastoral fantasy.

James's ultimate escape, after spending part of a tense night in the brownstone (during which we acquire some sympathy for his young exploiters as well) seems sure. We also expect him to fulfill his responsibility to Gladys by taking her home first—which he does at the expense of a long and frightening walk. James has earned the name "Prince," which the boys have begun to call him, in earnest before the long journey is over.

His return to his own tenement is also celebrated by his aunts and neighbors in the traditional heroic way: "We thought you was dead" (p. 113). "He's back. Look! He came back" (p. 115). And, of course, his mother is there waiting for him, brought back from *her* "funhouse" by his ordeal. Again, the Persephone myth of the return from a trip to hell and back into the arms of a parent is invoked, at a number of different levels. And again, by the time he finds his parent, he is as ready to help his parent as his parent is to help him. James enters the room and walks toward his bed:

> A small woman was sitting on it. . . . She was hardly bigger than Gino.
>
> James stood still. But where were her long white robes? Her long black hair? Where were her servants, her crown? . . .
>
> Why, she was hardly any bigger than he was! . . .
>
> How *could* she be his mother? [p. 117]

The process of role reversal can begin even at the age of ten, but his mother still has the power and responsibility, in this case, of granting him the birthright of his own identity:

> He thought, who am I? I'm not a prince. How can I be a prince? Who am I?
>   As though she had read his mind and heard his question, his mother held out her hand.
>   "Hello, Jimmy," she said. [p. 117]

Slake and James are both heroes, not anti-heroes. The city is not the end of them. Take away their fresh air, lock them in the funhouse, and yet they have the internal strength to make it anyway. If there is an irony in these endings, it is not a bitter one but a gentle irony—and the joke is on the cosmos, not the protagonists.

And what is this strength inside? It's the same strength of which pastoral dreams are made, albeit at first distorted. It is no mere chance that our heroes are at first incompetent, bumbling dreamers. James has a moment early in his captivity by the boys when he realizes the power of his own mind:

> They hadn't known what he had been laughing about, James realized. They couldn't tell what he was really thinking. They could make him go where they wanted and they could search him. But they couldn't get inside his head where his thoughts were. Maybe he'd have a great thought that would show him how he could get home. [p. 46]

James gets home. Again, *Slake's Limbo* carries out this theme in a more encompassing way. Holman shows us that she is concerned with the concept of the human soul when Willis's country grandmother tells him an anecdote about the Montana sheepherder who, when she complained that he smelled like his sheep, replied: " 'The only difference between me and a sheep, ma'am, is that I've got a soul.' " (p. 37). Willis is about to lose his soul in distorted fantasies. Slake has a soul that is developing; it appears, as it does in much traditional literature, in the metaphor of a bird. The bird first gnaws our hero from within and then, being freed, becomes a talisman and a leader. From the beginning of the story, and even after his rebirth, Slake felt hunger combined with anxiety, and then anxiety alone, as if a bird had settled in his gut and was pecking him from within. In the hospital, he feels a release from this bird, as if he has finally coughed it up. And then, when he leaves the hospital, he envisions it soaring above him toward the rooftops and wants to follow where it leads him. The last words of the novel, as upbeat as James's mother's greeting, are, "Slake did not know exactly where he was going, but the general direction was up" (p. 117).

I should reemphasize that the concern here with baring both the pastoral skeleton and the soul has largely ignored the very interesting urban flesh with which both are clothed. This depiction of the city is not only interesting but extremely realistic. These are urban novels written by urban writers who know New York, in all its terror, its shabbiness, and its wit, very well indeed. They are also writers who clearly, consciously play with specific types of settings—the underground subway, the Coney Island funhouse—that, in adult literature, have served as metaphors for the disturbed minds of anti-heroes, beginning with Dostoevski's narrator in *Notes from Underground.* Such settings are, in adult literature, permeated with bitter irony.

This bitter irony, which neither Holman nor Fox evokes, is not particularly suitable for a child audience, but it has certainly not been avoided entirely in pastoral books for children or young adults such as *Julie of the Wolves* and *A Wild Thing,* where the female protagonists learn pastoral skills to no seeming, lasting avail in the modern world.[6] Holman and Fox, however, seem determined to confirm the value of the pastoral dream in an urban reality and to assert the possibility of realizing it, even when growing up poor and / or black in a polluted city that has already obviously defeated many adults. It is a message that is conveyed not just by the relative triumph of the protagonists, but by the assertion that the young protagonist can redeem some of these defeated (or corrupted) adults, as Slake, in some way, saves Willis, and James, in some way, saves his mother. In classic children's pastoral, as in pastoral romance, the old can be redeemed by the young, as is Colin's father by Colin and Mary, and Heidi's grandfather by Heidi. Part of the irony of *Julie of the Wolves* and *A Wild Thing* comes from the fact that neither Julie nor Morag can influence the old, who may, or do, respectively destroy them.

Both Slake and James move from distortions of their pastoral needs into living out, within an urban context, true pastoral adventures of primitive survival or dangerous journeys—seemingly to redeem some adults along with themselves. Holman and Fox know that both children and adults are haunted by such frightening questions as "Where has all the fresh air gone?" Yet these authors also seem to say that we still must breathe and can even be *in*spired.

Notes

1. Felice Holman, *Slake's Limbo* (New York: Charles Scribner's Sons, 1974) and Paula Fox, *How Many Miles to Babylon?* (New York: David White and Co., 1967). Future references will be cited parenthetically in the text.

2. "Fresh-air kids" refers to recipients of charitable funds and services designed to get city kids into country summer camps and suburban home-stays.

3. The didacticism that dogged the heels of Rousseau's *Émile* (which found *Robinson Crusoe* the one acceptable book) was in favor of giving children a wealth of practical details of an everyday life close to nature, as in works such as Thomas Day's *History of Sandford and Merton* (1783–89) in which pastoral Sandford, a farmer's son, is always favorably compared to aristocratic young Merton.

4. See Erik H. Erikson's *Childhood and Society,* 2nd ed. (New York: W. W. Norton & Co., Inc., 1963), chapter 7, especially pp. 258–61.

5. The title of Fox's book is specifically related to the journey motif in the nursery rhyme, "How Many Miles to Babylon?" But the Biblical Babylon is an urban image associated with destruction in the Old Testament books of Isaiah and Daniel. It is, in addition, the place where Daniel and his righteous companions barely escape martyrdom. Babylon is also part of the apocalyptic imagery of Revelations. It is hard to believe that Fox was not aware of these associations, although she refrains from specifically evoking them. In the same vein, it seems probable also that Holman was aware of the theological associations with Limbo, that portion of Hell to which helpless unfortunates such as unbaptized babies are sent to await Judgment Day.

6. In a previous paper on "The Female Pastoral Journey in *Julie of the Wolves* and *A Wild Thing,*" delivered at the MMLA Convention in Indianapolis, November 1979, I examine these two books about runaway girls as pastoral variants of Joseph Campbell's "monomyth." I argue that the issues of both feminism and environmentalism are invoked yet handled differently in the two books, and I briefly explore a link between these issues as postulated by Dorothy Dinnerstein in *The Mermaid and the Minotaur: Sexual Arrangements and Human Malaise* (New York: Harper and Row, 1957). These two issues, I contend, lend a bitter irony to both books.

Reviews

And the Prince Turned into a Peasant and Lived Happily Ever After

Perry Nodelman

Breaking the Magic Spell: Radical Theories of Folk and Fairy Tales, by Jack Zipes. Austin: University of Texas Press, 1979.

For a radical theoretician like Jack Zipes, fairy tales have to be worthwhile; they represent "the collective, active participation of the people," and the people know best. But fairy tales are fantasy, and radical theoreticians usually consider fantasy an escapist diversion from the necessary consideration of things as they are. Darko Suvin, a Marxist critic of science fiction who admires just that one sort of fantasy enough to insist on its political usefulness, has nothing but disdain in *Metamorphoses of Science Fiction* (Yale University Press, 1979), for what he calls "the Great Pumpkin antics" of most fantasy. Fairy tales are filled with Great Pumpkin antics; some of them even describe how Great Pumpkins are turned into great coaches. Even worse, fairy tales originated back when a repressive aristocracy held all power, and even a bourgeois, pseudo-intellectual, would-be capitalist like myself can see that the values they express are feudal, outmoded, and not likely to promote the revolution. A radical theory of fairy tales is bound to be unwieldy, and Zipes does not bring off the impossible acrobatics he attempts in *Breaking the Magic Spell.* But following him as he tries to do so is stimulating and suggests much about fairy tales as children's literature.

Zipes claims that socio-historical forces express themselves in fairy tales in different ways at different points in history. As the collective creation of a precapitalist people, folktales express "their wishes to attain better living conditions." Later, literary fairy tales such as "Beauty and the Beast" show how the superficially bestial aristocracy is morally superior to the "crass, vulgar values of the emerging bourgeoisie," while the witch in "Hansel and Gretel" represents "the entire feudal system or the greed and brutality of

the aristocracy." In our own century, the dragon in Tolkien's T
Hobbit is "the capitalist exploiter," and folktales, refashioned by th
mass media, merely confirm the passive values of a consume
society.

Zipes's attempts to allegorize the evil characters of fairy tales ar
not convincing. Using the same specious logic, businessmen migl
see the dragon as the AFL.-CIO.; women might see it as me
children as their parents, dopers as the narcs. We all have ou
dragons.

But having located the specific meanings of fairy tales in histor
Zipes can perform the operation basic to his argument: he ca
separate their distasteful values from their thrust as a *kind*
literature. He can admit that folktales affirm dangerous feud
values but still say that they have "emancipatory potential." He ca
acknowledge the solipsistic escapism of the fairy tales written i
Germany in the early nineteenth century, but he can see it as
socially valuable refusal "to be formed by the powers of domin
tion." And he can insist that those old stories that once ha
emancipatory potential now merely co-opt our individual imagina
tions when communicated by mass media.

Zipes doesn't always present these ideas clearly. He rarely di
cusses individual tales, preferring instead to summarize in abstra
jargon the abstract arguments of numerous German leftist theor
ticians. He assumes that his analysis of a few German fairy tal
allows him to draw general conclusions about the history of a
European folktales. He seems to confuse the way in which folktal
were created with the values they express, so that any collectiv
creation is assumed—incorrectly—to promote collective value
And he doesn't make clear whether he dislikes the co-opting pow
of the mass media in general or something specific to mass-med
versions of fairy tales. He claims to argue the second of thes
possibilities but only writes about the first.

With good reason—mass-media culture is popular culture, en
joyed by the mass of the populace. Zipes could not attack the valu
it promotes without attacking The People. Not surprisingly, h
discussion of mass media never mentions demographics—the i
sidious way in which the communications industry figures out wh

most of us want and then gives it to us. He will not admit that there is junk on television, simply because most of us like junk; instead, he insists that "the audiences are the underdogs in the fight against the mass media which expertly exploit their humble daydreams to protect the vested interests of corporate capitalism." Similarly, he wants to admire the collective humble daydreams of the folk of the Middle Ages, but he has to admit that what those folk collectively probably dreamed of was becoming rich kings with the power to lord it over other humble peasants.

The essential flaw in Zipes's argument is that he uses the words *wishes* and *hopes* to mean two different things at the same time: not just dreams or daydreams, but also aspirations. Peasants in the Middle Ages did enjoy dreaming about being kings, but only because they knew they would always be peasants. And I suspect it is still true that the people convinced of their continuing powerlessness are those who most enjoy films and stories in which losers win. "Humble daydreams" are just that, ways of imaginatively purging our frustrations about the things we feel humbled by: escapist wish-fulfillment, not utopian aspiration.

But Zipes insists that folktales represent events that might actually happen. For him, even the worst of popular films expresses a utopianism that offers viewers "some small amount of hope for a qualitatively better future." In turning fairy tales into descriptions of achievable utopias Zipes has a disconcerting effect on them; he really does break their magic spells, by dissipating their magic. Those wonderfully illogical happenings that allow foolish or passive underdogs to triumph over their smarter enemies were not so illogical after all; no, "the magic and miraculous serve to rupture the feudal confines and represent metaphorically the conscious and unconscious desires of the lower classes." So Zipes saves fairy tales for socialism by denying that they are fantasy.

Bruno Bettelheim does that, too. But according to Zipes, Bettelheim's rigid Freudian interpretation of the stories foolishly disregards both Zipes's political prejudices and his revisionist Freudianism, which, unlike the Freudianism of both Bettelheim and Freud, does not confuse adjusting to reality with accepting repressive, bourgeois, capitalist values. Even worse, Bettelheim believes the old tales in their original versions have a permanent, true meaning, always understood by the human unconscious, and automatically will have a therapeutic effect on children who hear them. But having located the meaning of the tales in the shifting sands of history, Zipes assures us that imposing the feudal values of the old tales on the unconscious minds of contemporary children will be anything but good for them. We must instead choose the *right* tales, the ones "which suggest means by which children can implement their imagination to promote collective action."

In other words, fairy tales are useful. Zipes and Bettelheim both defend fairy tales, not as good stories, but as stories that are good for people. Both are convinced of the dangers of children's literature containing values of which they don't approve. So Zipes's discussion of Bettelheim offers the instructive spectacle of one angry utilitarian attacking another angry utilitarian; it shows how even the most liberal-minded adults are perfectly willing to limit the freedom of children. Neither Zipes nor Bettelheim has enough respect for children to allow them access to a variety of values, so that they may themselves discover and invent their own world.

As it happens, fairy tales are a good way for children to do that—as Zipes and Bettelheim both unintentionally make clear. Zipes's radical interpretations appear just as possible as Bettelheim's Freudian ones, or, for that matter, as Madame de Beaumont's aristocratic ones or as contemporary anti-sexist ones. But that the tales support such wildly different interpretations suggests that the interpretations are just variants, other ways of telling stories whose main characteristic is their openness to being told in different ways, with different meanings. What really matters about fairy tales is not their meanings, for we all are capable of devising different ones. What matters is that fairy tales allow us to do so, that they offer us a gift of interpretative freedom, a way to explore and discover ourselves and our own stories. Wise children respect and enjoy that gift; so should wise critics.

Eighteenth-Century Prefigurements

Robert Bator

John Locke and Children's Books in Eighteenth-Century England, by
Samuel F. Pickering, Jr. Knoxville: University of Tennessee
Press, 1981.

In the mid-1780s, the *Critical Review* found children's books
"scarcely objects of criticism" but urged that they be "perused . . .
with some care." Two centuries later, the Georgian storybook is still
scarcely an object of criticism. While there have been some recent
dissertations and several articles, books on the subject would include only Florence V. Barry's *A Century of Children's Books* (1922,
rpt. 1968), Sylvia W. Patterson's *Rousseau's "Émile" and Early Children's Literature* (1971), and now Samuel F. Pickering, Jr.'s *John
Locke and Children's Books in Eighteenth-Century England.*

Children's literature historians have examined the eighteenth
century when, in Harvey Darton's words, juvenile literature really
opens up, but often with one eye on the upcoming century. For
example, Darton found in Dorothy Kilner's *Life and Perambulation
of a Mouse* a pre-Alice fantasy framework. The eighteenth-century
book becomes mere prefigurement to be lamented and disposed of
before one gets to the more fanciful creations of the following
century.

What eighteenth-century writers were about, not what they
prefigured, is the focus of Pickering's book. It shows the two men
who were mainly responsible for what amusement was sanctioned
at all in children's books—both named John, one a physician-
philosopher and the other a small-town printer who married his
boss's widow and moved to London.

John Locke's *Some Thoughts Concerning Education* (1693), as Pickering shows, urged that nothing be overlooked that would form
children's minds. Finding little beyond Aesop, primers, and psal-
ters, Locke suggested that pleasant books suited to a child's capacity
be made available. Within a generation, Isaac Watts's *Divine Songs*
(1715) became *the* book of poetry for English children, popular for

more than a century. Watts, Pickering explains, followed Locke's denial of innate ideas and consequent fervor for forming the impressionable child, and, although not always heeding Locke's caution against "being unreasonably forward" in religious education, softened somewhat the Puritan compulsion to literally scare the hell out of children.

Forty years after Locke's death, when British parents had long taken in Locke's educational theory, as Pickering shows, John Newbery published his first juvenile, *A Little Pretty Pocket-Book.* Its preface to parents is an extensive paraphrase from the pediatric sections of *Some Thoughts Concerning Education.* Here is the kind of book "the great Mr. Locke" would approve, Newbery seems to be saying. And Newbery was, as Locke urged, making sure that children were "cozen'd into a Knowledge of the Letters" by encasing his sixpenny publication with shiny paper covers and by associating task work such as learning the alphabet with children's games like hopscotch.

Pickering plays a bit of literary hopscotch himself in taking the reader from Locke to Watts to Newbery. While Newbery is lauded for using gilt flowery Dutch boards, Thomas Boreman's books— which were sold a few years earlier—were bound, we are told in an appendix, "like Newbery's books." I agree with Pickering that Newbery's books were "shiningly superior" to Boreman's *Gigantick Histories,* but Newbery capitalized on a feature employed by earlier publishers, a point emphasized by the title of the appendix, "John Newbery's Predecessors." Pickering is on target in labeling the *Gigantick Histories* pedestrian tour-books, but Boreman did copublish a miscellany with Mary Cooper, another Newbery predecessor tucked away in the same appendix. Her preface to *A Child's New Play-Thing* also leaned heavily on Locke. To be told that Boreman's or Cooper's books resembled the typical Newbery book can confuse. There was no typical Newbery book when Mary Cooper published *A Child's New Play-Thing,* which was, as Pickering notes, in its second edition in 1743. Admittedly, Pickering is not employing a strict chronology. Yet while it is valid to view Boreman and Cooper over the shoulder of John Newbery, given the fact that literature historians such as Darton did not include Boreman at all, a corrective focus might be requisite to show Newbery as Boreman's (and Cooper's) more gifted successor.

Another minor focal adjustment I would propose is in Pickering's study of yet another John, the publisher John Marshall. Never has the publishing output of John Marshall be so effectively screened. Marshall began his publishing career in the 1780s with *The Renowned History of Primrose Prettyface* and other works in the Newbery (and therefore Lockean) mold. His more original, and more serious, publications featured Ellenor Fenn and the Kilner sisters, Dorothy and Mary Ann. But the group portrait of these authors as Marshall's "literary associates" makes for some forced images. For example, Pickering scolds John Marshall for the eye-for-an-eye punishment meted out to children who disobey, but it is mainly in the Kilner cautionary tales where girls inevitably knock out several teeth in falling out of forbidden window seats and boys are tied down and whipped for abusing a cat. Lady Fenn was more interested in natural science than were the Kilners, and she was never so sadistically punitive with her child-characters.

Pickering describes how Lady Fenn wrote anti–fairy tales and fables, the latter with the imprimatur of Locke. But Fenn defended herself against the proscriptions of Rousseau, who, like Locke, never sanctioned fairy tales, but who, unlike Locke, banished fables as well. While Locke's influence can be cited through the entire eighteenth century, at what point, if ever, does Rousseau become the ironic begetter of the increasingly popular book for children? Where Locke ends and Rousseau begins and where the two overlap would warrant an interesting study. *Émile* was already translated into English by the time *Goody Two-Shoes* appeared, but that book, Pickering demonstrates, is a thoroughly Lockean text.

Questions of focus do not mean the book has not developed its subjects. The description on the dustjacket claims that Pickering uses the ideas of Locke as a lens to survey the field. While a lens will pull some primary objects into focus, it often blurs backgrounds; actually Pickering has used more than a single lens to pull together a tremendous amount of material. He has consulted more than one hundred juvenile books in rare eighteenth-century editions, plus numerous chapbooks and dozens of Boreman and Newbery titles.

This is quite an impressive improvement in primary source study over both the Patterson and the Barry texts.

Lack of space seems to have truncated Pickering's bibliography of modern secondary sources. Neither the Patterson nor the Barry text is mentioned and only four periodical entries are listed, only one of which is on children's literature. Surely some noteworthy scholarly articles have appeared since Charlotte Yonge. For example, Pickering's own excellent articles, which often appear in publications other than children's literature journals, might have been cited. Listing such a wealth of primary source material, especially those with protracted subtitles, does take up space. Summary of fewer chapbooks, which were seldom meant for children (as their often bawdy and scatalogical contents reveal), would have allowed for a more amplified modern bibliography.

What Pickering does make room for is often superb, such as "Biographies of Animals and the Inanimate," in which he shows how, a generation after the adult novel began to feature talking banknotes and confessions of lapdogs, the juvenile novelists offered perambulations of pincushions and ponies. Pickering is a scholar who never makes the reader pay for all the toil of research that went into containing the contributions of a century. Like all enthusiasts, however, he sometimes gets carried away. For instance, Locke's comments on kindness to animals he posits as a major influence on Newbery and his successors. But if Locke (not Rousseau) is the dominant influence on the depiction of animals and the kindness-to-animals theme, why do the juvenile humane society tracts like *Keeper's Travels* first appear almost a century after Locke? And Pickering deals with the school stories of the 1780s without treating Sarah Fielding's *The Governess*, the first of such stories, although he provides a valuable study of the unique pastoralism of another often-neglected early female writer, Anna L. Barbauld.

By moving the focus on the eighteenth-century juvenile book from what it succeeded to to what it proceeded from, Pickering has demonstrated that what has been mostly the object of mere perusal can be the subject of genuine criticism.

Hearn on Huck

David L. Greene

The Annotated Huckleberry Finn: Adventures of Huckleberry Finn, by Mark Twain. Edited, with an introduction, notes, and bibliography, by Michael Patrick Hearn. New York: Clarkson N. Potter, 1981.

Clarkson Potter's series of annotated classics is deservedly well-known. It began with Martin Gardner's superb *Annotated Alice* and has continued primarily with children's books, although it also includes Thoreau's *Walden,* Stoker's *Dracula* (written for adults but read mostly by morbid adolescents), and even an *Annotated Shakespeare.* The strengths and weaknesses of these books grow out of a policy that has clearly guided each annotator: to provide notes on practically everything from the outrageously obscure to the painfully obvious. One cannot read these books simply for the text, unless he is able to ignore note numbers beside every column of text, dozens of added illustrations, and annotations often much longer than the passages they explain. But if he uses the books to elucidate obscure points or to gratify the antiquarian pleasures of scholarship, he will find them interesting and often valuable.

Michael Hearn's *Annotated Huckleberry Finn* is one of the best of the series. Hearn's research into published material has been exhaustive; he has even found unreprinted newspaper interviews with Twain. His introduction, which covers Twain's life in outline and the history of the book in detail, is enlightening and judicious; it could have been improved only by a full discussion of the various interpretations of the book, and that would certainly have made the introduction disproportionately long. At only one point do I disagree with Hearn's introduction: on page 24 he says that contemporary reviewers who accepted "local color only reluctantly and only when written by James Russell Lowell found Twain's bad grammar and slang merely coarse and inelegant." If we take this statement literally, it says that those who tolerated dialect only in

179

Lowell (*The Biglow Papers*?) did not tolerate it in other authors, which is akin to saying, "Those who like this sort of thing will find much here to like." But if we read into it the implication that most critics did not like local color and the attempt to reproduce dialect, I must disagree, for during this period such writers as George Washington Cable, Sarah Orne Jewett, Mary E. Wilkins, and others used dialect with little critical complaint. Hearn is surely correct that reviewers objected to Twain's use of dialect in *Huckleberry Finn*, but probably this was because the entire book is in dialect, rather than just scattered conversations. As Hearn points out, *Huck* must have seemed to superficial readers something like the works of Artemus Ward and his successors and was damned for that reason; the condemnation of Twain's novel was not, however, part of a general rejection of dialect.

The annotations are fascinating; there is little that Hearn does not clarify and there is evidence on practically every page of his extraordinary ability to discover obscure information. The publisher's policy of annotating everything has prevented the editor from developing a single coherent critical theory in his notes, but that is the fault of Potter, not Hearn; series policy has also forced the editor to annotate the obvious, such as a definition of "two bits" and an identification of King Solomon, and occasionally to include information that is interesting but does not help us to understand Twain: the note on "two bits" goes on to explain that this term originated in "the Spanish milled dollar of eight *reals*, or 'bits,' " an intriguing piece of information that focuses attention away from Twain's "bran-new Barlow knife worth two bits in any store," despite the praiseworthy additional note that tells us what a Barlow knife is.

Hearn's notes on the Duke and the King are especially fine. He surveys the stories about the lost Dauphin and provides a full explanation of the implied obscenity of the King's performance in the "Thrilling Tragedy of THE KING'S CAMELOPARD or THE ROYAL NONESUCH!!!" Throughout the notes, the editor uses comments from Twain's correspondence and interviews. Unlike Hearn, I do not like Kemble's illustrations. To me they seem badly drawn and grotesque rather than humorous; moreover they do not hint at the seriousness of the work. I was amused, however, at Kemble's illustration of "Indignation," a fine parody of the then-ubiquitous photographs of the "Delsarte Method of Elocution," photographs which showed a woman demonstrating such emotions as fear, aversion, and so on. (This identification of Kemble's drawing as a parody of Delsarte is the only thing I would have added to Hearn's notes.)

Hearn's superb investigation of *Huckleberry Finn* will lead readers to ask again: Did Twain, as Roger Sale concluded about another author, "create better than he knew"? Is *Huckleberry Finn* a master-piece despite Twain? Is this the explanation for the terrible falling-off of the last chapters, in which Tom Sawyer takes over and makes a game, rather a cruel one, out of Jim's desire for freedom? If Twain realized the significance of what has become one of the world's great novels, why did he prostitute his creation with *Tom Sawyer Abroad* and "Tom Sawyer, Detective"? And why did he consent to turn *Huck* into a musical extravaganza and allow his name to be used, falsely, as one of the authors of the musical? Twain's letters are ambiguous, but they support the view that Huck's creator knew the significance of his creation.

Hearn's careful, scholarly, and amazingly comprehensive investi-gation is an invaluable aid to understanding Twain's masterpiece. *The Annotated Huckleberry Finn* is a major compilation. We owe it to the publisher to add that Clarkson Potter has given it a format worthy of the text.

A Trio of Poetry Books for Children

Marilyn Nelson Waniek

A Visit to William Blake's Inn: Poems for Innocent and Experienced Travelers, by Nancy Willard. New York: Harcourt, Brace, Jovanovich, 1981.
A Day in Verse: Breakfast, Books, & Dreams, selected by Michael Patrick Hearn. New York: Frederick Warne & Co., 1981.
Pink Lemonade, by Annie M. G. Schmidt, translated by Henrietta Ten Harmsel. Grand Rapids: Wm. B. Eerdmans, 1981.

Nancy Willard's *A Visit to William Blake's Inn*, inspired by Blake's *Songs of Innocence* and *Songs of Experience*, is handsomely illustrated by Alice and Martin Provensen and opens with a curiously misleading introductory anecdote, about how Willard first heard Blake's "Tyger, Tyger" when she was seven years old and received shortly afterward a mysteriously autographed volume of Blake's *Songs*. One might assume from this that Willard will offer, because of her own childhood fascination with Blake, an edition of Blake's *Songs* for children. This is not the case. Instead, she has written seventeen poems for children, many in the familiar cadences of Blake's best-known lyrics, about an imaginary inn staffed by dragons, angels, and a rabbit and owned by (to judge by the poems) a prosperous, cleanshaven William Blake, who (to judge by the poems) is a sort of spiritual guide to children and animals.

Despite Blake's presence as personage and cadence, one has the uneasy feeling, reading these poems, that their author has somehow lost sight of William Blake in the grand plan of her book. The second poem, for example, introduces "Blake's Celestial Limousine," in which the speaker (a small boy in the illustrations) travels to Blake's Inn. The limousine, we find out in the last lines, is "a wish that only flew / when I climbed in and found it true." We reach these lines, however, after hearing from the driver, apparently an angel clad in a mackintosh and boots, that "all luggage must be carried flat / and worn discreetly on your hat / or served with mustard on a bun." The absurdity here is more Edward Lear than William Blake, and this jarring juxtaposition is characteristic of several poems in the collection. Blake's tiger, of course, makes several appearances, but so do the king of cats, a wise cow, a bear, a rabbit, and an assortment of small animals. The tiger, whose energy, strength, and cruelty led Blake to wonder about its Creator, has here been domesticated, contritely confessing to Blake that it has eaten "half the roast and all the bread" and "the three / lumps of sugar by your tea" and sweetly asking Blake for a bedtime story which will cure its stomach-ache, in a poem which ends:

> Now I lay me down to sleep
> with bear and rabbit, bird and sheep.
> If I should dream before I wake,
> may I dream of William Blake.

As these two poems indicate, Willard is reaching for larger meaning than one is accustomed to in poems for children: her poetry is about the power of the imagination, about the power of poetry to heal. Yet too often the poems try to achieve meaning by echoing or mentioning Blake. "Two Sunflowers Move into the Yellow Room" does both, to a much diminished end:

> "Ah, William, we're weary of weather,"
> said the sunflowers, shining with dew.
> "Our traveling habits have tired us.
> Can you give us a room with a view?"
>
> They arranged themselves at the window
> and counted the steps of the sun,
> and they both took root in the carpet
> where the topaz tortoises run.

Unfortunately, the echo wil be lost on the child unfamiliar with Blake, and the child will wonder: How do sunflowers travel? How will they cease to travel in the inn, since they are at the window? A longer poem, "The Wise Cow Makes WAY, ROOM, and BELIEVE," comes closer to offering real meaning. Here the Wise Cow, when told to "make" the abstractions named in the title, interprets the request literally, making WAY a nest of grass and hay, ROOM a loom on which weather can be weaved, and BE-LIEVE a boat rather similar to the "celestial limousine" of the earlier poem. Here again, however, neither the echo of Blake's cadence nor the mention of his name makes this a successful poem. The poem ends:

> The Wise Cow said, "My dear,
> BELIEVE shall be a boat
> having both feet and fins.
> We'll leave this quiet moat.
> We'll welcome great and small
> with WAYS and ROOMS for all,
> and for our captain let us take
> the noble poet, William Blake."

Even a young child will wonder why there is suddenly a "moat" in the poem, and the ear sensitive to rhythm will notice that the different meter of the last couplet, meant to echo Blake, is the only instance of tetrameter in the thirty-six line poem.

The strongest poems in the collection are those which are least influenced by Blake's meter and myth. "Blake Leads a Walk on the Milky Way" describes a life-long walk, on which the tiger, the cat, and the child learn to value the stars, and presumably the imagination. Blake gives

> . . . silver shoes to the rabbit
> and golden gloves to the cat
> and emerald boots to the tiger and me
> and boots of iron to the rat.

Thus unequally outfitted from the beginning, the characters gain wisdom unequally during their walk. While the others gather stars the "sullen" rat says, "What's gathered by fools in heaven / will never endure." At the end of the walk Blake gives

> . . . silver stars to the rabbit
> and golden stars to the cat
> and emerald stars to the tiger and me
> but a handful of dirt to the rat.

No reason is given in the poem for this injustice dealt the poor rat: is Blake as uneven-handed as the One who made the tiger and the lamb? Willard does not consider this question, which weakens what is otherwise a lovely poem. Nevertheless, this poem and the accompanying illustration are the best pages of the book, and this poem, with "Blake Tells the Tiger the Tale of the Tailor," may be worth the price. The latter poem, a long ballad that similarly uses Blake as a character, describes in rather oblique fashion the development of a tailor from one who builds his house of the wool and fur of living things,

> of wool of bat and fur of mouse,
> of moleskin suede, the better part
> of things that glimmer, skim and dart.

Kept awake at night by the "cries and chirps" of the creatures whose "fur and fury, wool and wings" he has stolen, the tailor moves with his wife to Blake's Inn. There he becomes Blake's own tailor:

> On windy days and moonless nights,
> Blake wears a suit of shifting lights.
> The tailor now has grown so clever
> he stitches light and dark together.

We are told by her publishers that while she was writing these poems Nancy Willard built a six-foot model of the inn, decorated with moons, suns, stars, and prints of Blake's paintings and filled with the characters that appear in the poems. The evident delight can be seen in all of the illustrations and a few of the poems in the book. But the danger implicit in the apparently burgeoning popularity of the book is that for a generation of children the poetry of William Blake—which is, after all, the "celestial limousine" in which Nancy Willard was flown at the age of seven to the world of her fantasy—will be diminished to these too often condescending and jingling echoes of its greatness.

A Day in Verse: Breakfast, Books, & Dreams, an anthology of twenty poems by fifteen authors, edited by Michael Patrick Hearn, is appealingly illustrated with etchings by Barbara Garrison and organized around the average schoolday of an ordinary child. For *ordinary* read suburban, middle-class, white, untroubled. Like the poems in Willard's collection, these are uneven in quality, but the unevenness here is justified because they describe different aspects of the day. Some are delicate, evocative free-verse poems about quiet dreamtime; others are rollicking sing-songs about more mundane matters. The free-verse poems are the more successful, but Russell Hoban's couplet about eggs "Sunny-Side-Down" is inventive:

> Lying face-down on the plate
> On their stomachs there they wait.

An anonymous schoolyard rhyme is also witty and clever:

> Why,
> You—
>
> Double-barrelled,
> Disconnected,
> Supersonic
> Ding-dong-bat:
>
> Don't you dare come
> Near me, or I'll
> Disconnect you
> Just like that!

Often, however, the formal verse in this collection is of no particular linguistic interest, describing—sometimes at great length—familiar childhood scenes. Especially strong is Jane Yolen's "Crazy Quilt," which lists quilt-patterns and describes how the quilt on one child's bed comforts her.

Some of the free-verse poems recall more sharply and evoke with more force childhood and its moods. Kenneth Gangemi's simple "Classroom" captures the intense boredom a schoolchild can feel and makes the imaginative leap to freedom:

> I stare at
> The number 2

I stare at
The number 2

I stare at
The number 2

It looks
Like a swan!

In Joanne Ryder's "Inside the Lab," a bored child transforms the classroom into a sea where "Silver fish / nibble sweetly / at a piece of fallen chalk," and "shy seahorses bob / up and down and up" behind the teacher, and "sharks slide by" the child's desk, so close "I can almost touch them." Charlotte Zolotow's delicate little poem, "In Bed," captures in a few well-chosen words both fear and reassurance:

When I am in bed
I hear
footsteps of the night
sharp
like the crackling of a dead leaf
in the stillness

Then my mother laughs
downstairs

The final poem in the book, Nancy Willard's "Dreaming," describes a child's dream in a repetitious chant that reminds me of tribal poetry, and that would, I think, be a marvelous bedtime poem to be read aloud to a child. The child dreamer goes to the

. . . watchtowers of morning,
. . . I took the morning train to my own country,
and it stopped in my own room where nothing changes,
where the mouse sleeps in its hole and the cat sleeps on my
    bed,
where the dog at the door twitches, dreaming of wolves,
where wolf, hunter, and horse fold up with the shadows,
and I brought back nothing except this story.

Although several of the poems in this collection are either sufficiently amusing or sufficiently evocative to make a child return to them, I suspect that, despite the power of some of Garrison's etchings, this book is one that a child will read once, then put at the bottom of the books piled on the shelf. Had Hearn chosen to include a few less safe, more provocative subjects among them, his anthology might have avoided this fate. None of the poets he has included seems to have been an unhappy child, or to have had unhappy friends, or to have tormented other children, or to have had cruel teachers, or to have wondered about life and death. Or to have read Judy Blume's novels for children, whose popularity can be partly explained by her ability to remember.

Pink Lemonade, the first collection of the Dutch poet Annie Schmidt's to be published in English, is translated by Henrietta Ten Harmsel and vividly illustrated by Linda Cares. Most of the forty-two poems in the volume are long narratives, several unfortunately crammed onto a double-page spread, together with one or more drawings, resulting in some almost illegible pages. Nevertheless, this collection contains some very amusing and fanciful verses that succeed in conveying thoughtfulness and even in teaching something, with wit and charm. The collection is over-long: it might work more effectively with only the better poems included. But some of the poems included here will be enjoyed by both adults and children.

There is, for example, the tale of three imaginative mice and a very dull giraffe, who go for a walk together. When the mice see a wall or a hedge, they imagine all sorts of wonderful things on the other side, but the giraffe tells them "there's nothing at all." The mice finally desert the giraffe, preferring their imagined images to the dull reality that the giraffe sees. There is also the tale of the pig who said, " 'Oh, no,' " and " 'Oh, dear! / I want to be different, I want a career.' " There are three thieves who steal the moon from the sky and drop it: luckily, the "Committee for the Space-Age Preservation of the Moon" happens to see the moon as it sizzles and sinks in the Adriatic and hangs up a new moon created in a laboratory. There is "Weeping Willie," who drowns in his own tears; and Lily Jo, a Mexican fly who is very proud because she once bit a Spaniard in the arm, so now she has Spanish blood; and John, a boy who drives to New York every night in his bed. These stories are told at a galloping pace, which perfectly suits them.

In the best poems in this collection language is more than a means by which a story is conveyed; it is delightful for its own sake. When, for example, in "The Ducks," the ducks on the pond decide to turn the tables and feed Johnny, one of them observes that "this is ducky to do." After shopping for, preparing, and feeding Johnny his breakfast, the ducks offhandedly "called out as they walked through the gate, / 'Tomorrow it's your turn; be sure you're not late.' "

In "Doll Party," the queen of the dolls "plans the dolly follies" that all dolls attend one night a year, to dance the "boogie-woog" and drink "dolly pop." A boy named Jimmy Jingaling, in "The Magic Wand," changes all the grownups in town into other things:

> He changed the mayor of the town into a big red fox,
> And Mrs. Green—the florist's wife—he changed her into
> phlox.
> And all the children followed him—you should have heard
> them laugh
> Whenever Jimmy made a duck, a peacock, or giraffe.
> Then they would shout, "Hurrah, hurrah!" at each new
> mouse or fawn,
> And after fourteen hours or so the grown-ups all were gone.

The children, free from adult supervision, play in the park until "way after dark," but then, lonely for their parents, they persuade Jimmy to bring the grownups back. The poem ends:

> They all came back, that is, but one: the teacher, Mr. Blake;
> Yes, someone must have eaten him, for he had been a cake.

The translations are not perfect; occasionally Ten Harmsel lapses into a phrase which is awkward or impossible in English. Of twin boys she tells us, "They were exactly even old"; when the thieves plan to take the moon from the sky they say, "We're off to rob the moon!" Three towers piled on top of each other are "higher than the highest dome." In spite of these lapses and a

tendency to pad the line ("but yet she said she couldn't stop"),
Henrietta Ten Harmsel has produced a collection of poems which,
for the most part, seem as if they might have been written
originally in English.

What emerges from the stronger poems in this collection is the
sense that there is a poet who has written them. That poet has a
twinkle in her eye, and she knows how to talk to children and to
play games with them in a language that they can understnd and
appreciate. She tells them her fantasies, but she also speaks to them
of their concerns, complaints, and dreams through imagery which
transforms but does not distort its true subject. Nor is she afraid to
be serious with them on occasion. In "The Proud Little Light," an
electric Christmas-tree light flies out the window and over the
countryside, so that the people who see it believe it is a star. When
it falls before the force of wind, sleet, and snow, the people wish
on it:

> The people all felt very glad;
>   they all felt warm inside,
> And all of them began to work:
>   "We must work hard," they cried,
>
> "So that the peace for which we wished
>   will really come about."
> As for the star, he fell to earth,
>   and glowed, and faded out.

Perhaps no American adult writing today can risk the simple
sentiment of these lines. Yet the electric light has become a symbol, the falling star is a childhood talisman, and the poem's
straightforwardness makes it accessible and meaningful, while at
the same time encouraging the child to understand it on more than
the literal level. I'd like to have had *Pink Lemonade* to read when I
was a child.

Running Risks with Language: Contemporary Prose and Poetry for Children in West Germany

Jack Zipes

Dimension, vol. 12, no. 1, edited by Karlhans Frank. University of Texas Press, 1979.

During the last fifteen years in West Germany there has been a remarkable development of experimental children's literature. Whereas German writers had shied away from dealing with thorny problems of childhood experience in the immediate postwar period, they rose to the forefront of a general European reform movement in the late 1960s that sought to make children's literature socially more realistic and emancipatory at the same time (see my essay in *Children's Literature,* 5 [1976]). It is difficult for an English-reading public to obtain translated texts of this new German children's literature, so that the special issue of *Dimension,* edited by Karlhans Frank and containing stories and poems, fills a need by helping us to gain a sense of the experimentation in West Germany. Frank's anthology is the first to appear in English with the German originals on the opposite pages.

Frank is a gifted writer of children's books in his own right. Since 1968 he has produced numerous volumes of poetry and prose for children, written television scripts for children's shows, and developed four "Sesame Street" paperbacks for educators. His most recent children's book is *Was macht der Clown im ganzen Jahr?* (What Does the Clown Do All Year Long?), published in 1978. Here, as the guest editor of this thematic issue of *Dimension,* he has gathered together approximately twenty-two texts in prose and poetry—along with several unique illustrations—for children between the ages of six and fourteen. He does not presume or want to pretend that this is a "representative" volume of the best texts for children by West German authors; rather, he has made a careful and sensitive selection of provocative stories and poems that challenge young readers' minds. All of them are admirably translated by different persons under the guidance of A. Leslie Willson, th general editor.

To begin, the thematic issue of *Dimension* is introduced by Rut Lorbe's insightful essay on West German poetry for childrer Lorbe presents several interesting examples of recent experimen tation with motifs, rhymes, sounds, and structure to indicate how poems can make the young reader "aware of all the possibilitie that lie in the language, and . . . invite him to have confidence i the language, to run risks with language." This sets the tone for th rest of the volume, for Frank has collected stories and poems tha reflect how the authors themselves run risks with language an how young readers can follow these risks. In the course of readin all the texts, one learns not only about artistic endeavors on beha of children in West Germany but also about social conditions in th Federal Republic.

Since it would be difficult to summarize all the fine contribution to this volume, I want to cite some of the more interesting concern of the authors and the expressive forms that they have developec Three stories—Gina Ruck-Pauquet's "Red Man and Red Girl, Iring Fetscher's "The Frog Prince—How It Continued," and Gun ter Herburger's "The Cement Dwarf"—exemplify the ways i which numerous West German authors have reutilized fairy-tal motifs to question the irrational and unjust conditions in moder society. Frank's own contribution, "The Really Sad Story of th Smart Pig," borders on the fairy-tale genre, but it is more a shor fantastic and symbolic speculation about the nature of oppresse creatures. On the realistic side, there are penetrating sketches c family and social life in the Federal Republic—all drawn with sympathetic eye for the difficult situation of youngsters. Han Christian Kirsch's "Quarreling" is a sensitive portrayal of a brothe and sister who develop stronger bonds of love while observing how the relationship between their parents becomes more bitte Wolfgang Fienhold's story, "Fatso," deals poignantly with unwar ranted prejudice against odd-looking children. Carola Ber ninghoven's "Ilona Doesn't Go Home at Noon" allows readers t gain insight into the sufferings of a child who is neglected by he mother and feels isolated in a daycare center. "Elke, and Fear Too" by Wolfgang Gabel describes the discrimination experienced by an adolescent boy who has been abandoned by his parents and is disparaged as an orphan. The poetic first-person narrative allows the reader to grasp the boy's conscious awakening to what it means to be stamped an outsider by society. Sophie Brandes's portrait of Fritz in "Fritz Castaldo's Guardian Angel" is just as skillfully drawn, but her protagonist is presented ironically as a boasting male chauvinist who is afraid of women.

Most of the stories are summed up in the long poem by Theodor Weissenborn, "Get Ready for Life," toward the end of the volume. It begins this way:

> and live,
> feel,
> perceive,
> sense,
> sit in a school
> and be glad,
> jump up suddenly,
> yell, overwhelmed, quick happiness: The sun's coming!
> At once be warned to be quiet,
> talk back,
> get punished with extra work,
> be quiet.

The tension between encouragement and discipline is maintained throughout the poem to provoke and challenge readers to question the normal routine of life. It is indicative of the unusual rhetoric in some of the best West German prose and poetry for young people, which seek reversal of the ordinary. In fact all the stories and poems in the thematic issue of *Dimension* demand that the readers question the general run of life and that they run risks not only with language but with their own lives. This is not to be done haphazardly. One of Frank's own poems from *Der fliegende Robert: Viertes Jahrbuch der Kinderliteratur* (Fourth Yearbook of Children's Literature) points to the direction risks should run:

Fly If Possible
Not Without a Net

The Flying Flamingos
are flying up high
turning spirals and saltos
they tumble and fly.

Two catchers, four fliers,
their team's like a dream.
They twirl like propellers,
not a fall, not a scream.

You gaze and you stare
and would like to fly too
like a ball in mid-air
in everyone's view.

But before you go flying,
let me repeat a wise saying:
success comes only to those
who learn to take risks

if possible not without a net,
and here's the reason why:
many are the stars and acrobats
who've fallen from the sky. [my translation]

Two Illustrators

James B. Best

Edward Ardizzone: Artist and Illustrator, by Gabriel White. New York: Schocken, 1980.
The Work of E. H. Shepard, edited by Rawle Knox. New York: Schocken, 1979.

Books dealing with children's book illustration appear in a limited number of formats: they focus on one illustrator and explore his or her life, career, and artwork in detail; they analyze a number of illustrators working during a given period or in a common style; or they compare and contrast how a number of illustrators in different times have dealt with the same book or genre of material.

Both books reviewed here fit the first format. Gabriel White's book on Edward Ardizzone is an excellent biography and analysis of his artwork. However, the analysis is seriously unbalanced; between 1929 and 1976 Ardizzone illustrated 170 books, yet only two chapters are devoted to a discussion and analysis of his book illustrations. What is written is instructive, but it merely serves to whet the appetite for a more definitive work.

White begins with a discussion of Ardizzone's childhood, suggesting that his keen visual awareness, appetite for small detail, and retentive memory served as a source of inspiration for his art. The relationship between these childhood gifts and his book illustrations then waits while the author discusses Ardizzone's early drawings of Maida Vale and his work as a military artist in World War II. The analysis of Ardizzone's illustrated books begins with a statement of his philosophy of illustration: the illustrator is both stimulated and constrained by the textual material he is illustrating, but his primary task is to create a visual world that corresponds to that which the author is describing. Powers of observation and recollection, as well as a knowledge of the processes by which the artwork will be reproduced, are central to the fulfillment of this task.

White divides Ardizzone's work into three periods to show the development of his style of illustration. The first period, 1929–47, established the basic characteristics of that style, particularly his pen and ink work—a simple line, contrasting areas of black and white, and open edges. The illustrations are appealing in their simplicity and their ability to communicate with children in a style similar to one a child might employ. The second period, 1947–65, produced some of his finest work, notably the illustrations for Victorian classics by Dickens, Thackeray, and Trollope. At the same time Ardizzone was illustrating the works of four contemporary authors—Maurice Gorham, James Reeves, Eleanor Farjeon, and Mary Lewis. Unfortunately, the analysis of Ardizzone's artistic contribution to books by all these authors is limited to seven illustrated pages. Obviously little more than a line or two can be said about each, rather sad since this period is Ardizzone's richest in scope and versatility. The second chapter on his book illustrations includes a brief discussion of only four books from Ardizzone's third and most prolific period of children's book illustration, 1965–76.

While Knox's book also attempts to show the relationship of the artist's early life to his illustrations, it is less successful than White's. Perhaps the family members who contributed to the book were too close to their subject; the finished product is a detailed biography that does surprisingly little to link E. H. Shepard's life to his work, except to note that he was the son of a middle-class English family and that he illustrated books for his middle-class peers.

The two best chapters in the book were written by Penelope Fitzgerald and Bevis Hillier; they deal with Shepard's development as a black-and-white illustrator. Fitzgerald discusses English illustrators of the 1860s, particularly Charles Keane, and their impact on Shepard's work. Hillier defines for the first time the characteristic style of Shepard's drawings and attempts to mark his place in the history of English illustration. These two chapters are too brief to serve as more than an introduction to the study of Shepard's work, but when they are taken in conjunction with his two autobiographical pieces on his childhood, one can develop a suitable sense of why his art developed as it did.

The chapter focusing on Shepard's period of greatest critical acclaim, 1920–40, is one of the weakest in the book. Although there are numerous pencil sketches and color plates from *Winnie-the-Pooh, The House at Pooh Corner,* and *The Wind in the Willows* reproduced in this chapter, there is very little analysis of the artistic development of the characters which generations of adults and children have come to know and love as Pooh, Robin, Toad, and Badger. For *Winnie-the-Pooh* and *The Wind in the Willows* Shepard visited the locales described by Milne and Grahame, and the book illustrations flow from the story lines and Shepard's knowledge of scene, visualized in terms that children understand. But Knox's assertion that Shepard "understood Christopher Robin's loneliness as Milne did not" (p. 113) is not substantiated by a comparison of Milne's text and Shepard's illustrations. In fact, very little attention is paid to how or why Shepard approached the Milne and Grahame works as he did. Considering the seminal importance of these two works and their illustrators for children's literature, Knox's failure is regrettable.

Consequently, when Bevis Hillier judges Shepard as the last of the great Victorian black-and-white illustrators, there is little in the earlier sections of the book to confirm or deny this evaluation. It is to Hillier's credit in the concluding chapter that he is able to bring convincing evidence in support of his judgment. Unfortunately, however, Hillier's judgment of Shepard's place in history does little to increase our understanding of his importance to the Milne and Grahame classics.

Both books contribute to our understanding of each illustrator, but they suffer from defects common to books of their format. With the exception of one chapter in the book on Shepard, there is little effort to place the illustrator's work within the broader context of children's book illustration, or to compare one illustrator with others working at the same time or in the same genre. Both books stay firmly fixed in their format. The emphasis in each book on the relationship between childhood experience and illustration content and style, although important, neglects the influence of artistic peers. No illustrator is an artistic island, but one would never know it from these books. Ardizzone's style seems to have been unaffected by any other illustrator, while Shepard's style was derived from that of his artistic predecessor Charles Keane. Child-hood events undoubtedly had an impact on the artistic lives of these men; however, it is hard to believe that their artwork is merely a reflection of their childhood. Similarly, these books provide little evidence of any interplay between English and American children's book illustration; the style and content of each seems curiously reflective of only his own national culture. Nonetheless, Shepard's illustrations for *Winnie-the-Pooh* have proved popular in the United States, indicating that cultural content and illustration styles can transcend national boundaries.

As good and as useful as these two books are, they could have been better, and more valuable, had the authors taken a somewhat broader perspective on their topics and spent less time defining and defending the uniqueness of their illustration and more time placing their illustrators within cultural, historical, and artistic contexts. These books also point to the still-needed definitive work on children's book illustration, focusing less on the works and talents of individual artists (as does Barbara Bader's excellent book, *American Picture Books from Noah's Ark to The Beast Within* [1976]), and more on tracing the evolution and development of the field. Some of this has already been done, but no one has yet brought the material together and synthesized it in one volume. Until then, works on individual illustrators will exist without a cultural context to provide a basis for assessing and comparing the contributions of the artists under study.

Varia

Naomi Lewis is a British writer, critic, and broadcaster. She holds the Eleanor Farjeon Award for "distinguished services to children's literature," is a fellow of the Royal Society of Literature, and has written extensively for the (London) *Times*, *New Statesman*, and *The Observer*. Her recent books for and about the young include an annotated translation of selected Andersen stories, a collection of poems with illustrations by Leo Lionni *(Come With Us)*, and an annotated anthology on dolls *(The Silent Playmate)*. The editors feel that she is particularly suited to illuminate the meanings of fantasy and its developments in children's literature, both past and present.

The Road to Fantasy

Naomi Lewis

Some years ago—seven, maybe: that seems a fitting number—I was asked to take part in a broadcast discussion on fantasy. Fantasy . . .? Strangely, though I had written often enough on Carroll, Le Guin, all those mages, I had never really defined the term to myself. Unscripted talks need a headful of ordered thought and proper reserves of data. I wandered into the National Book League[1] and glanced at the splendid array of pamphlets. "Have you," I asked, "a thing on fantasy?" "No," replied Jenny Marshall sweetly, "but you will write one."[2]

My mind leaps over the following months or longer and lands at a point when a list was at last compiled (about 200 titles, in print or almost so), and a paragraph—factual, succinct, freshly evaluating—was due to be written on each. The whole thing was to be the N.B.L.'s Christmas exhibition, and time (as always) was running out. Each day I would calculate that, working from dawn to dawn, I might complete a further ten or twelve entries. The average was nearer three. But somehow it was done; the introductory essay was finished, typed, and put in the messenger's patient hand. The exhibition was held; the little book was kindly received by the critics, and presently it was sold out. A second edition has also gone. The third is on the way.

Problems? Findings? Many of both. But the main ones at the outset concerned the term itself. For is not *all* our reading fantasy? It is Middle Earth; it is also the seed catalogue, the travel brochure, the do-it-yourself handbook. It is the child's dream of being an orphan, a foundling—even more than the orphan's dream of being a "family" child. It is the king over the water, Bonnie Charlie, a fellow who in life, I believe, scarcely deserved the marvelous "fantasy" songs that his cause inspired, songs that move us still. It is the exile's dream of the homeland. Edward Thomas, who never left his native England until he went to his battle-death in France in 1917, listened to soldiers speaking of home. For him, their easy fantasy covered a deeper one. What is that place? he mused. And where?

> I would go back again home
> Now. Yet how should I go?
>
> This is my grief. That land,
> My home, I have never seen;
> No traveller tells of it,
> However far he has been . . .

John Masefield reproached himself for writing fantasy poems about the sea ("All I ask is a tall ship") when he knew too well how harsh and mentally dulled could be the life of a working seaman of his day. (He came to the sea as a boy, and left it forever before he was twenty—thus, both the knowledge and the nostalgia. For the truth of the fantasy, read his great poem *Dauber*.) *Jane Eyre*—and *Villette,* too—are wish-dream fantasy raised to the level of genius.

Fantasy lies down a rabbit hole, but even there it needs the presence of Alice herself, a non-fantastical girl if ever there was one. It is the ballad of Percy and Douglas, that stirred the young Philip Sidney more than a trumpet; it is the battle trumpet itself, and the harp song of the minstrel boy, marching out to death. It is the pretty pastoral theme of a hundred poems ("How sweet is the shepherd's sweet lot!"), already an absurdity when Shakespeare wrote *As You Like It,* where a whole summer court plays at greenwood. It is Samarkand if you do not live there—and equally, to many a child, the home life of *Little Women.*

Enough. A limiting line to the list had to be somewhere drawn. I saw this line at just beyond the furthest edge of the probable—and then as far on as need be. What did the *New Collins English Dictionary* say? *"Fantasy. n.* A creation of the imagination unrestricted by reality . . . a series of pleasing mental images, usually serving to fulfill a need not gratified in reality . . . an illusion, hallucination or phantom." Yes, yes, the definition would serve.

With the second edition (in which several mistakes were mended and one or two others crept in: such is the wayward nature of words) came a welcome bonus—the offer of a picture on the cover. Which? No hesitation—I knew at once: almost any of Arthur Hughes's illustrations to George MacDonald's books. Here was a likely one: North Wind, an awesome beauty, filling the midnight sky with her swirling hair, while, far below, birdlike against her vastness, the child Diamond clings to her classic foot. *How* likely it was I did not realize until the whole publication appeared. In the MacDonald texts the engravings are quite small, about the size of a playing card. Our designer boldly enlarged this one to fill the page—about four times the size of the original—and the impact was startling. You saw the hand of engraver Dalziell at work, the occasional tremble, even. But you saw as well, almost too clearly, how Hughes had entered MacDonald's mind what he found.

And so to the third edition. What themes, what names, what landmarks to report? Major ones—too soon, perhaps, to say—but after all, two or three of these odd and seminal surprises in any decade is a handsome quota. The 1970s had about that number; the 1960s rather more. The 1980s have time yet. Themes? Various (that's good). Names? Often unexpected Books of notable quality? Yes, they arrive. Dahlow Ipcar's magical novel *A Dark Horn Blowing* grows out of legend and ballard. (The dark horn lures the young wife to the midnight sands and into the eerie boat for Elfland . . .). Jan Mark's *The Ennead* needs an intelligent reader, but it seems to me the outstanding other-planetary novel of many a season. Delia Huddy's *The Humboldt Effect* is a quite exceptional time-switch story. *Playing Beatie Bow* (for rather young readers) is another notable time-play fantasy. The picture book *Tilly's House*—pictures and story both by Faith Jacques—is a born classic, the best of quite a number of doll tales: life seen in miniature, Andersen-fashion. In *Charmed Life* and *The Magicians of Caprona,* Diana Wynne-Jones writes with wit and assurance of the range, limits, and expertise of magicianship. *The Path of the Dragons* by Jean Morris is a remarkable book on the old gods and the new men (is progress always upward?), on what was lost with the loss of Atlantis and its rare people. (What would have been the opinion of Keats on *this* Hyperion?) But the novel is also one of a growing number of "older" books to give new thought to the great mythic beasts of the

The North Wind. Etching by Arthur Hughes for George MacDonald's *At the Back of the North Wind.* Courtesy of the Special Collections Department, University of Connecticut Library.

title. Le Guin has shown this advance already—see the magnificent Earthsea chapter in which Ged and the great Dragon of Pendor have courteous confrontation, parrying wit with wit, the victor gaining the day with verbal moves of power. Stevie Smith, who made her own doors into most assumptional strongholds, supplies a dragon note at once wry, elegiac, and sadly topical in her poem *Fafnir*. She concludes:

> Take thy rest in the green grass
> Too soon, mild Fafnir,
> The time will come
> When thy body shall be torn
> And thy lofty spirit
> Broken into pieces
> For a knight's merit.
> Fafnir, I shall say then,
> Thou art better dead
> For the knights have burnt thy grass
> And thou couldst not have fed.

Other books, other paths. In Lionel Davidson's *Under Plum Lake*, a boy attempts to set down an intensely realized magical experience, in a place where every joyful facet of boy-life, as he knows it, is heightened, speeded, and magnified. This is not all, for he passes over the frontier of death—then returns. Something of this kind—a passage through death—also befalls a boy in John Rae's *The Third Twin*. Discovered hiding at night in Westminster Abbey, this boy remains as hostage with the Abbey's irate (and famous) ghosts while his brother returns to put certain ghostly grievances to Authority. But the hostage boy is not to be found. Days pass, then weeks . . .

New but not new, is this fantasy theme of death. Though tacitly banned from children's "modern" fiction for much of our own century, it has always waited in legend, ballad, and tales of history, in countless Victorian novels, and never failing to draw and hold child readers. Read again the words of little Paul Dombey (never mind about Wilde); see how MacDonald inteprets Diamond's death in his great North Wind story. "To die will be an awfully big adventure," said Peter Pan; but he never believed that it would happen. C. S. Lewis's *The Last Battle* (where it *does* happen) was still a taboo-breaker in 1956. Today the taboo has gone and the theme lies open, all the more beguiling because it is unresolvable.

Time, ghosts, and myths relived; dragons, dolls, and death . . . How strange, by contrast, that (with rare exceptions) works of fantasy make so little use of dreams. I do not mean merely as plot device; this is frequent enough. What is in the N.B.L. list? *Tom's Midnight Garden*—yes, for sure. And of course William Mayne's *A Game of Dark*. And Catherine Storr's *Marianne Dreams,* and Alison Uttley's *A Traveller in Time,* lyric and mournful: "Many of the incidents in this story are based on my dreams, for in sleep I went through secret hidden doorways in the house wall, and found myself in another century." These are outstanding books, and the dream-motif, differing in all, is intrinsic to the matter of each. But of real dream-fantasy, whose scenes are both sharply surreal yet fast-dissolving, *Alice* remains the prime example. What's more, the other two most striking instances I can find also belong to the day before yesterday. Few books in the genre are so rich in dream-sequence as the first of these, that flawed pre-Raphaelite master-piece, Jean Ingelow's *Mopsa the Fairy* (1869). In one such episode Mopsa and the boy Jack, in flight from certain primitive beasts, reach their boat and are offered the protection of a Craken's coils, arch after arch, endlessly reaching away. The boat trembles, "either because of its great age, or because it felt the grasp of the coil underneath." Then, as they sail on, they perceive the arches closing in; soon they have to crouch down in the boat. (C. S. Lewis must have recalled this scene in *The Voyage of the Dawn Treader*.) "The next arch almost touched the water. 'No! that I cannot bear!' cried Jack. 'Somebody else may do the rest of the dream!' " "Why don't you wake?" says Mopsa, as if amused.

Other echoes of *Mopsa* are, I suspect, in the second book, Nesbit's *The Magic City* (1910), now newly in print again. Though less well-known than her earlier fantasy tales, it is of extraordinary inter-est—more so, indeed, than its author could have realized. A parentless boy, morose because his loved older sister, his guardian ally, and chum, is marrying, builds a city from books and bricks and candlesticks and his old Noah's Ark—and finds himself caught in it "on the other side of a dream" with a series of noble deeds to undertake before release. Except for two unattractive episodes (one concerning a dragon, the other some wretched lions), the book is a feast of invention, a remarkable interweaving of fact and fantasy based on dream. It also supplies the quotation: "Everything in the world is magic, until you understand it."

Does anyone now read George du Maurier's *Peter Ibbetson*? Here, in dreams, for many years, a man meets a long-vanished childhood friend. Du Maurier himself preferred this book to *Trilby*. It wasn't written for children, but I read it much as a child, and its haunting sense of dream stays with me still. With du Maurier, of course—his own artist—pictures and text are inseparable. Which are the greater purveyors of fantasy, words or pictures? They interrelate more than we think. Illustrators at best can be true magicians, and our debt to them cannot be calculated. Unfortunately the worst—especially the popular, vulgar, slick—have also power. A significant answer comes from the child who preferred radio to television because, as he explained, "in radio the pictures are better." Here I look up my note to Frances Browne's *Granny's Wonderful Chair*. This ends:

> The stories leave an intensely visual impact: the mer-creatures all in green, but "everyone with the same colourless face and the same wild light in their eyes," the ladies in rose-coloured velvet with crystal lamps, the field full of grass and violets, with snow-white sheep. This is strange. The author was blind from infancy.

Where is our richest fantasy area? In picture books for the very young, of course—a region where no law of the adult cosmos (the "real") need have any hold, whether of sun, moon, gravity, time, and space, where unlikely fauna, feral, extinct, or fabulous, crocodile, dragon, dinosaur, can comfortably join the domestic home—well, look for yourself. The entire fantasy list could be filled from the under-eight picture-book section. Many of these are based on nursery rhymes—the wildest form of verbal fantasy that numbers of humans are ever likely to meet—silver nutmeg, golden pear, night and distance, poverty, grief, gossip of history, rags of ballads, all the old meanings long dissolved; Babylon a candle's burning away and the moon no further. Should we be surprised that, given such a diet in infancy, the student and near-adult young should so often turn to science fiction and fantasy?

And now I am back once more with the opening question: which books, what borderline? That working definition (beyond the line of the probable) isn't an absolute. Should I include after all *The Secret Garden*? It could slip in through its one supernatural moment—that voice (a direct Brontë borrowing) heard by the moody father in far-off foreign parts. But the real fantasy is the thing itself: the wild hidden garden, the buried key, the echoing house on the moor with its secret child. Yet these are on *this* side of the probable—just. What of historical fiction, the daydream choice for some? We can reach the moon, but all the skills in the world cannot take us into the *living* past, where Shakespeare walks and talks. And yet, however guessed at, imagined, tidied up, novels of history deal with possible fact. So for most of these (there *are* some exceptions) our fantasy door is closed.

Wait—there is one more problem, and it lurks under all the rest. If fantasy is not all good fantasy, why is this? How? Where do the paths divide? Well, with all those permissive shops and movies to hand, we need not look far for some of the answers. But to keep within our own terms, and with child-reading in mind, I would start by saying that fantasy which imprisons the mind in a mesh of superstitions, imposed assumptions, rituals, codes, taboos, which blocks out thought and distances ("We've always done it, so it can't be wrong"), is evil fantasy. For a demonstration read Shirley Jackson's brilliant tale "The Lottery," surely one of the best short stories in the world. Theology is not blameless, allotting spiritual privilege (a mind, a "soul") to some living things and quite as arbitrarily denying it to others, a willful form of fantasy which has long served to justify the unjustifiable—to women, to slaves, to the handicapped, to the nineteenth-century laboring poor, to animals all the time. As an easily recognizable instance, fantasy (legend, story, obstinate superstition) has almost achieved, in the ugliest of ways, the genocide of the wolf, one of the most maligned of sentient creatures. We all know that child-readers, the voracious ones especially, have a natural rejection mechanism. Religious dogma and other abstracts can slip right through them, totally unabsorbed. But the same children do remember positives: that spindles prick (whatever a spindle might be); that the wolf is bad and deserves a hideous end, unsparingly described. Look at your own children's shelves and see how, today as always, this terrible myth persists. I, for one, never pass on a book where wolf is villain.

The *best* of fantasy—ah, that's a different matter. If you have the luck to meet the right rhymes and stories early enough, you should have in your mind for life the freedom of time and space and seasons, of skies and seas and distances, of turret stairways that lead to a fairy being, all-comforting, all-advising, prepared to give you the longed-for answer, interpret it as you may—and a bonus of words and images besides. What's more, sage counsel and wise examples may rise up shrewdly at needed moments, even in adult life: promptings of courage, hope and endurance, of advised politeness to spider, toad and crone. Your private forest of silver leaves will later lead to profounder forests and they will not seem strange. Good fantasy grows from the real, not least the humdrum real; it illuminates that reality.

Wrote Francis Thompson:

> Where is the land of Luthany
> And where the region Elenore?
> I do faint therefor. . . .

And with equal visionary longing, may not some dreamer in Luthany yearn for the fabled metropolitan London or New York? The desire itself, the mind's journey, is the gift. Thus, Louis Simpson's "singular Columbus" sets his airy sail

> For a country that cannot fail,
> Since there's no finding it.

The great sustaining fantasies of Avalon, Paradise, Tir-Nan-Og, the Celestial City, the Land of Heart's Desire—where have they ever been found outside the human mind? "I've always been expecting things to be more wonderful than they've ever been," says Lucy in *The Magic City*. "You get sorts of hints and nudges, you know. Fairy tales—yes, and dreams . . ." "Suppose we *have* only dreamed," says C. S. Lewis's Puddleglum, "or made up all those things—trees and grass and sun and moon and stars and Aslan himself . . . Then all I can say is that, in that case, the made-up things seem a good deal more important than the real ones." Emily Brontë rarely moved, and never by choice, from her austere home area; but she knew more than most of the boundless reach of imagination. In poem after poem—most hauntingly in that extraordinary narrative ballad "Julian M. and A. G. Rochelle" ("Through the dungeon crypts idly did I stray")—she writes of the ranging freedom of the mind in all adversity. The invented Gondal fantasy land of her childhood grew with her as she grew, a great terrain in which the aspects of life that occupied her could be endlessly played out—endurance, self-sufficiency, the relations of humans with nature, visionary experience, the implications of death.

She was a genius, and this is an extreme example. Yet our primal ancestors could never have sensed the living nature of Eden until it had become irretrievably lost. In place of the beautiful, unapprehended real, they were given the power of imagination, of fantasy, if you like.

Some might think that a fair exchange.

Notes

1. The National Book League is an independent British non-commercial trust and organization to promote books and reading.

2. Jenny Marshall, editor of the first two editions of *Fantasy Books for Children*, was then in charge of children's books at the N.B.L. Since the N.B.L.'s move to Book House, London SW18 in 1979, the director of children's books has been Beverley Mathias.

Dissertations of Note

Compiled by Rachel Fordyce

Adelman, Richard Parker. "Comedy in Lewis Carroll's *Alice's Adventures in Wonderland and Through the Looking-Glass.*" Ed.D. diss. Temple University, 1979. 285 pp. DAI 41:257A.

Adelman contends that Bergson's essay on "Laughter" (1900) is a good standard for evaluating comic elements in *Alice* and *Looking-Glass.* "In fact, the essay may also prove invaluable to the understanding and appreciation of comic devices utilized by contemporary writers of children's literature." Adelman applies Bergson's principles to both works, as well as to the suppressed "Wasp in a Wig" from the latter work and to the Tenniel illustrations, while emphasizing the repetition that is fundamental to Carroll's humor. The last chapter of the dissertation "presents the full text of the parodies which Carroll created . . . as well as the text of the poems which inspired them."

Alberghene, Janice Marie. "From Alcott to *Abel's Island:* The Image of the Artist in American Children's Literature." Ph.D. diss. Brown University, 1980. 206 pp. DAI 41:5100A.

This work, in four chapters, studies the "domestication" of the artist in children's fiction from Alcott through *A Bridge to Terabithia* and concludes that children, by example, are given very little incentives to become artists based on the portrayal of artists in American children's fiction. The first chapter illustrates the theme of familial affection linked to the artist in Alcott's *Little Women, Jo's Boys,* "Psyche's Art," and "A Country Christmas." The second shows artists as naturally gifted and learning the "lessons of domestication regarding the role of the artist in society." Works studied are *Dobry, Johnny Tremain, Adam of the Road,* and *The Silver Pencil.* The third chapter, a study of *The Door in the Wall, A Bridge to Terabithia, The Trumpet of the Swan,* and *Harriet the Spy,* suggests that the artist uses art as therapy. The last chapter, and the most complex, portrays art as a component either of discipline or of experience. Alberghene treats, among others, *Charlotte's Web, Abel's Island, The Second Mrs. Giaconda,* and *The Cat Who Went to Heaven,* concluding that "the child reader [is not encouraged] to identify with the artist; the reader is instead encouraged to identify with a character who is dependent on the domestic or self-sacrificing aspects of the artist's personality." Those few authors who allow the child to sympathize or empathize with the artist stress "the artist's discipline and loyalty to family and friends."

Bedard, Roger Lee. "The Life and Work of Charlotte B. Chorpenning." Ph.D. diss. University of Kansas, 1979. 185 pp. DAI 41:23A.

At her death in 1955 Charlotte Chorpenning was probably the most influential person in children's theatre in the United States. She is recognized as a writer of plays for children and adults, poet, teacher of a well-known class in play-writing, director, and dramatic theorist. Bedard's dissertation explores her early life, her work with George Pierce Baker and his Workshop 47, her influence on the Goodman Theatre programs for children in Chicago, her tenure at Northwestern University, and, preeminently, her major role in the Children's Theatre Press, the Children's World Theatre, the Children's Theatre of Evanston, the former CTC, and her influence on the Junior Leagues' touring companies for children.

Bedard concludes that "through her work with a wide scope of children's theatre organizations, and the large number of popular plays that she wrote, her influence touched virtually every facet" of the children's theatre field. His study is based on correspondence, interviews, archives, and Chorpenning's many works for children and adults.

Botsford, Antoinette. "The Toone Marionette Theatre of Brussels." Ph.D. diss. University of California, Los Angeles, 1980. 435 pp. DAI 41:3781A.

Botsford traces the history of the Toone Marionette Theatre from the early nineteenth century to the present, basically dividing her study into two parts: early history through the influence of Michel de Ghelderode, the famous Belgian playwright, and recent history under the influence of Jose Geal, an intrepid modernizer and innovator. It is likely that the Toone Marionette Theatre would have succumbed in the early twentieth century if de Ghelderode, in his teens, had not "transcribed a number of Brussels folkloric puppet plays from oral vernacular tradition into a written French format." Botsford translates these works for the first time into English and appends them to her dissertation. De Ghelderode's influence and assistance continued until his death in 1962, but by that time Brussels and the theatre had been ravaged by wars, the plays had not kept pace with changing social and cultural patterns, and without the revitalization that Geal brought to it, it is likely that the theatre would have gone under. Geal modified epic dramas like *The Three Musketeers*, stressed technique and accuracy, and "introduced structured, written scripts which helped to develop a faster-paced show that still left room for spontaneous improvisation," while maintaining links with tradition. Botsford stresses that it is possible to maintain a theatre that is modern, goes beyond mere entertainment, and still has strong ties with the past.

Bourgholtzer, Joey Marie. "A Pony Ride." Ph.D. diss. State University of New York at Binghamton, 1980. 100 pp. DAI 41:2598A.

Dissertations that are examples of original, creative writing are becoming more frequent but by no means common. Several dissertations, from Lowell Swortzell's through those he has directed in theatre departments, include original plays for children. But Bourgholtzer's may be the first to be a work of prose fiction for children. A quasi-deconstructionist work, Bourgholtzer's dissertation takes the child into the experience of reading and thinking a book. It "employs the idiosyncrasies, confusions and word-play inherent in the language in a seriocomic approach" by "making it progressively more obvious that the story bears no relation (and, therefore, need not conform) to anything other than its own construction." One hopes that a book intended to show that confusion is a natural state for a reader does not merely portray confusions of its own.

Copley, Deana Kay Wilson. "Creating and Directing a Musical Play for Children's Theatre, *Fabulous Aesop* (Volumes I and II)." Ed.D. diss. University of Northern Colorado, 1980, 256 pp. DAI 41:1841A.

In lieu of a strictly defined thesis, Copley's dissertation is a three-part work that analyzes the writing of a play for children, the performance of that play, and includes, in Volume II, the script, music, and choreography for her play *Fabulous Aesop*, which is the development of various Aesop fables. "The style of the language in the dialogue and song lyrics is somewhat formal"; the play's theme is "compromise," and the "message" is that the "pursuit of the arts is a worthwhile endeavor." Copley wrote and directed the play, designed the choreography, and composed the music.

Freeman, Ann. "A Comparative Study of Hans Christian Andersen and Charles Dickens: The Relationship Between Spiritual and Material Value Systems as Defined by Their Treatment of the Child." Ph.D. diss. University of California, Berkeley, 1979. 220 pp. DAI 41:236A.

Freeman's dissertation is predicated on the fact that Andersen and Dickens both viewed the world as being "divided into two competing realms of experience: an outer, everyday world where adult institutions demanded a high degree of conformity and where materialistic values prevailed, and an inner, fantasy world which contained a more elementary value-system based on immediate sensory perceptions." She stresses that each author is consumed with showing that child characters are of immense value in "expressing the unrest of an entire historical period obsessed with fragmentation and self-division." Through comparative analysis she shows how the two authors, similarly and differently, treat bifurcation of character and individuality in various works.

Grove, James Paul. "Mark Twain and the Dilemma of the Family." Ph.D. diss. Illinois University at Carbondale, 1980. 369 pp. DAI 41:3580A.

Grove's thesis is of interest for his study of *Tom Sawyer, Huckleberry Finn*, and *The Prince and the Pauper*. Historical and critical in approach, discussions in the dissertation center around the ambivalent and transitional nature of domestic life in the late nineteenth century, the image of marriage that Twain portrays in his novels, and Twain's "inability to resolve his dilemma concerning the family," particularly in terms of mother, father, and orphan characters. In *Huckleberry Finn*, Grove sees Twain "drawn to images of the disintegrating family" in his depictions of "forced separations, betrayals, madness, bereavements, and catastrophes."

Hensley, Charlotta Cook. "Andre Norton's Science Fiction and Fantasy, 1950–1979: An Introduction to the Topics of Philosophical Reflection, Imaginary Voyages, and Future Prediction in Selected Books for Young Readers." Ph.D. diss. University of Colorado at Boulder, 1980. 240 pp. DAI 41:3580A.

Hensley's is the first lengthy work on Andre Norton, a prolific and generally popular writer of children's fantasy and science fiction. Hensley explores forty-five books for Norton's treatment of philosophical reflection, imaginary voyages, and future prediction. She contends that Norton is more than a writer of "fast-paced adventure" because Norton delves into a wide range of themes that are central to human experience in a world where individuals struggle against "both human and social oppression. Her protagonists return from their adventures to instruct their communities that social endurance and growth is contingent upon individual freedom and cultural diversity as well as upon the mutual cooperation of all intelligent life." Much of Hensley's dissertation is devoted to the analysis of specific works to demonstrate that Norton is a "superb storyteller" who "presents complex ideas and plot structures in a deceptively straightforward writing style."

Hoilman, Grace Dona Gubler. "Voices and Images of the American Indian in Literature for Young People." Ph.D. diss. Ball State University, 1980. 464 pp. DAI 41:3566A.

In a deep and rich dissertation, Hoilman analyzes both the stereotypical Indian in literature for children as well as the contemporary Indian writers of poetry that has special appeal to children through its vivid imagery, optimistic tone, and ties to the past. Initially she discusses the racism in literature about Indians and the "neglect" of literature by Indian writers. Four stereotypes are demonstrated: "the noble redman, the ignoble savage, the comic buffoon, and the helpless victim." In addition, Hoilman discusses traditional information books and fiction for young readers, contemporary changes in attitudes toward Indians, books specifically published for Indian children and, most interestingly, compares collections of children's folktales "with the sources from which they were adapted." These reveal "the kinds of changes that have been made and determines that some are justifiable in the interests of making the Indian oral heritage comprehensible to non-Indian youngsters and that some are not because they violate the integrity of the tales." An analysis of translators of traditional Indian poetry and of contemporary Indian poetry rounds out the dissertation.

Hoyle, Karen Anne Nelson. "The Fidelity of the Text and Illustrations of Selected Danish Children's Fiction Translated and Published in Great Britain and the United States, Excluding Works by Hans Christian Andersen." Ph.D. diss. University of Minnesota, 1975. 539 pp. DAI 36:1880A.

Hoyle began her stylistic analysis with 154 Danish fictional works translated into English, sometimes under variant titles. By applying criteria suitable for evaluating excellence in translation, she ultimately worked with twenty-three titles, only eleven of which met her highest standards (for example, they retained the author's exact name and acknowledged the illustrator while changing the format of the book only minimally or not at all). Other criteria that she applied were these: character names and places should be retained; there should be no "expansion, change, or deletion of episodes"; illustrations should be the same; the appearance of the translated work should be "similar to the original book in terms of size, type of binding and cover and inclusion of book jacket"; and all original bibliographic material should be contained in the front material of the book. That Hoyle found so few examples of works that met these standards is significant and highly suggestive for future translated book awards and for book publishing in general.

Kash, Graham Stephens. "Humorous Folk Ballads in America: Themes and Techniques." Ph.D. diss. Indiana University, 1980. 579 pp. DAI 41:2718A.

Kash acknowledges that American folk ballads have frequently been included in anthologies and collections based on "region, occupation, or ethnicity" but contends that rarely are they studied critically as thematic groups. By focusing on the humor in titles, plots, themes, diction, and dénouement, Kash analytically compares and contrasts thematic elements in the ballads. He notes that most ballads center around the topics of "love, greed, cleverness, and the frontier" and in general "the folk balladist is a promoter of orthodoxy; however, the underlying conventionality is often presented in a subtle manner," thus presenting interesting problems of interpretation for the folksinger or critic of ballads.

Leaf, Linaya Lynn. "The Identification and Classification of Educational Objectives for Creative Dramatics When It Is Done with Handicapped Children and Youth in the United States." Ph.D. diss. University of Oregon, 1980. 544 pp. DAI 41:3328A.

Much of Leaf's lengthy dissertation is concerned with educational objectives that ultimately lead to further suggestions about appropriate areas of investigation. However, her definition of creative dramatics with handicapped children, and the various methods for allowing handicapped children to participate, are of value. She finds significance in the knowledge and awareness the handicapped child gains from participating in creative dramatics, if motor skills are not overly emphasized.

Miller, Katharine Fraser. "The Archetype in the Drawing Room: Fairy Tale Structures in the Novels of Jane Austen." Ph.D. diss. Brown University, 1980. 342 pp. DAI 41:5109A.

Miller, using the Campbell and Eliade formula for heroic initiation and Bettleheim's analysis of the didactic method in fairy tales, shows clearly the structural similarities between archetypal fairy tales and the major novels of Jane Austen. Miller divides Austen's heroines into two types—impetuous and self-willed "peasant girls" such as Marianne Dashwood, Elizabeth Bennet, and Emma Woodhouse, and "true princesses" such as Elinor Dashwood, Fanny Price, and Anne Elliot—to illustrate that "the specific growth ordeal" of each heroine "nearly parallels that of a popular fairy tale protagonist." Through a careful analysis of fairy-tale tradition and the Austen novels Miller concludes that "in each case the novel's fidelity to archetypal pattern invests its narrative with a thematic and structural backbone that serves to ground its ironic energy in timeless moral/social values and to focus its romantic power in a traditional comic vision of constructive growth and change."

Oldham, Jeffrey Thomas. "A Comparison of American Photo-Illustrated Children's Books for Early Childhood Years Published in the 1950–1960–1970s." Ph.D. diss. Southern Illinois University at Carbondale, 1980. 134 pp. DAI 41:3585A.

The purpose of Oldham's dissertation is to compare and contrast the aesthetic and technical aspects of photo-illustrated children's books over the past three decades, "to identify the type and subject of books on which authors center their efforts; and to examine to what extent the photos and corresponding text (when used) are related." He demonstrates that most photo-illustrated texts for children used black-and-white photography, that the photos were realistic, accurate, and straightforward, that they were faithful to the text, and that they did not "overemphasize either the child's or the adult's world."

Petersen, Bruce Thorvald. "No Shadow of Another Parting: Dickens' Concept of the Family." Ph.D. diss. Indiana University, 1980. 377 pp. DAI 41:264A.

Petersen's dissertation focuses on *Pickwick Papers, A Tale of Two Cities, Little Dorrit, David Copperfield, Dombey and Son, Great Expectations,* and the Christmas books, stressing the biographical nature of *David Copperfield* and the role Dickens's youth played in forming the social and ethical themes considerd particularly Dickensian. He concludes that the "concept of family becomes an essential ethical philosophy implicit to all" of Dickens's work. See also Freeman and Grove, above.

Posner, Marcia Joan-Weiss. "A Search for Jewish Content in American Children's Fiction." Ph.D. diss. New York University, 1980. 338 pp. DAI 41:2339-40A.

Posner's study encompasses seventy-three books with scenes set from the 1880s to 1950, all of which are realistic fiction that focus in varying degrees on religious or secular, formal or informal aspects of Jewish life. She analyzes "the effect that being Jewish had on [characters] and their responses to world and national events of particular relevance to Jews" as well as "the attitudes, values, concerns, and goals . . . attributed to them by the authors." While most books had positive content, not all were perceptive, accurate, or noncondescending in their portrayal of authentic Jewish characters and values.

Ronning, Kari Ann. "Above All a Nice Girl: The Heroines of Bestsellers 1895–

1920." Ph.D. diss. The University of Nebraska, Lincoln, 1980. 291 pp. DAI 41:1588A.

Ronning's dissertation is important not only because it is eminently readable and well-developed, but also because of its approach to the stereotypical treatment of female characters. While Ronning is concerned with bestsellers for adults from 1895 to 1920, her analysis of formulaic stories, heroines sculptured by the demands of popular clichés, and "rigidly patterned" types as an outcome of contemporary life has much to say about female child characters in books of the same period and much later, as well as about characters who are mothers in children's novels. She categorizes a wide range of stereotypes and shows how stereotypical ideals emerge and how they are eventually affected by time and changing norms.

Shail, George Ellsworth. "The Leningrad Theatre of Young Spectators, 1922–1941," Ph.D. diss. New York University, 1980, 860 pp. DAI 41: 4889-90A.

Shail traces the early history of the Leningrad Theatre of Young Spectators from its inception in 1922 through the prewar years to 1941. This theatre, the most child-oriented and certainly one of the best of the Russian children's theatres, is notable because of the inspired direction of its founder Aleksandr Briantsev, because of its link "with the small, but significant children's theatre movement in the Russian Empire before the 1917 Revolution," and because it is the first theatre in the world to train actors specifically to work for a child audience. Shail concludes that the "Leningrad Tiuz . . . had a strong commitment to the concept of art and education as a unified force for the moral enlightenment and aesthetic nourishment of the child spectator."

Stockard, Janice Lynn. "The Role of the American Black Woman in Folktales: An Interdisciplinary Study of Identification and Interpretation." Ph.D. diss. Tulane University. 212 pp. DAI 41:1166A.

Contrary to general perception, black women do play a major role in American folklore, signified by the sixty-one works that Stockard analyzes in her dissertation. An interdisciplinary study, it is an analysis of "cultural group identification, literary themes and style, historical validity, and socialization and role-specific definitions." She reveals a female black folk hero "who has been popularized since the period of American slavery" and who basically plays a religious or familial role in the folktales.

Sucke, Greer Woodward. "Participation Plays for Young Audiences: Problems in Theory Writing, and Performance." Ph.D. diss. New York University, 1980. 963 pp. DAI 41:853A.

This lengthy dissertation includes the texts of three participatory plays by Sucke: *Johnnycake/Gaspee, Don't Sleep under the Mapou Tree!,* and *Bakalu Baka.* Sucke analyzes the problems of writing participatory plays for children, the unique situations that arise from performing them, and how one allows children to participate in staged drama. Specifically, he is concerned with "shared problems related to participatory cycles, audience stimulation, feelings that hindered participation, suitability to age level, special benefits to participants, and spatial design," all of which he directly relates to the performances of his three plays.

Wolf, Virginia Leora Bouham. "The Children's Novel as Romance." Ph.D. diss. University of Kansas, 1980. 413 pp. DAI 41:2107A.

Wolf's dissertation is a refreshingly clear and detailed study of a difficult, vitally important, but frequently ignored subject; she describes "the formal characteristics of the children's novel, to relate it to the adult novel, and thereby to define it as a genre." Covering a wide range of generally contemporary children's literature, Wolf reviews criticism of the children's novel and "establishes that this criticism has relied only inconsistently and partially upon modern criticism of the novel as a genre." Concerning realistic novels for children, she concludes that they fail because "their formal, thematic, or narrative incoherence render them popular romance," although she does survey some successful "realistic romance." The final chapters of the dissertation trace "the increasing reliance" on the conventions of romance. "It is the conclusion of this study that the children's novel is very much like those adult novels identified as romance and should be understood and evaluated accordingly."

Also of Note

Batchelor, Ronald. "Creative Dramatics and Theatre Arts among Socially and Emotionally Handicapped Inner-City Adolescents: A Description and Analysis of a Drama Project." Ed.D. diss. Columbia University Teachers College, 1981. DAI 41:143A.

Biagini, Mary Kathryn. "Measuring and Predicting the Reading Orientation and Reading Interests of Adolescents: The Development and Test of an Instrument." Ph.D. diss. [in Library Science]. University of Pittsburgh, 1980. 243 pp. DAI 41:4871A.

Breiner-Sanders, Karen Elizabeth. "The Child and the Adolescent as Protagonist in the Post–Civil War Spanish Narrative." Ph.D. diss. The George Washington University, 1980. 448 pp. DAI 41:4053A.

Bromnell, Gregg. "Fairy Tales and Their Possible Use as Instructional Materials: An Empirical Study." Ph.D. diss. University of Kansas, 1979. 203 pp. DAI 41:919A.

Burke, John Joseph. "The Effect of Creative Dramatics on the Attitudes and Reading Abilities of Seventh Grade Students." Ph.D. diss. Michigan State University, 1980. 104 pp. DAI 41:4887A.

Calabrese, John Anthony. "Elements of Myth in J. R. R. Tolkien's *Lord of the Rings* and Selected Paintings of Paul Klee." Ph.D. diss. Ohio University, 1980. 204 pp. DAI 41:3303A.

DeBacco, Ronald Eugene. "Dickens and the Mercantile Hero." Ph.D. diss. Indiana University of Pennsylvania, 1980. 262 pp. DAI 41:1062–63A.

Fertkin, Marian I. "The Use of Literature and Library Resources in Creative Dramatics." Ph.D. diss. University of Illinois at Urbana-Champaign, 1980. 179 pp. DAI 41:462A.

Hasse, James Joseph. "The Effect of Reading Ability, Content Organization, and Recall Context on Children's Identification of Main Ideas and Retention of Prose." Ph.D. diss. Purdue University, 1979. 108 pp. DAI 41:166A.

Hedahl, Gordon Orlin. "The Effects of Creative Drama and Filmmaking on Self-Concept." Ph.D. diss. University of Minnesota, 1980. 159 pp. DAI 41:851A.

Hollwitz, John Charles. "The Mythopoetic Art of C. S. Lewis." Ph.D. diss. [in Speech]. Northwestern University, 1980. 235 pp. DAI 41:2352A.

Hughes, Larry Raymond. "The World View of C. S. Lewis Implicit in His Religious Writings." Ed.D. diss. Oklahoma State University, 1980. 150 pp. DAI 41:3613–14A.

McDaniel, Henry Arwood. "A History of Drama in Recreation from 1969–1974 in

Five Florida Municipal Recreation Programs: Tallahassee, Hollywood, Delray Beach, Dunedin, and Sarasota." Ph.D. diss. The Florida State University, 1980. 206 pp. DAI 41:3328A.

Pillar, Arlene M. "Dimensions of the Development of Moral Judgment as Reflected in Children's Responses to Fables." Ph.D. diss. New York University, 1980. 196 pp. DAI 41:2441–42A.

Ransom, Velez Hayes. "Transactions Between Traditional and Modern Life as Shown through Alaskan Northwest Arctic Folklore and Legends." Ph.D. diss. United States International University, 1980. 120 pp. DAI 41:1166A.

Rossman, Florence Patricia. "Preschoolers' Knowledge of the Symbolic Function of Written Language in Story Books." Ed.D. diss. Boston University School of Education, 1980. 169 pp. DAI 41:2039A.

Sharp, Patricia Tipton. "Children's Literature Collections in Fifty-Four Colleges and Universities: What They Are and What They Might Be." Ph.D. diss. The University of Iowa, 1980. 106 pp. DAI 41:1265A.

Snyder, Philip Jay. "Stories and Storytelling in Dickens." Ph.D. diss. University of Minnesota, 1980. 233 pp. DAI 41:2128A.

Stone, John Vandegore, III. "The Fairy Lover: A Literary Analysis of Norwegian and Icelandic Local Legends." Ph.D. diss. The University of Wisconsin, Madison, 1979. 618 pp. DAI 41:4127A.

Tajeran, Zarentaj Taji. "A Content Analysis of Iranian Children's Story Books for the Presence of Social and Moral Values." Ed.D. diss. University of the Pacific, 1980. 175 pp. DAI 41:1017A.

Wang, Yu Jung. "An Analysis of Male and Female Roles in Chinese Children's Reading Materials Published in Taiwan, China." Ph.D. diss. New York University, 1980. 146 pp. DAI 41:661A.

Contributors and Editors

ROBERT BATOR, a professor of English at Olive-Harvey College in Chicago, has recently edited *Signposts to Criticism in Children's Literature* (American Library Association, 1983).

JAMES J. BEST, a professor of political science at Kent State University, has taught for several years a course on the history of American illustration in the American Studies Program. He is currently completing *Illustration: A Bibliographic Reference Guide* for Greenwood Press, and two essays on the relationships between illustrators and art editors during the period 1890–1920.

HAMIDA BOSMAJIAN chairs and teaches in the English Department at Seattle University. She is the author of *Metaphors of Evil: Contemporary German Literature and the Shadow of Nazism.*

FRANCELIA BUTLER teaches English at the University of Connecticut, where she will be directing an NEH Institute on Children's Literature from June 20 to August 12, 1983.

ELIZABETH CRIPPS, a Recognised Teacher of London University, teaches at the Chelmer Institute of Higher Education in Essex. Her essays include studies of Lewis Carroll and Kenneth Grahame, and she is currently working on an edition of Charles Kingsley's *Alton Locke Tailor and Poet* for Oxford University Press.

PAUL DOUGLASS teaches in the Writing Program at UCLA. His essay on Bergson's philosophy and modernist aesthetics will appear in *Thought* in 1983.

RACHEL FORDYCE is associate dean of the College of Arts and Sciences at Virginia Polytechnic Institute and State University. She is currently on leave with an American Council on Education Fellowship.

THOMAS H. GETZ teaches English at the York Campus of Pennsylvania State University. He has published articles on contemporary poetry and fiction.

DAVID L. GREENE chairs the English Department at Piedmont College in Georgia. He is coauthor of *The Oz Scrapbook* (Random House, 1976) and is working on a series of articles on Salem witchcraft.

ANN HILDEBRAND teaches in the English Department at Kent State University and has published on religion studies in public education.

ELIZABETH KEYSER teaches English at the University of California at Santa Barbara. She has published essays on Hawthorne, Melville, and James, has an article forthcoming on Charlotte Perkins Gilman, and is at present completing a book on Louisa May Alcott.

U. C. KNOEPFLMACHER, professor of English at Princeton, has written extensively on the Victorians, including an essay on the Wordsworthian Child of Nature as presented in later nineteenth-century literature. He is presently engaged in a study of Victorian fantasies for children.

LOIS R. KUZNETS, recently in the English Department at Lehman College, CUNY, has moved with her husband to Ann Arbor, Michigan, where she teaches English at the Kingswood School in Bloomfield Hills. She has published widely in children's literature and is particularly interested in the realistic novel for children.

NAOMI LEWIS holds the Eleanor Farjeon Award for "distinguished services to children's literature."

THOMAS J. MORRISSEY teaches English and directs the writing program at SUNY at Plattsburgh. He has published several essays on literature and writing pedagogy and is completing a book on Pinocchio with Richard Wunderlich.

PERRY NODELMAN teaches children's literature and science fiction at the University of Winnipeg and is the associate editor of the *Children's Literature Association Quarterly*. He is currently working on the iconology of children's picture books.

HARRY C. PAYNE, a professor of history at Colgate, is the author of *The Philosophes and the People* (Yale University Press, 1976), and has recently edited Volumes 10–12 of *Studies in Eighteenth-Century Culture* (University of Wisconsin Press, 1981–83).

COMPTON REES, who teaches English at the University of Connecticut, has written on archetypal approaches to the teaching of children's literature.

JON C. STOTT, a professor of English at the University of Alberta, was the first president of the Children's Literature Association. His numerous essays have appeared in such journals as *Children's Literature in Education, Language Arts, Signal,* and the *Walt Whitman Quarterly*.

HENRIETTA TEN HARMSEL, a professor of English at Calvin College in Grand Rapids, Michigan, has published a book on Jane Austen and various articles on fiction. Her translations of seventeenth-century Dutch poets include *Jacobus Revius: Dutch Metaphysical Poet* (Wayne State University Press, 1968) and translations in *Essays on P. C. Hooft* (Amsterdam: Querido, 1981). She is presently translating *Good Friday* by Jeremias De Decker on a Fulbright grant in Holland.

MARILYN WANIEK teaches English at the University of Connecticut and has published her poems widely, including the book *For the Body* for Louisiana State University Press.

RICHARD WUNDERLICH teaches sociology at the College of Saint Rose in Albany, New York. He has delivered and published a number of papers on the sociological implications of children's books and is completing a book on Pinocchio with Thomas Morrissey.

JACK ZIPES is coeditor of *New German Critique* and a professor of German and Comparative Literature at the University of Wisconsin in Milwaukee. His numerous essays and books on children's literature and fairy tales include the recent *Fairy Tales and the Art of Subversion* (1982) and *The Trials and Tribulations of Little Red Riding Hood* (1982).

Index to Volumes 6–10

Compiled by Lance Tatro

Essays and Varia

Book Reviews